An Introduction to Religious Language

Windsor and Maidenhead

95800000169252

ALSO AVAILABLE FROM BLOOMSBURY

An Introduction to Sociolinguistics, by Sharon K. Deckert
Contemporary Critical Discourse Studies, edited by
Christopher Hart and Piotr Cap
Discourse Analysis, by Brian Paltridge
Spoken Discourse, by Rodney Jones
The Semiotics of the Christian Imagination,
by Domenico Pietropaolo

An Introduction to Religious Language

Exploring Theolinguistics in Contemporary Contexts

Valerie Hobbs

BLOOMSBURY ACADEMIC
LONDON • NEW YORK • OXFORD • NEW DELHI • SYDNEY

BLOOMSBURY ACADEMIC
Bloomsbury Publishing Plc
50 Bedford Square, London, WC1B 3DP, UK
1385 Broadway, New York, NY 10018, USA

BLOOMSBURY, BLOOMSBURY ACADEMIC and the Diana logo
are trademarks of Bloomsbury Publishing Plc

First published in Great Britain 2021

Copyright © Valerie Hobbs, 2021

Valerie Hobbs has asserted her right under the Copyright, Designs
and Patents Act, 1988, to be identified as Author of this work.

For legal purposes the Acknowledgements on p. xvi constitute
an extension of this copyright page.

Cover design: Rebecca Heselton
Cover image: Salvation Mountain, Slab City, California, USA @alexradelich/Unsplash

All rights reserved. No part of this publication may be reproduced or
transmitted in any form or by any means, electronic or mechanical, including
photocopying, recording, or any information storage or retrieval system,
without prior permission in writing from the publishers.

Bloomsbury Publishing Plc does not have any control over, or responsibility for,
any third-party websites referred to or in this book. All internet addresses given in this
book were correct at the time of going to press. The author and publisher regret
any inconvenience caused if addresses have changed or sites have ceased
to exist, but can accept no responsibility for any such changes.

A catalogue record for this book is available from the British Library.

A catalog record for this book is available from the Library of Congress.

ISBN: HB: 978-1-3500-9575-5
        PB: 978-1-3500-9574-8
        ePDF: 978-1-3500-9577-9
        eBook: 978-1-3500-9576-2

Typeset by Integra Software Services Pvt. Ltd.
Printed and bound in Great Britain

To find out more about our authors and books visit www.bloomsbury.com
and sign up for our newsletters.

For Andrew, Max and Martha

CONTENTS

LIST OF FIGURES

LIST OF TABLES

PREFACE

My interest in religious language began to take shape when I first became a student of linguistics, over twenty years ago. But my path into scholarship in this area has had many twists and turns, and it has come at some personal cost. My PhD research, for example, involved an ethnographic investigation of the Trinity College London TESOL Certificate course, a largely market-driven short course which serves as one of the key entrance points to the profession of English language teaching. Such courses are big business, and key figures in this industry tried to get my work banned from one international conference because of concerns about damage to their reputation and their business. The conference organizers stood their ground and subsequently invited me to be plenary speaker at a special event. This disconcerting experience was nevertheless significant in forming my identity as a scholar. For as long as I have been an academic I have focused my work on examining the ways in which seemingly inclusive large institutions, both religious and seemingly secular, establish community boundaries. In many cases, sadly, I have witnessed these institutions marginalize and exclude vulnerable members.

In 2015, I had been researching and teaching on the topic of disciplinary discourse for around ten years, focusing recently on the language of philosophy. Around this time my work on religious language began in earnest. As a result of a short project on representations of feminism in Christianity, Dr Bill Dennison, a Christian minister and scholar, invited me to attend an ecclesiastical trial in the United States involving a minister who refused to require his disabled wife to attend a weekly church service. Following a guilty verdict, Dr Dennison asked me to attend the appeal to a higher ecclesiastical court that same year. At both events, I collected court documents and took extensive field notes and transcriptions of court speeches and, using this data, wrote a series of articles which appeared on a popular Christian news site. My first article received the most hits of any article on that site in its history. Not long after, I was interviewed about this project on a popular weekly Christian podcast series. The hosts notified me that several members of the prosecution in the trial had written letters and e-mails asking that the airing of my interview be cancelled on the grounds that my reports were 'untrue and prejudicial'. Several key individuals also involved in the proceedings wrote to the hosts to attest to the validity of what I had written. Yet again, I was witnessing the policing of significant community boundaries by powerful members. Unlike my PhD research, this was now taking place in an overtly religious context. I had nevertheless encountered the same behaviour and even some of the same language in both places. I began to make connections I hadn't before seen and ask questions I hadn't before considered. This led me to approaches to the study of religion and religious language which start not with boundaries but with possibilities.

I currently convene one of the few modules in the world which equip students with tools to identify and analyse religious language. Theologians and those working within religious studies more broadly often discuss the role of language in religion, and many volumes have been written on core religious texts, such as the Bible and the Qur'an. But few scholars, even linguists, have paid attention to religious language in the many and varied contexts where it occurs. As I aim to do each year with my students, I hope to convince you of the pervasiveness and significance of religious language in all of our everyday lives, individually and collectively. This book is the result of many years of research and teaching about the role that language plays in creating, fostering and revealing what we hold most sacred. Religious language reveals what we love, what we cherish, what we protect, what we hate and what we fear. Thank you for reading this book. I hope it honours your investment.

FOREWORD

The study of language always needs two perspectives, which are sometimes summarized under the headings of 'structure' and 'use'. The first looks at the nuts and bolts – the sounds, spellings, structures, words and so on. The second looks at how these elements are put to use in real situations. Some people talk about a 'bottom-up' approach for the first and a 'top-down' approach for the other, or 'micro' and 'macro'. The terminology varies, but the insight is constant: the study of a language, dialect, or – as in this book – variety (or genre) needs both, and the trick is how to bring them together. Should one start at the bottom and work up, or the other way round?

Rare indeed is it to find both perspectives neatly integrated in the study of a genre, but that is what this book manages to do. I have found my understanding of religious language greatly enhanced by the combination of the two perspectives. How has Valerie Hobbs done it? By placing the notion of context centre-stage. And by recognizing one of the central facts about language variation: that there are no sharp divisions between the conventionally recognized genres. Language users pay little respect to boundaries. We may hear echoes of sports commentary, advertising, journalese, science, law and so on, in everyday conversation at any time, and any one of these varieties might borrow from any of the others. And so it is with religious language.

But on what a scale! I already knew that the language used within the confines of a particular religious text regularly bursts its cerements and can be encountered in all sorts of unexpected settings, from advertising to zombie films. I brought together hundreds of examples in my *Begat*, an exploration of the influence of the King James Bible on the English language, written for the 400th anniversary. But what I did not do in that book, and which is done so beautifully here, is to step back and see how that kind of diffusion leads us to a deeper appreciation of the role of religious language in life and thought. As Valerie Hobbs puts it in her final chapter, she wants to propose 'a theory of religious language which extends beyond the language of devotion for a sacred supernatural to the depth and breadth of language that encodes what we value and what we hate and fear the most, both as individuals and as communities.' In my view she has admirably succeeded.

Much of the success is due to the way she has brought corpus linguistics into the arena. I have not seen this done before, except sporadically in the occasional article. Certainly never in an introductory book, and so systematically. Yet it is essential, for it provides the empirical basis for observations that otherwise would be ungrounded impressionism. It is easy enough to claim that religious language, however defined, spreads into other domains. The trick is to prove it in ways that go beyond the anecdotal. Her exploitation of the various corpora is a major feature of this book and provides the kind of evidence we need to test hypotheses about the presence of the sacred in everyday life. And an extra level of conviction comes from her own anecdotes, which – in its references to such topics as Brexit and Donald Trump – adds an up-to-date dynamic to her argument that corpora dating from a few years ago cannot provide. 'Contemporary' is another important word in her title.

But there is a rhetorical dimension to all this. All studies of language varieties are, in their individual way, minefields, for as soon as we ask why a variety is the way it is, we encounter questions to do with the nature of society that go well beyond the linguistic. Valerie Hobbs does not shirk addressing these issues, and it is the honest and open-minded account she gives of the way people vary in their use of and response to religious language that is a hallmark of this book. It is all done with an enviable clarity of exposition. I especially like her thematic anticipations and recapitulations, her thoughtful follow-up questions, and her reiteration of signposts to show the reader how the argument is evolving. She is somewhat apologetic about doing this, but she does not need to be, for it helps readers to keep their heads above water, in a subject where it is all too easy to drown.

I have learned so much from *An Introduction to Religious Language*. It is a book that takes the study of religious language to a new level. Having worried a few years ago about where theolinguistics was going, I am now convinced that it has a bright future.

David Crystal

ACKNOWLEDGEMENTS

If this book is of any value to anyone, my students are largely to thank. I especially appreciate my religious language students whose questions and projects have surprised and pushed me in the most helpful of ways. Thank you to Gurdeep Mattu for commissioning this work for Bloomsbury and to Andrew Wardell, Becky Holland and Helen Saunders for assisting me throughout. Thank you also to the anonymous reviewers who provided just the sort of feedback I was hoping for.

I am also appreciative of the generosity of Professor Jean-Pierre van Noppen, who stepped away from his retirement to travel to Sheffield in 2017 and give several guest lectures at the University of Sheffield. I thank Professor David Crystal and Dr Laura Paterson, who wrote letters of support for grant applications and provided feedback at various stages on the content of this book. Finally, I owe a great debt to my dear friend Dr Bill Dennison. His scholarship, his professional and personal advice, and his friendship have empowered me to think more critically and, more importantly, to remember and rest in what is infinitely more important than any professional success. One such place of rest is Andrew, whose company I will always prefer.

If this book is a failure, I wish I could blame the many people who have dragged my name through the mud as I've observed and written about the experiences of vulnerable people in various institutions. But the truth is, they have had no negative effect or influence. If no one buys this book, if it meets with harsh critique, if scholarly work on religious language goes in a different (even better) direction? Ah well. My joy and gratitude will remain intact.

I gratefully acknowledge the permission granted to reproduce the copyright material in this book. Thank you especially to Lisa Bennett for the use of her photograph of an Atlanta billboard. I also thank Paul Rayson, David Tollerton, the Diocese of Worcester, Orion Publishing Group, Elsevier, Cambridge University Press, Equinox Publishing, Taylor and Francis, and *The Telegraph* for their permission to use copyrighted material. A full list of copyright material is available in the Permissions section. Every effort has been made to trace copyright holders and to obtain their permission for the use of copyright material. I apologize for any errors or omissions and would be grateful if notified of any corrections that should be incorporated in future reprints or editions of this book.

The third-party copyrighted material displayed in the pages of this book is done so on the basis of fair dealing for the purposes of criticism and review or fair use for the purposes of teaching, criticism, scholarship or research only in accordance with international copyright laws, and are not intended to infringe upon the ownership rights of the original owners.

PERMISSIONS

Unless otherwise indicated, all Scripture is taken from the Holy Bible, New International Version®. Copyright © 1973, 1978, 1984 Biblica. All rights reserved throughout the world. Used by permission of Biblica.

Portions of this book contain my own research previously published, as below. This material is used with the permission of the publishers.

Hobbs, Valerie. 2018. 'Disability, the "Good Family" and Discrimination in the Dismissal of a Presbyterian Seminar Professor.' *Journal of Language and Discrimination* 2 (2): 133–61. @ Equinox Publishing Ltd 2018.

Hobbs, Valerie. 2019. 'The Discourse of Divorce in Conservative Christian Sermons.' *Critical Discourse Studies*, September, 1–18. https://doi.org/10.1080/17405904.2019.1665079.

Figures

Figure 1.1 In Design We Trust. Kaboompics. Licensed under CC0.

Figure 2.1 Inner Street Preacher, 2018. Courtesy David Tollerton and @ rllyquitetired.

Figure 3.1 Jesus Saves, 2006. Courtesy Lisa Bennett.

Figure 3.2 Charles Street. Baltimore, Maryland, 2016. Elvert Barnes. Licensed under CC BY-SA 2.0.

Figure 3.3 Let There Be Meat, 2015. Courtesy Orion Publishing Group.

Figure 4.1 Ivory Soap. Christian *Herald*, 1913. Courtesy Wikimedia Commons.

Figure 4.2 Clean Eating, 2018. Kobisnir. Licensed under CC BY-SA 4.0.

Figure 4.3 Wedding Invitation, 2014. Chris Wanjagi. Licensed under CC BY-NC 4.0.

Figure 4.4 Wedding Invitation Design. Alaina Kraning. Licensed under CC BY-ND 4.0.

Figure 5.1 Foreword from Bishop John, 2019. Courtesy Diocese of Worcester.

Figure 5.3 Let It Be. Andy Roberts. Licensed under CC BY 2.0.

Figure 6.1 Kanye West's 'Yeeezus' Tour. Peter Hutchins. Licensed under CC BY 2.0.

Figure 6.2 Jesus Light of the World, 1974. xdd869. Licensed under CC BY-ND 2.0.

Figure 6.3 Too Stupid to Understand Science? Try Religion! 2016. Osseous. Licensed under CC BY 2.0.
Figure 6.4 In Cod We Trusted. Francesjane, 2007. Licensed under CC BY-NC-ND 2.0.
Figure 6.5 God's Billboard. wuji9981. Licensed under CC BY-NC-SA 2.0.
Figure 6.6 Extract from Greenville Presbyterian Theological Seminary Board Report, 2018. Courtesy Equinox Publishing Ltd.
Figure 7.1 Food Prayer, 2013. Cornelia Kopp. Licensed under CC BY 2.0.
Figure 8.1 A Life Well Lived, 2017. Fæ. Licensed under CC BY-SA 4.0.
Figure 9.1 Bite Me, 2005. Ryan Glenn. Licensed under CC BY 2.0.
Figure 9.2 Boris Johnson, Let My People Go, 2019. ©Telegraph Media Group Limited 2019.
Figure 9.3 Remembering Steve, 2011. Pspechtenhauser. Licensed under CC BY-NC-SA 2.0.
Figure 9.4 Don't Fear Cancer. Fight It! 1938. Courtesy Wikimedia Commons.
Figure 10.1 Blasphemy! Chanel Bag on the Street, 2011. mckrista1976. Licensed under CC BY-ND 2.0.

Appendices

Appendix 2 The Complete Theological Wordlist. Copyright © 2010 Elsevier Ltd. All rights reserved
Appendix 3 The USAS S9 'Religious and the Supernatural' Lexicon. Courtesy Paul Rayson

1

Why religious language?

In the last ten years or so, numerous books and news articles have reported that religion is back. Writing about his recent book *Living with the Gods*, Neil MacGregor argues that while the advance of science caused religion to retreat over the last fifty years, the world is now putting its faith back in religion (MacGregor, 2018). Recent figures indicate that worldwide, 84 per cent of us identify with a religious group, some of the largest being Christianity, Islam, Hinduism, Buddhism, Folk Religion and Judaism (Pew Research Center, 2017). 'Religion is surging', write John Micklethwait and Adrian Wooldridge, editor and Washington bureau chief of the *Economist* (Micklethwait and Wooldridge, 2010), pointing to phenomena like Californian megachurches, exorcism in Sao Paolo and mosques in Nigeria. Religion is even back in Sweden, according to a series run by highly respected morning paper, *Svenska Dagbladet* ('Guds återkomst [The return of God]', 2010).

Although numerous scholars have debated the rise and fall of religion as well as the complex question of what counts as religion, religious language more specifically has not attracted anything close to the same level of attention. Granted, religious language is only one of many methods by which we perform religion. Religion traditionally understood also involves places of worship and sacred landscapes, body language such as the sign of the cross and other gestures, sacred food, iconography and other artistic imagery, liturgical and otherwise special clothing and even keeping silent and still. Nevertheless, many religious activities require language. Prayer, religious songs, consecration, confession and preaching are just some of the examples we might think of straightaway. Although outside of the scope of this book, religious language is even in some non-Western religion closely intertwined with gesture, dance, chanting, music and other non-linguistic elements (see Beck, 1995; Bohlman, Blumhofer and Chow, 2006).

But beyond these explicit expressions, religious language is also embedded in unexpected places like advertising, politics, news media, popular culture and even healthcare, to name a few (see Figure 1.1). Politicians rely on it, pop singers tap into it, businesses benefit from it and sport fans invoke it. Yet most people are unaware of just how common religious language actually is. Professor of Bible, Society and Politics James Crossley writes, for instance, that many people are surprised at the amount of religious language that pervades political discourse in England (Crossley, 2018). And *The New York Times* recently reported Americans' shock at Attorney General Jeff Sessions's use of the Bible to justify President Trump's policy of migrant family separation (Jacoby, 2018), despite the frequent use of language like this in politics. Religious language is all around us. But it is also something most of us use, perhaps even without realizing it. Religious language is a visible and significant means by which we construct and reconstruct our beliefs about the world and our place in it. By it we both bless and curse. By it we manipulate and are manipulated.

In light of the pervasiveness of religious language in society and the need for skills to identify and critically examine it, the study of religious language has perhaps never been more important. In 1981, theologian F. W. Dillistone wrote, 'Theolinguistics is one of the most urgent and yet most demanding disciplines of our time' (Dillistone, 1981: 20). And yet, in his 2018 chapter 'Whatever Happened to Theolinguistics?' linguist David Crystal notes that the linguistic study of religious language, comparatively popular in the 1980s, has all but disappeared (Crystal, 2018). In fact, much of the scholarship

FIGURE 1.1 *In Design We Trust.*

on religious language has been done by philosophers, who consider what they call the 'problem' of religious language. Among the questions they've grappled with are: Is it possible to make truthful statements about invisible beings? Can religious language literally describe a deity? Does the use of metaphor mitigate the difficulty of describing the divine? Such questions are worth asking but don't really get to the heart of why we use religious language and what it does for us.

Early interest in religious language by linguists in the 1970s was bolstered by a growing interest in linguistics more broadly, largely thanks to the work of American linguist and political activist Noam Chomsky. Some of this initial work on religious language focused on glossalia, or speaking in tongues, a type of pseudo-language, which has a particular socio-cultural function in some religious movements such as Pentecostalism. In his book *Tongues of Men and Angels* (Samarin, 1972), William Samarin analysed the more technical aspects of the phenomenon of tongues speaking. Around the same time, Felicitas Goodman completed her cross-cultural and largely anthropological work *Speaking in Tongues* (Goodman, 1972). Her definition of glossalia as a hyper-aroused, disassociative state was heavily criticized by Samarin and also Walt Wolfram as a distortion of this complex phenomenon (Wolfram, 1974). In short, early work on religious language was characterized by a focus on what made the talk of religious people different, weird even.

Work on religious language by linguists was boosted again in the early 1980s. During this period, Belgian linguist Jean-Pierre van Noppen introduced the term 'theolinguistics', based largely on his substantial work on spatial metaphors and, more specifically, spatial theography (van Noppen, 1980). Van Noppen's ground-breaking work explored the question where is God? He also edited two volumes on religious language, the first including scholarship in the areas of semiotics, philosophy, theology, literary criticism, psychology and linguistics (van Noppen, 1981) and the second focusing on metaphor (van Noppen and Buscarlet, 1983).

Other scholars took up the mantle of theolinguistics, producing five volumes on metaphor and discourse analysis in a larger series published by Peter Lang in the 1990s. Noel Heather's volume 5 in the series, entitled *Religious Language and Critical Discourse Analysis*, for example, focuses on the religious language some Christians use in order to manipulate and control (Heather, 2000). Another scholar, Webb Keane argued for the necessity of an ethnographic approach and attention to intentionality and agency in religious language (Keane, 1997). Then there are the collections edited by Tope Omoniyi, one with Joshua Fishman, of work by various scholars on the sociology of language and religion (Omoniyi, 2010; Omoniyi and Fishman, 2006). These include work on the language of Hinduism in the United States, holy hip-hop and language and religion in Bethlehem, Melbourne and Singapore.

In recent years, linguistic analysis of religious language has diversified even further, from work on Christian, Buddhist and Muslim sermons (Esimaje, 2014; Malmström, 2016) and prayer (Shoaps, 2002), to Christian hymns and other religious music (Ingold, 2014), to wedding invitations in Jordan and Iran (Al-Ali, 2006), to religious language in everyday talk. Stephen Pihlaja has expanded the field by considering religious language online, particularly between Muslims, Christians and atheists (see Pihlaja, 2014). Pihlaja has several other books in the works which will enrich our understanding of methods of analysing religious language (Pihlaja, 2021) as well as the links between religious language and cognition (Richardson, Mueller and Pihlaja, n.d.).

Then there is the work by a wide range of scholars that explores religious language in contexts such as politics and advertising but without the theory and tools of linguistics. Richard Mocarski and Andrew Billings, for example, consider how Nike and the basketball star LeBron James co-constructed the legend of King James, tapping into a Messiah narrative (Mocarski and Billings, 2014). Scholarly work explicitly focused on religious language has been steady but nevertheless somewhat scattered and at times difficult to locate.

Aims and summary of the book

We have seen important advances in the study of religious language, and there is further work on the horizon. But when it comes to our knowledge about how such language is put together, we have such a long way to go. What counts as religious language? Who uses it? Where can it be found? What are its distinctive features? What purposes does it serve? These are all questions we have only begun to answer. Truly, the topic of religious language is gargantuan. This book aims to contribute to the study of religious language by exploring why people use religious language and what it accomplishes. It aims to present and study some of the common features of the language people use to talk to about what they hold sacred. It considers the use of religious language both in religious and in seemingly non-religious contemporary contexts. Over the next nine chapters, this book aims to raise questions that bring together and in some ways challenge the limited work on religious language, ultimately considering the question: Is it possible to be human without being religious?

This book does not claim to provide an exhaustive model of the ways religious language works. But then, the approach I use to study religious language would be inconsistent with such an attempt. Like all language, religious language is versatile and changeable. If I were attempting in this book to formulate rules that govern religious language, I'd trip over before I even began. Instead, my main aim in this book is to uncover at least some of what religious language does for us and what that tells us about ourselves as human beings. Only after considering why and for what purposes we use religious language will I begin to identify some of the common features we rely on to accomplish these purposes. In short, this book is an introduction to the topic of religious language. It focuses on some of the macro and micro features of religious language: religious vocabulary, archaic language, parallelism, metaphor and intertextuality, all operating within a set of contextual clues, text types and larger discursive strategies that often mark a text as religious.

My own research has focused on religious language in English within parts of the world where Christianity is prominent. So this book will substantially lean on what religious language looks like and accomplishes in this set of contexts. However, throughout the book, I will draw attention to scholarship on and examples of religious language in other contexts, wherever possible. I will consider the extent to which the ways people use religious language around the world support or undermine my overall theory, which is this: everyone, regardless of religious affiliation or lack thereof, participates in sacred-making through language.

I hope that this book will be useful for a wide range of readers, whether you have a passing interest in the subject, are undertaking academic study of religious language or are teaching in this area or a related one. Ultimately, what I want for every reader is that by the end of this book, you will be equipped with a few tools to identify and critically examine the religious language you encounter and perhaps even use and, ultimately, to reflect on what you hold sacred.

Chapter 2 will explore definitions of and debates around the concept of religion and what these mean for definitions of religious language. I'll first consider closed definitions of religion and their limitations, moving on to the open horizon that more inclusive definitions offer. I will put forward a functional approach to religion, which considers what religion does for us and why. Central to all of this are ideology and its relationship to language. I'll discuss this briefly, then end by explaining why I choose the term 'religious language' over other possibilities.

Chapter 3 begins with an overview of a functional theory of language and explains concepts like discourse and context. I'll then explore three functions of religion and religious language in greater detail, ending with an example of religious language at a funeral, where the functions of religious language meet.

Chapter 4 is the first of three chapters that comprise a toolkit for studying religious language. In each chapter, I discuss tools for identifying and analysing common features of religious language. This chapter will start by dividing religious language into two categories: explicit and implicit. This will take us to the exploration of contexts where religious language is likely to appear, both overtly religious and less so. I'll then concentrate on the ways a text's structure can communicate sacred meaning, moving on to common religious discourse strategies.

In Chapter 5, I get slightly more technical as I explain the different types of religious vocabulary and the ways that patterns in large collections of texts (corpora) can help us identify this vocabulary. This chapter also covers another common feature of religious language, archaism, which is old-fashioned or antiquated language. I hope you'll stick with me through this chapter, as I introduce (hopefully) helpful examples to make the technical explanations more concrete.

Chapter 6 is the last of the toolkit chapters. Here, I turn to religious parallelism, metaphor and intertextuality. My discussion here includes an overview of common types of religious parallelism, an overview of methods such as metaphor identification and an extended example of intertextuality in a text taken from religious higher education.

Chapter 7 is the first of three chapters that look specifically at religious language in various contexts. In this chapter, I consider prayer. Discussion begins with what is prayer, who does it and when. I review the purposes and directionality of prayer and how these can shape a prayer. The chapter then focuses on two prayers: the Lord's Prayer and the Atheist's Prayer. Taken together, these constitute a site of conflict, and I examine how their linguistic features point to fundamental sacred beliefs.

In Chapter 8, I examine religious language at a time of significant life transition: the time of human death. Specifically, I consider the discursive construction of a 'life well lived'. Whereas the previous chapter focuses on two short texts, in this chapter I use recently developed corpus linguistic tools to explore patterns in two large collections of texts, a corpus of obituaries from Legacy.com and the Corpus of Global Web-Based English (Davies, 2013). I also rely on critical, discourse-based approaches to investigate a selection of individual texts more closely. The chapter ends by considering the ways that the phrase 'a life well lived' marks certain lives as sacred and others as not so.

Chapter 9 is the final chapter that looks at religious language in context. Here, I move outwards to consider some of the many additional sites of conflict, crisis and life transition where people use religious language in sometimes unexpected ways. I review scholarship exploring religious language in international politics, sport, advertising, healthcare and conversion. In each, I point to opportunities for scholars of religious language to advance our understanding of the ways that people use language to sacralize spaces, people, objects, activities and, ultimately, beliefs.

The book concludes with a summary of the theory of religious language I have proposed, based on the many examples considered throughout the book. In the end, this book proposes a move beyond narrow characterizations of religious language as 'God-talk' to interaction with recent developments in various scholarly fields as well as engagement with empirical data from a wide variety of contexts. This approach speaks to the importance of a study of religious language which accounts for the porous boundaries between the sacred and the secular, and equips us to critique the religious language we all encounter and use.

Suggestions for use in teaching

I've heard some people say they dislike it when authors tell their readers how to use a book. If you are one of those people, please skip this section and carry right on to Chapter 2. For those of you who'd like to see how I use this material with my own students, please carry on reading!

I wrote this book primarily for my students, based on lectures and materials I created and have been testing and using in the classroom for years. To stimulate engagement and reflection, each chapter of the book begins with an image or short text and a set of questions. I discuss the text and answer these questions as the chapter unfolds. Each chapter ends with sections containing recommended reading and a variety of discussion and exploration tasks. These tasks can be used as the basis of a seminar. Suggested answers to these tasks can be found on the publisher's website.

When I teach on religious language, my module runs for twelve weeks, two hours each week. In the first hour, I lead a seminar group, based on a task and a set of questions that I've asked the students to prepare answers for, based on the previous week's lecture. In the second hour, I deliver a lecture on the next topic. A typical semester looks something like Table 1.1

The assessments give students the freedom to develop their analytical skills by choosing and analysing texts of their choice, taken from contexts that suit their interests. There are three assessments. The first two are text analysis proposals (one focusing on a text or texts from an overtly religious context, the second focusing on a text or texts from a 'secular' context; 750

Table 1.1 Sample Module Outline

Week 1	Introduction to the Module: What Is Religion? (Ch. 2)
Week 2	A Functional Approach to Religious Language (Ch. 3)
Week 3	Sites of Religious Language and Discourse Strategies (Ch. 4)
Week 4	Religious Vocabulary and Archaism (Ch. 5)
Week 5	Religious Metaphor (Ch. 6)
Week 6	Religious Parallelism and Intertextuality (Ch. 6)
Week 7	Religious Language in Prayer (Ch. 7)
Week 8	Religious Language at the Time of Human Death (Ch. 8)
Week 9	Religious Language in Other Contexts 1 (Ch. 9)
Week 10	Religious Language in Other Contexts 2 (Ch. 9)
Week 11	Religious Language in Other Contexts 3 (Ch. 9)
Week 12	Summary and Conclusions (Ch. 10)

words each, 20 per cent each). There is then a final essay/project (2,500 words, 60 per cent) which carries out the proposed analysis of **one** of the texts or sets of texts. The final project involves a critical analysis and discussion of religious language features in that text or texts, supporting the analysis and arguments with academic sources and empirical evidence.

2

What is religion? What is religious language?

FIGURE 2.1 *Inner Street Preacher, 2018.*

How would you define religion? What about religious language?
Now consider the photo in Figure 2.1, taken during the spring, 2018 industrial action across sixty-five UK universities. What questions, if any, does this photo raise regarding definitions of religion and religious language?

In this chapter, I attempt to answer the difficult question: What is religion? The aim of this chapter is to highlight the helpfulness of an approach to religion which doesn't attempt to set boundaries around religion but rather looks at all that religion does for us. After looking at closed and open definitions of religion, this chapter also discusses the relationship between ideology and religion.

Definitions of religion

What is religion? When historians and news reporters talk about the recent rise in religion's popularity, the kinds of examples that they tend to use often assume a commonly held definition of religion, as an institutionalized meaning system involving a supernatural being or some other invisible presence. But some followers of religion, such as non-theist Quakers and some schools of Hinduism, do not maintain belief in a supernatural deity. So some scholars add additional criteria, arguing that what differentiates religion from other meaning-making systems is its authoritative leadership who establish the boundaries of the religion, setting and systematizing the standards of orthodoxy and consecrating certain rituals. But even this is still a fairly exclusive way of thinking about religion since it disregards people who see themselves as spiritual but not religious. For example, what about people who don't attend overtly religious services but instead hold a more individualistic and less systematized set of beliefs?

Complexities like these have prompted inclusive definitions of religion. Consider, for instance, Jeppe Sinding Jensen's definition of religion, from his book *What Is Religion?*

> Not all religions share the same features, but typically they include ideas about superhuman agents, human fate after death, morality, ideas about the order of nature and the cosmos, conceptions of an 'other world' and – not least – how humans are to behave and think in this world.
>
> (Jensen, 2014: vii–viii)

Jensen's definition refers to an 'other world' but, as he says, this is only typical, not necessary. Definitions like his include a wide range of meaning-making systems, lived spirituality as well as organized religion.

But even definitions like these are still far from simple. Some have argued that the term 'religion' itself is fairly modern, largely Western and wholly unhelpful in getting to grips with the rich diversity, overlap and rapid change within the various streams of religious life and tradition (Smith, 1991). Although it is difficult to imagine a topic more widely studied and talked about than religion, the issue of what counts as religion is far from settled.

In this chapter, I explore in more detail this important but rather tricky question, what is religion? However, this chapter will quickly move away from attempting an exhaustive definition of religion. As Patrick McNamara famously quipped, 'Try to define religion and you invite an argument' (McNamara, 1984). My aim here is to sidestep this debate at least somewhat by adopting a functional approach to religion. This means my aim is to identify first what religion *does* and then, ultimately, the reasons people use religious language and where and why and how.

Closed definitions of religion

I've already mentioned the distinction between exclusive and inclusive definitions of religion. Another way of making sense of the numerous definitions of religion involves considering them as either closed or open. Closed definitions, rooted in a distinction between the secular and the sacred, attempt to mark out the boundaries of religion according to its core essence (see Hylén, 2014). Closed definitions are about limits, about supporting what is already known and using this to determine expectations for the future (Comstock, 1984). We can see this setting of limits in the following definitions:

1   '[Religion is] the belief in Spiritual Beings' (Tyler, 1873).
2   'Religious statements express the faith of persons, who as persons are involved in transcendence' (Smith, 1978: 183).

These definitions rely on the presence of something immaterial, a supernatural or otherwise transcendent entity. But a closed definition is any definition that aims to mark out religion's core essence.

Definitions such as these often require a distance between religion and the secular or non-religious world. It seems that often this distance operates as a kind of othering of either religion or the so-called secular world. In other words, it can allow those who consider themselves non-religious to maintain feelings of separation from religion and vice versa. Although of course there is variety among closed definitions of religion, in this way of thinking we define religion ultimately in terms of its opposition to the non-religious or the secular. Kim Knott and Matthew Francis explain this dominant way of thinking about religious-secular relations like this:

> Institutions, values, ideas, places, and people are assumed to fall into either one or another category – church or state, faith or reason, belief or science. Whether in the American constitution, the French educational system, or the British National Health Service, this separation leads to the marginalization of religion in the public sphere. Likewise, transgressions that threaten these boundaries are seen as impositions that should be forbidden: e.g. the opposition to public displays of religiosity in the clothing of nurses in the National Health Service in Britain and to school pupils in France.
>
> (Francis and Knott, 2011: 44)

In short, a closed definition of religion sees religion as equivalent to religious institutions and their adherents, beliefs, rituals, traditions and practices. The secular is anything else.

We can also find this religious-secular distinction in much of the scholarship on religious language. For instance, Noel Heather's book *Religious Language and Critical Discourse Analysis* focuses solely on overtly religious contexts, like a Christian hymn singalong and a pastor's Bible study (Heather, 2000). And so does the rich, interdisciplinary 2018 collection edited by Paul Chilton and Monika Kopytowska (Chilton and Kopytowska, 2018). In John Swayer and J. M. Y. Simpson's *Concise Encyclopaedia of Language and Religion* (Sawyer and Simpson, 2001), emphasis is on what Tope Omoniyi and Joshua Fishman call 'religion in the material sense which takes the form of institutions and establishments' rather than a spiritual sense which operates at the level of the individual (Omoniyi and Fishman, 2006: 1). Work like this tacitly characterizes religious language as talk to and about God by people affiliated with organized religion. The approach here involves locating members of organized religion and analysing their language.

But what about the uses of religious language by people who don't call themselves religious? For example, let's look at the word 'divine', which has fairly overt religious connotations and crops up in all kinds of places. Here are uses of 'divine' taken from the Corpus of Contemporary American English (COCA):

1   I heard the fresh sea bass is **divine** but you have to use an outhouse.

2   Tilda Swinton is **divine** as Amy's breezily cruel boss.

3   The marsh-mallowy texture of a well-made semifreddo is **divine** (Davies, 2008, emphasis mine).

In these excerpts, there's no reference to a supernatural deity. These utterances don't take place in an overtly religious context. But they do tap into well-established connections between food or celebrity and the sacred. So are they religious?

Often, when scholars using a closed definition of religion look at language like this, they assume that a process of secularization has occurred. In this way of thinking, the religious language is no longer religious per se but functions in a **new, largely different way**. Kevin McCarron argues, for instance, that even though religious language is common within the Alcoholics Anonymous (AA) community, AA is still wholly secular (McCarron, 2006). McCarron looked at 'recovery narratives' of former addicts who document their journey to sobriety. In these narratives, he notes that addicts regularly refer to explicitly religious concepts such as spirituality, resurrection and conversion. He concludes that religious language is used because it's comforting. It allows the AA community to talk about a deeply personal yet wholly secular experience using language that evokes mystery and complexity. But here's the clincher. McCarron also argues that using religious language like this is inappropriate. Even though the humanism of AA is a belief system and relies on religious language, it is not a religion, McCarron says. So people in AA should not be using religious language. When it comes to distinguishing between what is secular and what is religious, the sticking point here seems to be the 'God part'.

Other scholars share McCarron's view, that re-appropriation of religious language by 'non-religious' people and groups is a form of linguistic abuse. Some of these abuses are seen as more dangerous than others. Citing Steven Lukes's *Power: A Radical View* (Lukes, 1986), Jean-Pierre van Noppen takes this perspective, writing that to misuse religious language is to influence people's views, thoughts and preferences in such a way as to make them believe that these ways of thinking and living are divinely ordained[1] (van Noppen, 2011). Van Noppen gives the example of religious language in US politics, where references to God are commonplace and used to fuel nationalism. Here we begin to approach the territory of scholars who work on language and ideology. I'll come back to the topic of ideology in a bit, but what we see here is another distinction between religion and the secular. For some, it seems that the idea is that secular people should use secular language and leave religious language to the religious people (i.e. so long as the religious people keep their ideas to themselves).

In the meantime, let's go back to the examples of 'divine'. What can we make of language like this? Are these, put simply, secular re-appropriations of religious language? Even further, are these abuses of religious language? When I first began teaching on the topic of religious language, I treated them that way. But problems quickly arose, particularly as my students and I found evidence that religious language is used in strikingly similar ways across a variety of contexts, both overtly religious and seemingly secular. The lines between religious and secular were far from clear. I'll return to the relationship between food and religion later, but for now I'll say that as I studied religious language in more contexts, I began to embrace the ambiguity. Among many questions I pondered were:

1   Who decides what constitutes a 'proper' use of religious language and with what criteria?
2   What is the difference between appealing to the authority of a deity and to any other powerful authority figure or even authoritative concept (like food as sacred) when influencing others?
3   When does religion become an ideology?

In short, the question I faced was this: How can we differentiate between use and mis-use of religious language without drawing arbitrary lines? This led me to consider more open definitions of religion.

Open definitions of religion

Where closed definitions of religion are about identifying outer limits, open definitions of religion are about possibilities. These possibilities are what religious studies scholar W. Richard Comstock calls 'an open horizon', a path that leads to unanticipated understanding (Comstock, 1984). To help us get to grips with this, let's look at another example. In a special feature on religion in the journal *Sexualities*, Brian Duff compares the rites of pre-Vatican II Catholic mass and the rites of the modern strip club (Duff, 2010). In the former, he argues, we find priests in elaborate dress performing a ritual which gives the audience access to sacred truth. In the latter, the strip club audience finds another kind of elaborate dress, ritualized body movements and language and a form of individual and personal attention prompted by a monetary offering. He concludes that for many people sexuality functions as religion.

In order to see how well this comparison holds up, let's turn to Robert Cummings Neville's proposal for three criteria for religion, taken from the preface to the book *The Religious Dimensions of Confucianism* (Taylor, 1990). The first element is a **mythic, philosophical or theological cosmology.** A cosmology is a set of beliefs about the origins and nature of the universe and all it contains. It involves considering why things are the way they are and what this means. Returning to the strip club, Duff argues that in the pornographic, sex has ultimate meaning, and sexual desire is the means by which we can know our true selves.

The second necessary element of religion is **ritual,** that is, a set of deeply symbolic, repeatable sequences of activities that involve words, gestures or objects. Duff argues that the modern strip club enacts a ritual of male domination. Furthermore, he claims that the physical act of dominating women through sex acts as a kind of worship.

The final necessary element of religion, according to Cummings Neville, is a **path of spiritual perfection.** Religion changes people. It affects the way they live their lives. It is this last element that some scholars seem particularly to disagree on. Take Confucianism, for example. It is often perceived as a philosophical basis for living, a system of secular morality rather than a religion, not unlike the philosophy of AA. Still, philosophical movements like Confucianism and AA place followers on a path to a particular understanding of human life. Similarly, Duff argues that pornography draws participants into a path to sexual liberation, where men

> are called to a heroic role of the 'sexual liberator' and 'master' who initiates women into a knowledge of the 'truth' about their sexuality.
> (Duff, 2010: 692)

In short, according to Duff, the sexual domination of women is a means to achieving what it perceives as truth: sexual liberation. While some can (and probably should) question some facets to this analysis of pornography, Duff's comparison is nevertheless intriguing. It offers a good starting point for challenging dominant definitions of religion and considering more open definitions.

Duff and Cummings Neville are only two of many scholars from various fields exploring and challenging the boundaries between religion and the secular. Attempts at open definitions of religion include numerous definitions of spirituality as well as concepts such as the following:

1   Thomas Luckmann's 'invisible religion' (Luckmann, 1967)
    Invisible religion refers to the human tendency to transcend our biological selves and attempt to construct a set of meanings about the universe and ourselves.

2   Roberto Cipriani's 'diffused religion' (Cipriani, 2003)
    The values of organized religion spread throughout all societies through primary and secondary socialization. As a result, non-institutionalized forms of religion appear as instances of diffused religion.

3   Edward Bailey's 'implicit religion' (Bailey, 2010)
    Implicit religion is the set of beliefs and commitments people hold, regardless of their adherence to organized religion.

4   Karel Dobbelaere's 'meaning system' (Dobbelaere, 2011)
    Meaning system is an umbrella term that covers both religious and non-religious sets of meaning which consist of values and themes which give ultimate significance to individuals and priorities.

Each of these concepts considers religion as something far bigger and more widespread than belief in a supernatural being. Each offers us an opportunity to expand our minds when it comes to religion and to religious language.

Particularly important for the development of these open definitions is French sociologist Emile Durkheim's concept of the **sacred** (Durkheim, 1976). Durkheim argued that the sacred is simply that which is set apart from the ordinary, that which is treated positively with awe and respect or negatively with disgust or fear. The process of sacred-making is a universal phenomenon, not simply a feature of people who think of themselves as religious. And indeed, anything can be sacred, including food, as we saw in earlier examples from the COCA, and sex, as Duff argues. Key to Durkheim's argument are his definitions of other concepts, which flesh out the distinctiveness of the sacred. The **profane** are things that are ordinary and available for everyday use. **Religious beliefs** are articulations which distinguish the sacred from the profane. And finally, **religious rites** are fixed modes of action, rules guiding how a person behaves with regard to sacred things.

Building on Durkheim's theory of religion, Kim Knott's work on 'the secular sacred' (Knott, 2013) is especially useful in opening up the unstable categories of religion and the secular. Knott points to a notion central to open definitions of religion, **worldview**, most commonly credited to Immanuel Kant (Kant, 1987). Worldview refers to one's most basic presuppositions about the universe, knowledge and life. It comprises answers to questions such as the following, each of which is studied by various branches of philosophy:

1   What is prime or ultimate reality? (metaphysics)
2   What is the origin and nature of the universe and life? (cosmology)
3   What is the nature of external reality? What is our relationship to it? (teleology)
4   What is the nature of knowledge? How is it that we can know anything?(epistemology)
5   Does God exist? What is God's nature? (theology)
6   What are human beings and what is their nature? (anthropology)
7   What is the nature of value? How can we determine what is right and wrong? (axiology)

Put another way, the basic beliefs that make up our worldview are **axioms** (not to be confused with axiology), which *The Oxford Dictionary of Philosophy* defines as:

A proposition laid down as one from which we may begin; an assertion that is taken as fundamental, at least for the purposes of the branch of enquiry at hand.

(Blackburn, 2005: 31)

Because our worldview is axiomatic, we tend to argue from it, not for it, meaning that its truth is assumed. In her work on authority in religious communities, philosopher Linda Zagzebski puts it like this, 'We have no way to test that any belief we have is true without using our belief-forming faculties again' (Zagzebski, 2017: 98). Our worldview affects all that we do and say, and we see expressions of it even in the most mundane aspects of our lives.

Kim Knott's work focuses primarily on non-negotiable aspects of worldview, which are continuously reinforced, particularly in times of conflict or crisis. Knott uses the example of discussions around marriage and same-sex relationships to illustrate (Knott, 2013). For some members of institutionalized religions, the idea of marriage as a union between two members of the opposite sex is a sacred concern. For others, the human right to marry is fundamentally more sacred. In both cases, marriage is sacred but in different, competing ways.

However, as some have pointed out, even seemingly open ways of thinking about religion can be considered essentialist in some respects (see Schaffalitzky De Muckadell, 2014). For sure, the process of defining religion will always involve drawing boundaries for the purpose of identifying what counts as religion. These boundaries may be more or less inclusive, but they are nevertheless boundaries. And even institutionalized religions are constantly changing. So we need to account for the complexity and fluidity of religion. There is also the matter that followers of religion don't always behave in ways consistent with the religious tradition they identify with. And though I'll talk about the significance of authority in religion in a later chapter, people also have varying commitments to religious authority.

At issue here, as I hope you'll see as you carry on reading this book, is that worldviews can and do fluctuate and internally self-contradict. I mean, first, that the axioms that make up our worldview change over time, and some are more open to negotiation than others. And second, most worldviews are incoherent to some extent, meaning our axioms contradict one another.

The incoherency of our worldview may be because we are undecided about certain aspects of our views about ourselves and the world. Or it may be because it simply suits our own interests to conduct our lives inconsistently with our worldview, hence the platitude 'Practice what you preach'. Philosopher Angie Hobbs offers the following examples of these kinds of inconsistencies as they relate to money:

> It is perhaps not surprising how many unintentional anomalies there are in our thinking and practice, e.g. someone may say that they think money does not buy happiness and that being wealthy can be dangerous, yet exhaust themselves trying to make money to leave to their children, or they may say that they think investing in shares is wrong without bearing in mind that the banks they use or companies they buy from are doing exactly that.
>
> (A Hobbs, 2009)

Often, we may not even be conscious of our own worldview, living lives reliant on ways of thinking that we have absorbed from dominant norms around us but never fully examined, especially if our thinking has gone unchallenged. In this sense, worldviews are not just individually but also socially constructed. So we must be cautious about making claims about the extent to which a person is (1) aware of their sacred commitments and (2) wholly committed to them. But what we can say is this: our worldview comprises all that we experience and encounter and is in many ways socially, culturally, even supernaturally constructed. And our actions and indeed our language flow out of some aspect of our complex, often self-contradictory worldview.[2] As the Christian Bible puts it, "the mouth speaks what the heart is full of" (Luke 6.45).

Knott's notion of the secular sacred and other similar concepts expands our approach to investigating religion by considering the ways in which the lines placed around religion as a concept are in many ways arbitrarily drawn. Still, we must remember that the boundaries between closed and open ways of defining religion, like the boundaries between what is religion and what is not, are hardly clear-cut. Although this book argues for a functional definition, the aim is to approximate what Benson Saler calls a 'family resemblance' model (Saler, 2000). Rather than viewing a phenomenon as either religious or not (in a binary sense), my approach will be to map points of comparison between a particular phenomenon (like language in politics) and a clearer example of religious language (like language in a sermon). I aim to make a series of cases, based on these points of comparison, that a particular phenomenon resembles a religion.

Summing up, open ways of thinking about the secular, religion and the sacred offer an opportunity to study religion and religious language while accounting for the porous boundaries between the sacred and the secular. These open ways of thinking allow us to consider not just those looking to a sacred supernatural but those who ascribe ultimate significance to values and priorities without adherence to organized religion. But there are other concepts besides religion that we need to consider before we tackle the topic of religious language itself.

Ideology and collective identity

While religious language as a sub-field of linguistics is still in its infancy, there is substantial work in two closely related areas, ideology and collective identity. Such work takes a critical approach to language. This means that it considers in particular the power structures that language fosters, reflects and perpetuates.

Scholars such as Christopher Hart, Teun A. van Dijk, Veronika Koller and Theo van Leeuwen examine the discourse-ideology interface, considering the ways that belief systems manifest and are perpetuated through language. We'll look at this linguistic encoding in more detail later. When considering what counts as an ideology, van Dijk argues for the following criteria:

1 Ideologies are a set of beliefs.
2 Ideologies are axiomatic. This means they are a foundational set of beliefs, comprising a worldview.
3 Ideologies are socially shared. This means they comprise a group's set of beliefs about its identity, its existence and its reproduction. (On this note, an ideology differs from an individual worldview, which tends to be a mixture of the ideologies of various communities.)

4   Ideologies are gradually acquired, relatively stable and gradually
    lost, if group members disagree or leave a group (van Dijk, 2006).

Ideology controls all aspects of a group and manifests itself in the language
and social practices of the group. This looks a great deal like a religion,
doesn't it?

Interestingly, work on language and ideology has developed alongside
work on religious language, often without explicit acknowledgement of
their close relationship. For some scholars, what distinguishes ideology from
religion (as traditionally understood) is its resistance against mainstream
societal norms. In other words, a religion can become an ideology if it
runs counter to common sense, collectively held views in the surrounding
culture. So not all religion is ideological (see Rachik, 2009). However,
given the negative connotations associated with the term 'ideology', this
seems to imply (though perhaps unintentionally) that all resistance to
hegemony is problematic. In fact, some scholars argue that common sense
is itself a form of ideology. Within an overlapping area of scholarship
that focuses on language and collective identity, Veronika Koller's work,
for example, examines the linguistic resources that communities use to
'encode combinations of beliefs, values, norms, goals and emotions'
(Koller, 2012: 22). In Koller's model ideologies are networks of these socio-
cognitive representations that have achieved a sort of common sense status.
An example she gives is normative gender identity. Koller refers to religion
only as one contributing factor among many to the shared belief system
(what she calls socio-cognitive representation) of a particularly community.
But viewed through the lens of an open definition of religion, a social group
united around a belief system such as this is difficult to distinguish from a
religious community.

It seems that for most scholars working on language and ideology, all
religious communities (often not defined) are ideological but constitute their
own category. Van Dijk, for instance, mentions churches in his list of groups
that are ideological (van Dijk, 2006: 120). He argues for a typology that
distinguishes between a religious ideology and an ideology of, say, a pacifist
social movement. A distinguishing mark of religion, in this case, seems again
to be belief in a supernatural deity. In this way of thinking, some ideology
concerns itself with the material world, whereas religious ideology concerns
itself with the immaterial world (often but not only a deity). While we can
certainly agree that there are differences between a church and a pacifist
social movement, again, the boundaries between these two are not entirely
clear and, as we saw in the previous sections, they simply do not hold up.

Just like the question of what is religion, the question of what counts
as ideology has no easy answers. I've only scratched the surface of these
discussions. What I find helpful is to think of ideology broadly, as another
word for worldview, a term I will explain more fully in the next chapter. But

even this broad definition limits the extent to which the term 'ideological language' can apply to all religious language. Religious language does things other than communicate and enforce ideology. So while the discourse-ideology interface is helpful in some ways going forward, particularly in exploring collective sacred-making, it doesn't account entirely for religious language as a phenomenon.

In summary, work on language and ideology, broadly defined, concerns itself with the ways that belief systems manifest themselves in language. In Chapter 3, I'll discuss the specific ways in which categories of ideological discourse analysis can help our study of religious language. Indeed, scholarship exploring the ways that ideology encodes in language offers crucial insight for any investigation of religious language.

Ideological language, religious language or sacred language?

We've seen that the term 'ideology' is relevant for a discussion of an open concept of religion. However, as I've said, the term 'ideology' doesn't entirely suit my purposes here, for two reasons. First, religion (in an open sense) isn't one type of ideology. All overtly and non-overtly religious groups and indeed all individuals possess an ideology or worldview, which is both constructed through and reflected in part in their language. Second, religious language does more than encode ideology. It serves other purposes, as I will explain in the next chapter.

Still, is religious language the best term going forward? If it's true that everyone participates in sacred-making of some kind but not all people affiliate with organized religion, then why not use the term 'sacred language' rather than 'religious language'? After all, the word 'religious' in reference to those who consider themselves non-religious is problematic. The word 'religion' conjures up stereotypical images of the supernatural, of places of worship, of messianic and other religious figures, even of sacrifice, things that may not be shared by people who don't consider themselves members of widely recognized, institutionalized religion (see Lynch, 2014). In fact, uncertainty about the use of the word 'religious' has prompted a new term, the 'nones', which refers to people who claim no religion, for all kinds of reasons. They aren't just atheists. They are also people who may or may not believe in a god or the afterlife but who object to organized religion. There are therefore difficulties when using the term 'religious language' in such a broad fashion.

In addition, maintaining a distinction between the religious (institutionalized) sacred and the secular sacred, though not clear-cut, is still useful. Historically, the boundaries between religion and the secular have functioned as a means by which to establish an independent political arena and to navigate the relationship between organized religion and state institutions. Religious institutions and people of faith enjoy certain rights and freedoms under the law. In judicial courts around the world, there is constant debate surrounding who should have access to those rights. Animal rights advocates, for instance, have repeatedly argued that ethical veganism meets the criteria for institutionalized religion since the beliefs motivating a vegan lifestyle are religious in nature (Johnson, 2015). This issue came before the public eye again recently when, as reported in *The Telegraph*, ethical vegan Jordi Casamitjana claimed that he was fired from his job because of his 'philosophical belief in veganism' (Lyons, 2018). It is a political act to challenge the lines between religion and the secular.

Finally, there is the problem that scholars have either explicitly or implicitly defined religious language primarily as language connected with organized, institutionalized religion. To mark out my particular approach, should I therefore use the term 'sacred language', rather than religious language? But to complicate matters further, the term 'sacred language' has baggage as well. Although we encounter this term less frequently than the term 'religious language', it is commonly associated with an act of worship, that is, language used primarily in a religious service, a liturgy, for instance. It is also associated with the particular language of sacred texts. In Judaism, for instance, the language of the Torah is a 'sacred tongue'. And for (at least most) Muslims, knowledge of Classical Arabic as a sacred language is necessary in order to read the Qur'an, to pray and to carry out other religious duties and rituals (Haeri, 2003). In practice, then, the term 'religious language' is broader than the term 'sacred language' and so may be preferable.

There is further precedent for sticking with 'religious language' for my purposes here. Following in the footsteps of renowned sociologist of religion Edward Bailey, religious scholars frequently use the term 'implicit religion' when referring to the general human tendency to make sacred the world (Bailey, 1998). This, along with other similar terms like 'common religion' (Towler, 1974), 'surrogate religion' (Robertson, 1970) and 'quasi-religion' (Greil, 1993), shows that it is common practice among scholars to use the term 'religious' even to describe those who don't affiliate with organized religion. By choosing the term 'religious language', I am declaring myself to be in conversation with those scholars.

Finally, there is the matter of choosing a term that reflects the nature of sacred-making language. I will be arguing in subsequent sections and chapters that people talk about what they hold sacred in similar ways and for similar reasons, whether they are explicitly religious or non-religious. People take this sacred-making language from organized religions they are familiar with, for reasons we shall explore.

It is for all these reasons that I have chosen the term 'religious language' in this book. But I acknowledge that this decision is complicated and problematic in some ways. And I use this term without wishing to box anyone in against their will. At times, I'll rely on the term 'sacred-making' instead of 'religion' to acknowledge the complexity of this subject. This takes us to the next chapter, to another way of thinking about religion, according to what religion **does**.

Chapter summary

This chapter has introduced closed and open definitions of religion. These definitions reflect a debate around whether an otherworldly reality is what makes religion distinct. For the linguist, these distinctions aren't particularly helpful. An open viewpoint on religion allows for the possibility that anyone can use religious language, to suit their particular purposes. The approach to studying religious language I choose here continues in a tradition started by Emile Durkheim, who saw religion as an act of sacred-making. Since then, religious studies scholars have proposed many other open definitions, all acknowledging the fuzzy boundaries between religion and the secular. This chapter also briefly discussed terms related to religion: ideology and collective identity. Both are important for our work on religious language, as later chapters will explore. Finally, I explained my reasoning for using the term 'religious language'. In the next chapter, I will introduce a functional model of religious language.

Further reading

Bailey E (2010) Implicit Religion. *Religion* 40(4): 271–8. DOI: 10.1016/j. religion.2010.07.002.

Durkheim É (2008) *The Elementary Forms of the Religious Life* (Carol Cosman, Trans.) (2nd ed.). Oxford: Oxford University Press.

Hart C (2014) *Discourse, Grammar and Ideology: Functional and Cognitive Perspectives*. London: Bloomsbury.

Jensen J S (2014) *What Is Religion?* New York: Routledge.

Knott K (2013) The Secular Sacred: In-between or Both/And? In: Day A, Cotter C and Vincett G (eds.) *Social Identities between the Sacred and the Secular*. New York: Routledge, pp. 145–60.

Discussion and exploration

1   Some have argued that open definitions of religion are problematic because they normalize religion. What do you think this might mean? And why might this be a concern?

2   Read the article from *Vice* (https://www.vice.com/en_uk/article/8xpbvb/ we-asked-vegans-if-they-should-be-given-the-same-protections-as-religious-people), which reports on various opinions on the case for

classifying ethical veganism as a religion in legal terms. Then answer these questions:

   a   What competing definitions of religion do the various interviewees propose? What criteria for religion do the various people cite?

   b   Are there any instances of religious language in these articles, in your opinion? What criteria are you using for making that judgement?

   c   What do you think the religious language is doing in the text? What purposes is it serving?

   d   What issues do these articles raise that complicate the case for ethical veganism as a religion? Do you think ethical veganism could be considered a religion?[3]

3

Functions of religious language

FIGURE 3.1 *Jesus Saves, 2006.*

Consider the photograph of the billboard in Figure 3.1, taken in 2006 in Atlanta, GA. To what extent does this billboard have a religious message? Create a 'story' that explores the meaning of this billboard and particularly what the use of religious language means. Make sure you refer to aspects of the image that led you to your conclusions.

Now consider: Where did your story come from? How did you arrive at it? If you are working with others, to what extent did you arrive at a coherent interpretation of the billboard?

Many definitions of religion and religious language, like the ones discussed in the previous chapter, try to tell us what a religion is. They attempt to articulate the essence of religion, as well as whether that essence is fixed or whether it is flexible, even permeable. This discussion is important for any study of religion. But as we have seen, 'religion' is a slippery term. A functional approach to religious language helps us by considering the question: What does religion do? This is one way of opening up the study of religion and religious language, accounting for the possibility that indeed anything can be religious. This chapter will explore the usefulness of this approach and propose three main functions of religion: axiomatic, social cohesive and emotive.

A functional approach to language

Functional approaches to language have illuminated our understanding of the significance of contexts of language use. Broadly speaking, these approaches start by assuming that any feature of language, whether a word, a sentence, a text or an intonation pattern, exists in order to fulfil a purpose, relative to a specific context. In other words, language acts as social behaviour. This is not to say that all linguists taking a functional approach have agreed on what the term 'function' means. Some have argued that functional approaches place too much emphasis on social harmony, neglecting the powerful use of language to enact social change (Couture, 1991). The idea is that functional approaches look at how groups of people **tend to talk** and neglect how people **resist those ways of talking**. We'll come back to this in a moment.

In order to understand what it means to take a functional approach, a good place to start is the notion of **discourse**. The term 'discourse' is itself complex, defined in various ways by various scholars in various disciplines. One useful distinction is that between 'little d' and 'big D' discourses. 'Little d' discourse refers to language in stretches of text above the sentence level and 'big D' discourse refers to a combination of the text as an instance of language and the world(s) around that language, the context. James Paul Gee explains this distinction (Gee, 2004: 18) writing:

> The key to Discourses is 'recognition'. If you put language, action, interaction, values, beliefs, symbols, objects, tools, and places together in such a way that others *recognize* you as a particular type of who (identity) engaged in a particular type of what (activity) here and now, then you have pulled off a Discourse (and thereby continued it through history, if only for a while longer).

In his introductory book, *Critical Discourse Analysis*, Terry Locke introduces the notion of discourse by examining a photo of a billboard and inviting readers to come up with a story about the billboard (Locke, 2004). Following Locke's example, let's look again at the photograph in Figure 3.1 at the start of this section, which was taken in 2006 of a billboard in Atlanta, Georgia, in the United States.

This billboard constitutes a text, that is, it is a stretch of language, a form of 'little d' discourse. A linguist might begin by looking at the form that the language takes on the billboard. This is a text of just six words, possibly seven, depending on how you read it, and two sentences. When thinking about whether or not this text is religious, we might start by focusing on the overtly religious individual words and phrases in the billboard. The words 'Jesus' and the phrase 'Jesus saves' are the most obvious indications that something religious is going on here. These references to Jesus lend religious connotations to the words 'heal' and 'land'.

We might also consider the grammatical structure of the billboard's language, noting that the two sentences are simple in form. The first sentence contains one subject, 'Jesus', and one finite (marked by tense) verb, in this case intransitive, lacking an object, 'saves'. The second sentence contains a statement with a pronoun subject 'he' whose antecedent refers back to 'Jesus'. It has a verb with an epistemic modal 'will' and a noun phrase direct object (or nominal group direct object) 'the world'. These comments clearly utilize specialized linguistic vocabulary that allows me to talk about the relationship between the words in the text.

This is in some ways a good place to begin to understand this text. But comments like these don't fully engage with deeper questions such as: What does this text mean? What functions does it serve? In other words, **what is this text doing?** The text is made up of words, put together into chunks that are grammatically acceptable (ignoring for now the shared 's' in 'JESUSAVES'). But the text has also been put together in a particular way, in a particular place, at a particular time. On the face of it, the text might strike most people as religious. However, the name 'Jesus' and the phrase 'Jesus saves' have all sorts of uses in all sorts of contexts. For example, compare the use of phrase 'Jesus saves' in the billboard with the use of the same phrase on a T-shirt I saw recently:

Jesus saves. He goes to thrift stores.

Or consider the use of 'Jesus saves' in these lyrics of the Christian hymn 'We have heard the joyful sound':

We have heard the joyful sound:
Jesus saves! Jesus saves!
Spread the tidings all around:
Jesus saves! Jesus saves! (Owens, 1898)

In each of these, the same phrase serves different functions. The T-shirt example taps into and parodies historic links between American thrift stores (charity shops) and Christian community outreach. In the hymn, the phrase is more overtly religious, affirming and celebrating a belief in Jesus's sacrificial act memorialized in the Christian Bible.

So instead of starting with the language itself, we can choose to step back and consider bigger questions. Doing so would require investigating the category of billboards themselves.

1 What role do billboards play in this context?
2 What kinds of messages do they typically carry?
3 What events were current during the billboard's appearance?

In seeking to answer these questions, we might consider the religious and political landscape in Atlanta specifically and in the region more widely. To facilitate our understanding of this one billboard, we might compare it with other contemporary billboards containing religious and/or political messages. As our focus is on religious language, we would also need to ask about the functions of religion, including in political contexts like these. All of this would enable us to begin to construct a story about this billboard. What we want is a story that helps us understand how individual billboards like these, as instances of discourse, contribute to a larger set of meanings or Discourses. Table 3.1 contains one possible story about the billboard.

Table 3.1 A Story about the 'Jesus Saves' Billboard

Billboards, a type of outdoor advertising structure, are one of the oldest forms of advertising still in existence. They have both commercial and non-commercial uses. In the United States, non-profit, for-profit and government groups and even individuals use billboards to communicate overtly religious, political and other cultural messages. One of the most famous series of overtly religious billboards dates back to 1999, when an anonymous person started a campaign in Florida, called *God Speaks*, to use billboards to get people thinking about God (see here: https://godspeaks.com/about/). Although billboards are now banned in some states, the use of billboards to communicate religious and otherwise political messages is still fairly common.

Religious language in politics in the United States is well-established and linked to the notion of **civil religion, a set of shared beliefs, symbols and rituals which a society uses to make sense of its past in light of a deeper reality** (Bellah, 2005: 4). Civil religion binds a nation together and provides a transcendent justification for the state and its actions. Political leaders function as religious authority figures and make their authority and political policies sacred by invoking a sacred value or divine being. In the United States, as the dominant religion is Christianity, politicians draw on the language of Christianity. The United States is by no means the only country where politicians use religious rhetoric (see Chapter 9). In 2006, the American president was George W. Bush. According to some scholars, Bush invoked God in public speeches more than any American president prior (Coe and Domke, 2006).

Our billboard begins with the use of a phrase often repeated within the Christian faith to refer to Jesus's sacrificial death for His people. The use of present tense in the billboard's first statement and the lack of an object give this statement eternal significance and broad scope. This first sentence, on the face of it, expresses a belief that Jesus saves for all time. And his salvation is not offered exclusively to any one person or people. So far, this is an overtly Christian message. However, the red, white and blue stars and stripes of the American flag and the enlarged middle letters 'USA' are the first clear signal that this billboard is participating in and fostering civil religion, a close relationship between religion and nationalism. Note that this closeness is further accomplished by the shared 's' in the first sentence, which facilitates the enlarged 'USA'. This overt reference to the United States in some ways contradicts the timeless and expansive quality of Jesus's act of salvation. It suggests Americans occupy a position of privilege. We will come back to that in a minute.

The second statement in the billboard functions as a subtitle, reinforcing the extension of Jesus's salvific act to a specific geographical location. While the first statement uses present tense, the second uses an epistemic modal to demonstrate confidence in Jesus's salvation of 'Our Land'. We could possibly view this as having an apocalyptic meaning. There is no reference to the destruction of the world in the billboard. But entering the phrase 'will heal our land' into iWeb, the 14 billion word web corpus (Davies, 2018) produces texts about the terrible state of the world, expressing belief that God will rescue us all if we only turn to him, before it's too late. Here is an example from a news article reporting on a political prayer which American religious leader Glenn Beck posted on Facebook (Mansour, 2016):

I would like to ask that you, your family and friends join me for a day of prayers, fasting and humility. To beg the Lord to not remove His hand from us. To turn to Him and ask that He will heal our land.

The billboard's meaning is, however, open-ended and rather ambiguous. The word 'heal' indicates the land is wounded. But what is the nature of the wound? Let's return to that position of privilege Americans occupy in Jesus's act of salvation, according to the billboard. Who does the 'our' include? All Americans? Perhaps. But we could also see this as a message intended not to point individuals to the world religion of Christianity and to Jesus as Saviour but to point American Christians to the need for a government which privileges and legislates the values of Christianity. The reference to Jesus's salvific act may therefore be metaphorical, pointing to the state as the arm of Jesus. And the 'our' may therefore be exclusive. The nature of the wound is quite possibly the very existence of other belief systems.

All of this taken together points to the message's function: connecting with the observer-reader's feelings of nationalism and Christian religious conviction or even just familiarity, combining the two and imbuing them with a subtle sense of dread. Even more troubling than this is the billboard's veiled xenophobic meaning which privileges not just Americans but Americans of a particular religion. The billboard seems to be saying, ultimately, that Jesus will heal the United States from the blight of non-Christians. This is quite a political statement.

Already, the story I have told in Table 3.1 has far more detail than the short billboard. Note that in my analysis of this text, I took a multimodal approach, which means I considered visual imagery alongside linguistic choices. But there is still a great deal more we could say about this billboard. Again, this text taps into a tradition of linking billboards with religious and political statements. We might look in more detail at civil religion, that is, the close links between religion and nationalism in the United States and in other places worldwide. We could consider the extent to which xenophobia might be foundational to civil religion in this context. We could compare this billboard with others around the same time, which either contribute to or undermine this Discourse of civil religion. We could look at text types other than billboards. Overall, this approach involves considering the ways in which this text, as an instance of discourse, contributes to a larger set of meanings, Discourses, which function in a particular way at a particular time in history. This Discourse of civil religion affirms a layer of reality, a way of being in the world that is historically, culturally and socially situated.

By starting with the context and function of billboards, we consider what religious language in politics accomplishes as well as what billboards themselves do. Only then do we consider the linguistic choices that facilitate that. In this, we take a functional approach to the study of language. Note the word 'choice' in my discussion of the billboard. A functional approach defines language as a set of options, as a toolkit. As Geoff Thompson puts it, 'the exact nature of the tool used depends on the task at hand' (Thompson, 2013: 7). A functional approach starts with identifying that set of tasks, or functions, that we accomplish through language and the contexts in which those tasks take place. It then looks at the tools or features within language that speakers commonly use to accomplish those tasks. A functional approach to the study of language overlaps somewhat with the principles of discourse analysis in that they share a focus on the links between language and society.

It's important to note that the linguistic tools we commonly use when we produce a text are created collectively by users of a language. In essence, parallel to the relationship between discourse and Discourse is the relationship between an individual person and the culture(s) around them. The individual is always operating within a larger community, which both affects and is affected by the individual, particularly those individuals with authority and prestige. In the example of the billboard, I don't just mean that the billboard makers were using English in an English-speaking country. In this case, the makers relied on particular vocabulary, put into particular recognizable phrases, using a particular grammar and imagery that were recognizable to their audience and so facilitated their intended purpose. In doing so, they were able to tap into an existing story that is well-established in the wider social context. They exercised creativity but within constraints set by the larger social context as well as the nature of the text itself (billboard). Consider that without recognizability, the language choices that someone makes might be rendered largely useless. If we were to take this billboard out of its context and attempt to place it seamlessly into a different one, the audience would likely react differently, with apathy, confusion, even anger. However, a person might use this unfamiliarity to their advantage, in order to shock their audience or otherwise get their attention.

There are already established functional models of language, and these tend to be either formally neat and semantically messy or semantically neat and formally messy (van Leeuwen, 2008). For example, functional models can organize according to form (present tense, for example) and consider their many meanings (historical present, habitual present, instantaneous present, etc.). Barbara Couture refers to this as an approach which views reality as ordered, harmonious and stable (Couture, 1991: 271). On the other hand, functional models can start with a particular meaning and look at the many forms within language that people use to communicate that meaning.

Perhaps the most well-known, formally neat model is Michael Halliday's systemic-functional grammar, detailed in his book *Introduction to Functional Grammar* (Halliday and Matthiessen, 2014). Halliday's work has been complemented and expanded by many. Although models like Halliday's are primarily focused on grammar, as the name suggests, functional models do not isolate specific aspects of language. Rather, they look broadly at how grammar, vocabulary, information structure and other features of language and discourse combine and to what effect. This is because the various systems within language work together, not in isolation, as we saw in the billboard example. So while we may focus on one particular aspect of a text at any one time (like vocabulary), a functional approach always considers that language in its broader context, not only socially, culturally but also linguistically.

We face several problems in starting with formally neat models when considering religious language. Halliday's work, for instance, includes analysis of all kinds of text types, from overtly religious texts like an address by American evangelist Billy Graham at a National Prayer Breakfast to the poetry of Alfred Lord Tennyson. But Halliday approaches the analysis of all of these texts in a similar way, meaning religious meaning is not the central concern. He studies each text as one would any kind of language. Much of the work on religious language uses this Hallidayan model. What underlies such work is the assumption that religious language operates in most ways like any other type of language. Language is seen as the starting point, and religion the entity that makes use of it.

However, we do not mark all of our descriptions of the world and our experiences within it as sacred. For example, you might look out the window and remark that 'It's raining' to prompt a child to put on a raincoat. Encoded in this remark are grammatical and lexical decisions that point to an experience of the world and a desire to affect others. These are what Halliday refers to as the experiential and interpersonal functions of language.

But this remark isn't necessarily functioning as a statement of deeply held, sacred assumptions about the origins and order of the world.

On the other hand, what if you made the same statement, 'It's raining', after praying or perhaps just wishing for rain? Now the remark takes on deeper significance, and we can more convincingly argue that it is involved more directly in sacred-making. Functional models starting with form do not fully account for uses of language like these. As Tony Walter and Guy Cook put it, 'While rituals do in some measure fulfil these more fully researched functions, they have something else besides: a negotiation with the unknown' (Cook and Walter, 2005: 365). In some ways, it is this sense of mystery that existing models have failed to capture.

This book takes a semantically neat(ish), formally messy approach. I'll be drawing up a socio-semantic inventory of what religious does in this chapter, only then looking at some of the ways these functions are realized through language in the chapters to come. The advantage of this approach is that I can freely acknowledge that this introductory book only scratches the surface of the sacred-making potential of language. **What I propose here is simply a start to making sense of the ways that religion is accomplished through language.** Much more work needs to be done. The study of religious language necessarily involves investigating the ways that every feature of language (grammar, vocabulary, phonology, discourse) has the potential to encode religious meaning. Let's turn now to the functions of religion.

A functional approach to religion

In taking a functional approach to religion, the question we must start with is: **What does religion do and, in turn, what does religious language do?** In Chapter 2, I made the case for an open definition of religion as sacred-making. I argued, based on scholarship from various fields, that this is religion's primary function. Viewing religion through this lens has implications for what counts as religious language. Let's now explore what sub-functions we can identify within the broad category of sacred-making.

According to sociologist Emile Durkheim, religion has three sub-functions that combine to differentiate the sacred from the profane: **cognitive (or axiomatic), social cohesive** and **emotive** (Durkheim, 1976). Durkheim's model is a good starting point, but some have rightly criticized it for failing to account for religion's destructive action. The sections below maintain Durkheim's three-pronged inventory while expanding each category where appropriate.

The axiomatic function of religion

First, religion's **axiomatic function** participates in sacred-making by explaining the unexplainable, answering fundamental questions and providing meaning and purpose in a seemingly meaningless world. Paul Tillich posited that the function of religion is to express ultimate concern (Tillich, 1957: 5). Such comments tap into Immanuel Kant's notion of worldview. They point us towards the idea of religion as a quest for answers about fundamental questions about the world, life, morality and death, answers which declare what is sacred and what is profane or ordinary. More recently, as you'll recall, some scholars have adopted the word 'ideology' to refer to these axiomatic mental models of the world.

The axiomatic function of religious language, what some religious scholars call empirical usage (Binkley and Hick, 1962), involves making factual or historical claims connected to beliefs, people, things and events related to the sacred. These are what Durkheim refers to as beliefs or states of opinion. Overtly religious creeds such as the *Islamic Creed* and the *Four Noble Truths* in Buddhism as well as perhaps less overtly religious creeds like the *10 Principles of Burning Man* (Burning Man, n.d.c.) are a few obvious examples of texts whose main purpose is to articulate a set of axioms. But the axiomatic function of language can likewise be more deeply and more implicitly embedded in language, in systems of representation like transitivity and portrayal of social actors, as a later chapter will explore. One of the questions we will need to grapple with is this: Is all of our language use religious in some sense since it inherently reveals our perspective on the world? How can we answer this? Starting with Chapters 4 and 5, we'll look at some distinctions which can help us begin to mark out our territory.

The social cohesive function of religion

The second function of religion is its **social cohesive function**. Religion fosters community united around common sacred ideals, sacred people and objects, and sacred rituals. This community can involve people, animals or other living things or indeed non-living entities. It can involve a deity or some other invisible being or none at all. Religion involves connection and disconnection.

In terms of connection, the social cohesive function of religion reinforces group solidarity through shared ritual and can inspire people to altruistic acts. It acknowledges a religious community's interconnectedness by invoking a deity or other entity, through prayer, for example. It provides information about the sacred to others and influences their ideas about what is sacred. It attempts to bring new converts into the group via proselytizing. It resolves conflict. It controls and maintains conformity. Religion proclaims policies of behaviour and reinforces moral directives with the aim not only of meeting an axiomatic purpose but also of keeping the group's boundaries intact. Dominant members of the group may direct its members towards benevolent and beneficial thought and behaviour towards people and the world around them. In Figure 3.2, we encounter a Christian church's beliefs about the meaningfulness of love and influence

FIGURE 3.2 *Charles Street. Baltimore, Maryland, 2016.*

on the world. These are not just axiomatic statements but likewise social cohesive, directing its followers and potential converts to 'Love God. Love your neighbour. Change the world'.

Inclusion and exclusion go hand in hand, however. Particularly in times of conflict, religious language may serve to exclude sacred community members who transgress notions of the sacred and harm others. So boundaries can protect and serve. But religious language can also inspire people to destroy, to curse others and to commit violence and other forms of oppression. Indeed, history demonstrates that every religion, every community drawn together by shared notions of the sacred holds within it the potential for such devastation. Some have criticized Durkheim for not fully accounting for this particular aspect of religion. However, connection and disconnection are two sides of the same coin. Religion's ability both to unite and to divide (with or without violence) is consistent with the concept of social cohesion since there can be no community without boundaries. And we can learn a great deal about a community's sacred belief system by what constitutes a boundary violation. What are negotiable and non-negotiable? What beliefs, attributes and behaviours are necessary to remain part of an in-group? What constitutes rejection from that in-group? If you're part of the conservative arm of Christianity, feminism is a significant out-group marker, for instance (V Hobbs, 2015b). Indeed, some sacred transgressions have more serious consequences than others.

Some have argued that the social cohesive function of religion is what distinguishes religion from spirituality, which many see as more individualized and personal than religion. Some people would say that they believe in *something* but don't belong to organized religion. For example, in one study reporting lay definitions of religion and spirituality among older adults, religion was perceived as providing a community while spirituality was not (Schlehofer, Omoto and Adelman, 2008). However, people's notions of the sacred, even if more individual than institutionalized, are nevertheless constructed through interaction with others in the world. In their paper on the 'Spiritual Supermarket', Stef Aupers and Dick Houtman argue that

> spirituality is substantially less unambiguously individualistic and more socially and publicly significant than today's sociological consensus acknowledges.
>
> (Aupers and Houtman, 2011: 201)

The combination of various traditions into a mosaic of private spirituality is a socially and culturally constructed practice. In participating in such practice, those who consider themselves spiritual are building community. The Burning Man movement, a week-long festival held annually in the Black Rock desert of Nevada, now also a global cultural movement, is an example of this. The founders of the movement say that

> Burning Man is the sum total of the activities of its participants, and the ways to participate are as unlimited as one's imagination.
>
> (Burning Man, n.d.b.)

The community itself is founded on diversity of practice. It is the diversity itself which brings people together.

Consider also the act of prayer. Prayer is not just an act performed by so-called religious people or even people who call themselves spiritual. Prayer is often performed collectively with other people, but it can also be performed alone. For many different kinds of people from all walks of life, prayer is a means of reaching beyond the self, even to a community with no name. This community may not be made up of multiple people but may be simply an act of connecting with something external. Indeed, there is something deeply human about prayer. So while it may be useful at times to distinguish between religion and spirituality, the use of religious language to make connections outside oneself is not confined to institutionalized religion. The act of sacred-making is itself an act of social cohesion.

The emotive function of religion

The third function of religion is its **emotive function**. Faced with times of wonder and mystery, religion appeals to our imagination, arousing feelings and emotions that draw us close to what we hold sacred and to a sacred community. Religion is a means by which we can acknowledge human limitation or indeed affirm human aptitude. In his book *The Gold Bug Variations*, Richard Powers defers to religious language to celebrate the wonders and mystery of molecular biology beyond the grasp of human reason (Powers, 1991). About this, J.D. Thomas writes,

> Confronted by the complexity of life's smallest building blocks, the characters in *The Gold Bug Variations* recur to the language of religious devotion since the vocabulary associated with secularized scientific discourses cannot, for Powers, accurately illuminate the astonishing realities of evolution at the molecular level.
>
> (Thomas, 2010: 18)

Religious language gives us a means for appropriate response to the complexities we encounter in the world, in nature, in human experience.

Numerous studies have found that not only is religion a means to cope with mystery, but religion and religious language are also a powerful anti-stress mechanism. In times of amazement, unexplained phenomena, doubt, forgetfulness or uncertainty, articulation of and reflection on the sacred calm the mind. In times of grief and suffering, they offer solace. Religion is 'the refusal to capitulate to death, to give up in the face of frustration' (Yinger, 1957: 9). Articulating beliefs about what we hold sacred is a powerful means by which we cope existentially, with times of not only intense joy but also grief and loss. I'll explore this function of religious language in a later chapter when I look in more detail at language at the time of human death.

The functions of religious language: A brief example

In the next chapter, I'll begin to look in detail at some of the ways that these functions of religion are realized in language. For now, it's important to note that though one function might be more prominent than others in a stretch of language, religious language serves multiple functions at once. This means that analysis of religious language should therefore attend to all three functions. Here's an example.

Imagine you are at a funeral for a woman called Sarah. You see Sarah's father crying, and you wish to say something appropriate. There are of course many ways to go about doing this, but let's assume you and he believe in God and in heaven. In axiomatic terms, then, you decide to affirm, first, that Sarah herself is of great importance at this significant moment of life transition. So you choose to begin with a reference to Sarah. This places Sarah in a prominent position in what you say. Second, you want to articulate a set of deeply held beliefs about reality, as you see it. You believe that Sarah still exists beyond death. You believe in God and heaven and that Sarah now possesses the attribute of being in heaven with God. You want to articulate all of these truths, as you see them, in what you say. So on one level, you are choosing to articulate language that is axiomatic in its function.

But you also wish to acknowledge that this is a set of beliefs you share with Sarah's father. You wish your remark to function social cohesively. This reinforces your decision to put Sarah in a prominent place in what you say. Sarah is on everyone's minds, this being Sarah's funeral, and your mentioning her indicates that you are in solidarity with the group. This also leads you to choose to articulate only those things that communicate shared beliefs and to leave out any additional remarks that might divide you and Sarah's father. Note here that my analysis is considering not just what you say but also what you don't say.

Finally, and perhaps most importantly, your concern is comforting Sarah's father. You wish your words to have an effect on his emotive state and likewise on your own. So rather than asking Sarah's father whether he still believes in God or whether Sarah is in heaven, for instance, you choose a declarative sentence structure. This tells Sarah's father that Sarah's life after death is secure. So this results in your saying, perhaps among other things, that 'Sarah is with God now.'[1]

There are other ways to analyse this same utterance, but this particular utterance above requires a particular approach. This is because, first, it takes place in the context of a significant life transition, a key site for religious language. Second, it contains language with both strong religious connotations and implicit religious meaning. In the chapters that follow, I aim to offer an approach to the study of religious language that begins to capture its unique set of functions.

Chapter summary

This chapter has introduced a functional model of religious language, which starts with the question: What does religion do? In discussing the idea of function, I emphasized the importance of little-d and Big-D discourse in establishing context as our starting point for analysing religious language. I briefly considered other prominent functional models of language, noting that their main concern is not religious meaning. This means that we need a model of religious language that explores and accounts for its unique functions.

This chapter also identified three main functions of religion: axiomatic, social cohesive and emotive, each of which is present in any one stretch of religious language. These combine to construct a notion of the sacred in a way that taps into fundamental questions about the universe and life itself. Returning to the billboard example at the start of the chapter, we see these functions working together to:

1   articulate a belief in a sacred figure (Jesus) and his power to save the United States,

2   activate certain observer-readers' feelings of nationalism and Christian religious conviction, combining these to foster an in- and out-group, and

3   foster a subtle sense of dread but also hope in the sacred figure (or those who claim his authority) to 'heal' the United States.

The next two chapters will involve looking in detail at contexts where we are likely to encounter religious language, some of the more common discursive and linguistic realizations of the three functions of religion and advice on how to identify and analyse them.

Further reading

Besecke K (2005) Seeing Invisible Religion: Religion as a Societal Conversation about Transcendent Meaning. *Sociological Theory* 23(2): 179–96. DOI: 10.1111/j.0735-2751.2005.00249.x.

Fontaine L (2012) *Analysing English Grammar: A Systemic Functional Introduction*. Cambridge: Cambridge University Press.

Thompson G (2013) *Introducing Functional Grammar*. London, UK: Routledge.

Discussion and exploration

1   The image in Figure 3.3 is the cover of a recipe book associated with the restaurant chain Red's True BBQ, which until recently had locations in Sheffield and Leeds, United Kingdom.

As I did for the billboard at the start of this chapter, construct a story, which explores the use of religious language (and visual imagery) in this text in Figure 3.3. To help you do this, consider this quote from Wade Clark Roof's chapter 'Blood in the Barbecue? Food and Faith in the American South' (Roof, 2010: 109).

Anyone growing up in the American South ... knows that barbecue and Dixie go together like honey and flies. No other food is so distinctively southern, as obvious in the signs seemingly everywhere for barbecue, or simply BBQ, posted on billboards, the sides of buildings, and menus of restaurants, cafés, and honkytonks scattered from Mississippi to Virginia. By barbecue, I mean mainly pork ... cooked slowly and basted often with carefully prepared sauces; hence the word as southerners use it refers both to the food and its style of preparation. Anything less is not barbecue; indeed, southerners bristle when outsiders casually talk of barbecuing ... To defame the word barbecue in this way is not just a sign of ignorance, but a violation of a sacred regional norm. ... Food symbols are important

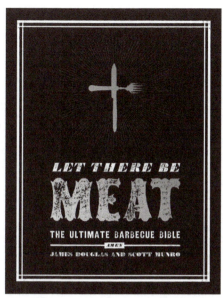

FIGURE 3.3 *Let There Be Meat, 2015.*

in any culture; more than just an object of curiosity or taste, they are bound up with a people's way of life, their deepest values and identities. That being the case, food symbols inevitably are implicated in religious and political matters. In fact, I shall argue that barbecue-and especially barbecue pork-is of crucial symbolic significance for the South.

You may also want to look at Red's True BBQ Facebook page or feedback from customers like these found here: https://www.tripadvisor. co.uk/ShowUserReviews-g186411-d3483712-r224647538-Red_s_True_ Barbecue_Leeds-Leeds_West_Yorkshire_England.html

2   Some have argued that Durkheim's concept of religion is so all-
    encompassing that what is essentially religious disappears. Consider, for
    example, this quote:

There are many things ... in our society that have a strong social sanction
but are not considered religious.

(Friedland and Mohr, 2004: 174–5)

What do you make of this claim? What are the differences, if any, between social borders and religious community borders?

4

Investigating religious language: Contexts, text types and strategies

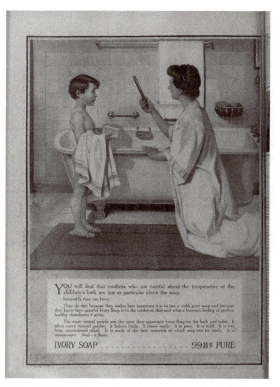

FIGURE 4.1 *Ivory Soap. Christian Herald, 1913.*

Figure 4.1 contains an advertisement for Ivory Soap. Is this a religious text? Why or why not?

Now consider the advertisement in light of the text below. Has this made you change your mind? Why or why not? What does this tell you about identifying and analysing religious language?

You love righteousness and hate wickedness;

Therefore God, your God, has set you above your companions

by anointing you with the oil of joy.

All your robes are fragrant with myrrh and aloes and cassia;

from palaces adorned with ivory

the music of the strings makes you glad. (Psalm 45.7-8)

In the previous chapter, I explored the question, what does religious language do? I presented a case for a semantically neat, formally messy approach to religious language and identified three functions of religious language: axiomatic, social cohesive and emotive.

In this chapter, we will begin considering the question: How do we go about analysing religious language? I'll start by differentiating between explicit and implicit religious language. Next, I'll identify contexts (both overtly religious and otherwise) where religious language is likely to appear. I'll then discuss two macro features of texts involved in sacred-making: information structure and discourse strategies. In the next chapter, I will hone in on some of the specific (micro) linguistic features often involved in communicating religious meaning.

Although this amounts to a kind of descending scale of macro units to micro units of a text, the approach I am using is not linear. Getting to grips with the use of religious language in a text will likely involve attending to all of the questions and features covered here, not necessarily in any particular order. Overall, the aim is to produce an introductory approach to identifying and understanding the ways language accomplishes religion.

The questions that this chapter tackles are:

1   What are explicit and implicit religious language?
2   In what contexts can we expect to find religious language?
3   What generic structures and discursive strategies do we often find in texts using religious language?

Explicit and implicit religious language

In the late nineteenth century, the manufacturer Proctor & Gamble published their first ad for Ivory Soap in a Christian weekly in the United

States. Seizing on the notion of Christian purity in Psalm 45 from the Bible and linking it with a cleaning product, Ivory Soap effectively marketized Protestantism. Cleanliness and tidiness, largely the work of women, were ritualized and inextricably bound with holiness through advertising. Industrial religion was born. It spread throughout the United States and beyond through advertisements like these but also through pamphlets, speeches and other textual tools by American Protestant reformers and industrialists (Callahan, Lofton and Seales, 2010). Industrial religion is not just an American phenomenon, either. In the UK, for instance, manufacturer *Out of Eden* now offers its own cruelty-free Eden Soap (Eden, n.d.).

Although we probably don't still consciously connect Ivory Soap with religion, in its original context it contained an example of **explicit religious language**. This is language with recognizable religious connotations and explicit references to sacred texts and people. Explicit religious language carries these connotations because it occurs more frequently in the context of institutionalized religion. Eden Soap is one we would more likely recognize as explicitly religious.

Explicit religious language is one of the most obvious signs that a text is likely doing religion. For instance, in August 2019, US President Donald Trump's claim, 'I am the chosen one', in trade discussions with China was immediately seen by many for what it was: messianic imagery (The Guardian, 2019a). This was a risky move, and the critical backlash was swift. But President Trump has filled his speeches with explicit religious language from the beginning of his campaign, testing his political base's receptiveness and laying a foundation for bold claims such as this.

Much of the scholarship on religious language focuses its attention on explicit religious language features in both overtly religious and so-called secular contexts. Examples include research on overt references to God by American presidents (Coe and Chenoweth, 2013) and on former Egyptian President Anwar Sadat's use of common religious expressions, verses from the Qur'an and other openly religious language in his political speeches (Abdul-Latif, 2011).

This work is crucial since explicit religious language like this is highly impactful. But language like this is also highly risky in certain contexts. It has the potential to provoke strong reactions and polarize an audience, either galvanizing or alienating them. Using Trump-like language in other political contexts can backfire, for instance. British politician Boris Johnson attracted ridicule in the run-up to the UK's exit from the European Union when he urged Prime Minister Theresa May to 'channel the spirit of Moses' and 'let my people go' (The Guardian, 2019b). Similarly, certain advertisements containing religious language work well in some contexts and spark outrage in others. Karen Mallia's article on religious imagery in advertising contains a rather long list of ads which were banned in some countries but not in others (Mallia, 2009). All of this points to the continuing importance of explicit religious language and our need to understand it.

This takes us to the second type of religious language, which is **implicit religious language**. This is language not specifically associated with or derived from a world religion but which functions as a form of sacred-making. Explicit religious language can gradually become implicit, as it is used en masse outside of institutionalized religion. Again, an example of this is the Ivory Soap advertisement. We no longer recognize that this language originally had explicitly religious meaning. But that meaning is nevertheless still attached, albeit hidden. We use and absorb implicit religious language often unconsciously. This means that typically language like this is more difficult to spot. However, if a text also contains at least some explicit religious language or is found in an overtly religious context, it can be relatively easy to locate implicit religious language. It extends the more explicit religious meaning in the text.

Implicit religious language can occur in overtly religious contexts as well as so-called secular contexts. For example, Hans Malmström's recent paper on sermons focuses on a particular linguistic feature known as 'hedging' within an overtly religious text type. Malmström examines the ways Christian preachers use hedging (non-assertive language like in the utterance, 'I am not sure if this is right, but ...') to engage listeners and acknowledge them as active partners in the context of a worship service (Malmström, 2016). He concludes that this linguistic feature in preaching helps highlight inclusiveness, blurring the boundaries between preachers and members of the congregation. In other words, it primarily serves a social cohesive function. Hedging also functions as a way of inviting listeners to come to their own conclusions, differentiating between the perspective of the preacher and the voice of the divine. This is hedging serving an axiomatic function, marking out non-negotiable and negotiable beliefs. Malmström's work reveals that hedging can serve religious purposes in an overtly religious context. We might expect to find hedging used in similar ways in other groups behaving religiously, even ones that don't call themselves religious.

But Malmström doesn't argue that hedging is particularly religious in and of itself, and this is a crucial point. People can use non-assertive language without participating in sacred-making. For example, as Ken Hyland has demonstrated, hedging is also used in academic writing to signal in-group membership (Hyland, 2005). Although academia can certainly behave like a sacred community (and believe me, for some people it does), it doesn't necessarily function that way in all circumstances for all people. **What matters when determining whether a stretch of language is religious or not is context.** Still, we could consider the extent to which hedging is more frequent in certain religious contexts.

So again, used outside of overtly religious contexts, implicit religious language can be rather elusive. Take, for example, increasing references to 'clean eating', 'clean living' and 'clean skincare', which were virtually non-existent before 2000 (see Figure 4.2). Although the word 'clean' does not appear more frequently in overtly religious contexts than in others, its use

FIGURE 4.2 *Clean Eating, 2018.*

to refer to purity and freedom from moral corruption is overtly religious. As we've just seen, in the late nineteenth century, soap makers capitalized on the belief system of Protestant Christian consumers, using religious language to link cleaning products with morality (Callahan, Lofton and Seales, 2010). This and other similar moves by advertisers and other industrialists have paved the way for any and all aspects of daily life to be imbued with moral meaning. So it is that a particularly religious meaning of cleanliness has become fairly common and used in a wider set of contexts to declare certain lifestyles and products sacred, as in Figures 4.1 and 4.2. This is a point I'll return to in later chapters.

Here is another example of implicit religious language in an often-tweeted quote from Sara Ahmed's popular book *Living a Feminist Life* (Ahmed, 2017: 4).

When did feminism become a word that not only spoke to you, but spoke you, spoke of your existence, spoke you into existence? When did the sound of the word feminism become your sound?

This text doesn't cite an overtly religious text or leader or use explicit religious words or phrases, but it functions as a solicitation of the reader's conversion narrative. It marks feminism as a sacred ideal in which you the feminist reader find your origins and to which you commit your very being. The assumption here is that to be a feminist involves an axiomatic depth of commitment. One's very identity is forged with feminism, and one's voice is united with (certain) voices of the movement. Ahmed taps into a creation narrative common to many world religions, which recounts the story of a deity who makes the world and everything in it. The suggestion implicit in her use of this narrative is that feminism is the god to which you commit. Not all feminists treat feminism as sacred, but clearly some do.

What all this demonstrates is that identifying and analysing explicit versus implicit religious language can be quite different processes. The problem we face is that any linguistic feature of a text can serve a religious function, given the right context. Truly, our task is gargantuan. One way of tackling this problem, when investigating implicit religious language, is to focus our attention **first** at the level of context and other macro features and **second** to the level of form or micro feature.

Sites of religious language

The difficulty we now face, as I hope you see by now, is this: How can we recognize and critically reflect not only on explicitly religious language but also on implicitly religious language like what we saw in the soap advertisement? Language like this has become so deeply embedded as to be almost unnoticeable.

Spotting overtly religious language in a text (a direct quote of a sacred text or reference to a religious authority, for instance) is often our first clue to answering the question: Is this text functioning religiously? But oftentimes, the religious language is more covert, as in the Ivory soap ad. To build a convincing case that a text is functioning religiously, we must consider context. This requires looking both at the text as a whole and at the world around the text. It involves considering the relevant characteristics that surround the text (both past and present), the set of circumstances surrounding the text, the author, the intended audience, the topic and perhaps even the audience response. Our understanding of the text also benefits from looking at other related texts, written on the same topic in a similar context or in response to the text we are looking at. All of this information helps us consider the text's overall functional purpose, what it is doing.

In the next section, I'll give an overview of places where we are likely to find religious language. This of course includes overtly religious contexts. But it also includes more universal sites of significance, where we are likely to encounter people talking about what they hold sacred.

Overtly religious contexts

Doing justice to the world around a text is quite a task. Still, our job is made easier by the fact that there are some sets of circumstances where we are sure to find religious language. First and most obviously, there are certain contexts that are overtly connected to organized religions like Christianity, Islam, Hinduism, Judaism, Buddhism, African traditional and many more. These contexts can be formal or informal, public or private, and carried out

Table 4.1 Examples of Explicitly Religious Contexts and Associated Text Types

Context	Examples of Texts
religious worship (public or private) or other ritual service	sacred text liturgy (mass, Eucharist) chant creed hymn and other religious song prayer prayer book sermon
significant life events in an overtly religious context (e.g. baptism, wedding, funeral, conversion)	sacred text hymn and other religious song liturgy prayer wedding invitation sermon, homily or message wedding vow eulogy obituary or death announcement conversion narrative sacramental books and other records
religious education (formal or informal, group or individual study)	sacred text theological and otherwise educational religious text religious lecture informal religious study group discussion creed
religious councils and other authoritative gatherings	sacred text canon law ecclesiastical court transcripts and documents ecclesiastical speeches ecclesiastical letters
everyday life of the individual follower of an organized religion	sacred text prayer religious talk online consultation with a religious authority figure profanity, blasphemy and praise religious music podcasts
religious news	newspaper, magazine and online news site

by a group or an individual. The language used in these situations can vary widely. Table 4.1 contains just some of the many overtly religious contexts and texts (both spoken and written) within those contexts.

Take religious worship, for example. Sermons are a particularly important text at this key site within world religion. Within many religious communities, sermons are delivered in a church, synagogue or a mosque. But they can also be delivered over the radio, on a podcast, via television or the internet. They tend to occur once a week, sometimes more often, and many people of faith download sermons during the week for extra listening. Lucy Rose, professor of homiletics, identifies four types of contemporary Christian preaching and their primary purpose, though these can combine in any one sermon (Rose, 1997):

1   traditional preaching, whose aim is to persuade the congregation of a truth claim.

2   kerygmatic preaching, communicating 'the unchangeable heart of the Christian gospel' (p. 42).

3   transformational preaching, where the 'purpose is to facilitate an experience, an event, a meeting, or a happening for the worshipers' (p. 60).

4   conversational preaching, whose purpose is 'to gather the community of faith around the Word where the central conversations of the church are refocused and fostered' (p. 4).

Whatever the type, the sermon is a time when members of a religious community are given instruction in a sacred text. The Christian sermon, within the larger genre of the religious sermon, is not unique in this way. The Friday sermon has an important place in communicating the message of Islam (Gaffney, 1994), and within Buddhism in Japan, the sermon is also central (Ishii, 1992).

The language of sermons tends to be particularly axiomatic, and sermons are a powerful influence on the people engaged. Linguistic work on sermons is limited but still rich. This includes study on politeness behaviour in sermons (Dzameshi, 1995) and genre analysis of fifteen sermons in Korea, the Philippines and the United States (Cheong, 1999). Some scholars have worked on Slovenian sermons, building knowledge about rhetorical units and lexical and grammatical features (Končar, 2008). There is work on evaluative language in evangelical Christian sermons (Ethelston, 2009) and on the use of contradiction (Singh and Thuraisingam, 2011). Most recently, Malmström's sermon study looks at words a preacher uses to mark the direction and purpose of a text in contemporary sermons (Malmström, 2016).

Religious language and even texts like sermons in Table 4.1 regularly occur in a wide range of situations outside of world religions or other overtly religious groups. For example, as I said in the last chapter, the act of prayer is something many people do, even those who don't consider themselves religious. Prayer takes place in response to a wide range of events. And profanity, blasphemy and other forms of 'bad language' are also found in all kinds of communities and often function in similar ways. Whether a person identifies as religious or not, profanity and blasphemy can bring a sense of control as well as intimacy and group bonding or, alternatively, signal out-group membership (McEnery, 2006; Stephens and Umland, 2011).

Over the years, I've found that some of my religious language students are initially sceptical that religious language is indeed all around us, not to mention that they themselves might use it. But before long, they are seeing it frequently in their everyday lives. My students have found religious language in all sorts of places, from the obvious places like a Church of England sermon archive to political speeches, from pop music to food advertisements, from football even to books on the art of handwritten letters. Once you learn to spot religious language, you don't have to look far.

Still, for the person just starting to explore religious language, there are places outside of organized religion where we are likely to find religious language. These places tend to have one or more of the following features: they will be moments of conflict and crisis, involve high stakes and/or entail significant life transition.

Moments of conflict and crisis

First, both within and outside of overtly religious contexts, we are likely to find religious language at **moments of conflict and crisis** (Francis and Knott, 2011). It is at these moments that a community's or an individual's notions of the sacred are called into question, requiring a re-affirmation of sacred borders. This involves rearticulating and reassessing what one holds sacred (axiomatic function), determining and declaring who is in and who is out (social cohesive function), thus galvanizing and affirming the in-group (emotive function).

'Conflict' is a broad term that refers to any breakdown in a community. This can involve violence but may not. Moments of conflict are also sites where different sacred communities may ally with one another because of shared sacred ideals relevant for that particular conflict. The different ways that feminists think about abortion rights is one example. A group of feminists and anti-abortion activists might work together despite disagreeing about other issues. Alliances like these reveal which aspects of their worldview each group treats as negotiable and non-negotiable. Indeed, other feminists may see such alliances as a betrayal of women's bodily rights, for them a more fundamental sacred ideal. So sacred borders are constantly in flux, being drawn and redrawn and overlapping at various times with other communities, as need or conviction requires.

Of course, these moments of conflicts can occur within and between different overtly religious communities as well. For example, in 2012, Greenville Presbyterian Theological Seminary in the United States terminated the contract of a professor close to retirement, claiming that he had violated their sacred ideal of the 'good family' by not requiring his wife to attend church. This conflict escalated as various Christians debated the legitimacy of their actions within a Christian belief system and asked themselves, just how sacred an ideal is the 'good family'? Alliances shifted and changed throughout as individuals and groups explored and tested the boundaries of their own belief system (V Hobbs, 2018a).

But thinking beyond conflict in and among organized religions, arenas like advertising, politics and sport are all sites of conflict where invoking sacred values is a powerful means to stir people's deepest-held convictions and convince them to buy, to vote, to support, to win. You may remember Kim Knott's example of debate around same-sex marriage from Chapter 2. And let's return to the UCU industrial action that I mentioned at the start of the same chapter. During this strike, religious language was a common occurrence. One union member tweeted a statement issued by Edinburgh University about its 'moral obligation to seek to minimise the disruption to our students' and asked, 'How about your moral obligation not to steal our pensions?'[1] The tweet not only referred to an axiomatic reality that this union member holds sacred but also challenged university management (via a question) to adopt this sacred value and change their policy. Uses of language like these demonstrate competing notions of what is morally required, according to a set of sacred ideals.

Religion and religious language also play a significant role in **moments of crisis**. These are times of extreme difficulty or danger, often requiring major decisiveness. Conflict and crisis share a close relationship. Crises are often instigated by conflict. They can emerge from conflict. A crisis can be at the personal or worldwide level. It can be existential or it can be material, precipitated by any triggering event, like illness, violence, economic loss or natural disasters like floods, famines, earthquakes or rising sea levels (Bugajski, 2011). Speaking about climate change, American politician Pete Buttigieg recently tapped into language like this to underscore the significance of activism in a time of environmental crisis.

> Let's talk in language that is understood across the heartland, about faith. You know, if you believe that God is watching as poison is being belched into the air of creation, and people are being harmed by it, countries put at risk in low-lying areas, what do you suppose God thinks of *that*? God would call it 'a sin.' (Miles, 2019)

Climate change in particular is a key site for religious language, used by people of varying positions to bolster their positions.

High stakes moments

The examples in the last section demonstrate that moments of conflict often involve **high stakes**, our next feature of situations where we are likely to find religious language. While everyone experiences conflict almost daily, high stakes moments or periods are intense, urgent, containing a large degree of uncertainty regarding the outcome. They are often complex and escalate quickly (Giebels, Ufkes and van Erp, 2014). In high stakes events, there is power, money, health, relationships and prestige at risk, and these factors fuel the use of religious language. Understandably, then, high stakes periods raise existential questions about personal and group identity, character and worldview. What do we believe? What has value? What do we stand to lose or gain as a result of this event? Who are we? Invoking sacred values helps to galvanize a group and convince others of the importance and meaning of a high stakes moment and even perhaps a particular outcome. The horrific Covid-19 pandemic of 2020 is an obvious example of a recent, even as I am writing, current crisis involving high stakes, when what was considered stable rapidly destabilized, when cultural standards and norms of standard operation are right now being constantly negotiated and renegotiated.

Significant life transition

The third feature of contexts likely to involve religious language is **significant life transition**. These include birth, marriage, death and other key life moments. Times like these tend to involve substantial change, which provokes reflection on fundamental questions about the world, who we are, where we are going, what we hold sacred. Considering the case of funerals, Guy Cook and Tony Walter point out differences in the language of traditional religious and contemporary secular funerals (Cook and Walter, 2005). Nevertheless, they write that the need for religious language,

> especially at times of transition, is by no means a monopoly of the [overtly] religious. It is apparently felt equally by the agnostic and the atheist. (p. 384)

They report that among the funerals they observed, whether traditional religious or secular, mourners used rhythmic and incantatory language in a way suggestive of humanity's powerlessness over death.

In addition to birth, marriage and death, religious language also appears at other moments of significant life transition. For example, conversion stories, also known as stories-of-becoming or change narratives, are more widely human that some might think. One example from the British National Corpus illustrates this, in an excerpt where a speaker uses the word 'conversion' to describe a newfound devotion to the Dutch-English sculptor and wood carver Grinling Gibbons. In this use of explicit religious language, the speaker marks Gibbons as sacred and set apart. The speaker goes on to compare himself to the apostle Paul whose conversion experience, as reported in Acts 9.18 in the Bible, involved a literal healing from blindness. The speaker is not just an admirer of Gibbons. He commits to him as if to a deity, as the use of religious language here demonstrates.

> 'It was a conversion experience,' he says, 'I had seen his carvings in a vague sort of way already ... but I found myself looking at them there in St James's as if for the first time. The scales fell from my eyes.' ('The British National Corpus,' 2007, A0X 1626, 1627)

In Chapter 8, I'll explore moments of significant life transition like these further, focusing on religious language at the time of human death. I'll also return to the act of conversion in Chapter 9.

Contexts and text types: Summing up

In summary, an important step when investigating religious language, using a functional approach, is to consider the text's context, the world around the text. If a text is intended for an audience that is or seems to be functioning religiously, the next steps involve considering who wrote it, to whom, about what, where, when and why. This helps us identify the Discourses surrounding a text and whether they are involved in doing religion.

We can of course expect to find religious language within organized religion. But there are other contexts where religious language is highly likely to be present. If a text connects to a highly charged topic, involving conflict, crisis and/or high stakes and/or occurs at a significant life transition moment, chances are that the text and the language therein are functioning religiously. Questions to ask about context and text type are:

1   Is the text used in an overtly religious context or at a key site of sacred-making?
2   What are the relevant characteristics of that context? Who is the text's author? Who is its intended audience? What is it about? What other texts is it in conversation with?

Religious text structure

We've looked now at contexts and text types in which we are likely to find religious language. But how can we identify these text types? Certain religious texts tend to be structured in particular ways, which make these texts easily recognizable to a reader or audience. Take wedding invitations, for example. As a significant life transition moment, weddings are one place where we are likely to encounter religious language. Occasions like these, historically linked with organized religion, often contain explicit religious references to sacred ideals, perhaps even a supernatural being. But they are also highly ritualized. Most people would immediately recognize a wedding invitation because of the look and feel of it, the quality of the paper, the lettering and the manner of delivery. But the structure of information on wedding invitations is our first clue that the text is indeed a wedding invitation. And more than that, a wedding invitation's generic structure reflects a sacred set of values, whether the organizers identify as religious or not at all.

The scholar Mohammed Al-Ali has carried out research on the structure and language of Jordanian wedding invitations (Al-Ali, 2006). He concludes that the way that the invitations are typically structured is heavily influenced by religious beliefs and, more specifically, masculine kinship authority. The father offers the invitation, and the father's name often appears first on the invitation. Other research has compared Muslim and Christian wedding invitations in the same geographical context, finding that in both sets of invitations, the father's name is prominent (Mohammed Sawalmeh, 2014). One difference, however, is that the Christian invitations mention the bride 100 per cent of the time, compared with 27 per cent on the Muslim invitations (Mohammed Sawalmeh, 2014).

In the United States, on the other hand, wedding invitations tend to name both of the bride's parents at the start, and the bride's name is always included and almost always before the groom's (Eslami, Ribeiro and Snow et al., 2016). This is true regardless of whether the wedding invitations contain other more obvious markers of religion, like a quotation from the Bible or a reference to God. Some scholars argue that these two features stem from a more egalitarian sense of parental authority but also a chivalrous 'ladies first' ideal (Otnes and Pleck, 2003). In short, wedding invitations (and other texts produced for a wedding) tend to follow a particular generic structure, which reflects a particular way of seeing the world and the people in it.

The study of the information structure and distinctive linguistic features of a particular text type is called **genre analysis**. This involves investigating the different functional components (called moves) of a text and the vocabulary and grammar of each component. This involves asking questions like: What information comes in what order? What language marks out each section of the text? What information comes at two significant points of emphasis in the text: beginning and end? What information is made prominent in the text through other means, whether visually or through repetition? What information is left out? As in the research on wedding invitations, answering these questions helps us understand what is made sacred in a text and in what ways.

Scholars who conduct genre analysis on religious texts often focus on a particular religious group and identify the contexts in which that group practises its religion. An example might be a formal worship service or some other special, ritualized gathering. They then identify texts from those contexts, like sermons, and compile large collections of that one type in order to trace linguistic and discursive patterns. This information helps them determine which texts are typical and which are unusual. In doing this, they build up a picture of what this type of text is usually like, in this particular set of contexts. Again, context is crucial, since any one type of text can vary across different cultural settings. Although there may be similarities across any one genre, a text's particular structure will move and shift according to its specific context and purpose.

In order to account more fully for context, scholars doing genre analysis often look at the world around a particular genre. Some conduct interviews with the people who create and use the texts. This creates a rich, insider description not only of the linguistic features of the texts but also of the ways a community uses them. A scholar might even become an observer-participant in the context where the texts were created. The aim is to paint as full a picture as possible of the religious language used in those contexts, considering its form, its function and perhaps even its distinctiveness. The benefits of this well-rounded approach are not just theoretical. The knowledge this approach produces helps people entering those contexts to acclimate to the kinds of interactions they will likely have and the kinds of texts (spoken or written) they will encounter and use.

Genre analysis has been criticized for focusing on larger patterns and not accounting for texts that depart from the pattern. When considering religious language, we want to consider not just what most people in a sacred community do with language but also what flexibility exists in those unspoken rules and what happens when someone breaks those rules.

Still, for those studying religious language, it's worth familiarizing yourself with scholarship examining the information structure of texts connected to organized religion. This will help you in a number of ways. First, you'll get a greater sense of the ways texts are typically structured in organized religion. This knowledge will allow you to identify more easily certain types of overtly religious texts and to spot copies and even parodies of these texts (see Chapter 7). Second, this scholarship often offers insight into the reasons texts are structured in a particular way, the sacred values that underpin them. All of this information will be useful as you encounter similar and distinct text types.

Although there are not many scholars conducting genre analysis (and other similar analysis) of overtly religious texts, a few recent examples are:

1   James Kapaló's work on Hungarian archaic folk prayers (Kapaló, 2011),

2 Robin Shoap's analysis of Pentecostal prayer, showing a rejection of ritualized prayer in favour of spontaneously produced prayer (Shoaps, 2002),

3 Mohammed Al-Ali's study on Jordanian death announcements (Al-Ali, 2005) and

4 Liliek Soepriatmadji's (Soepriatmadji, 2009) and Eun Ye Cheong's (Cheong, 1999) analysis of Muslim sermons in Singapore and Christian sermons in Korea, respectively.

Work like this helps us understand not just how texts are structured but also by whom and for what reason.

In summary, paying attention to a text's information structure can help us determine the extent to which it is doing religion. If a text adopts the information structure of a text type associated with organized religion and/or a significant life transition moment, it is almost certainly functioning religiously. But we must also consider that within other sacred communities (not overtly religious), texts can also be standardized. Once we've identified the text type that our chosen text is modelling itself on, if any, we can then ask in what ways the text follows the information structure of the genre, in what ways it departs from these and what the author of the text is making sacred. Questions to ask about the information structure of a text are:

1 To what extent does the text follow the information structure of an overtly religious text?

2 What does the information structure of the text reveal about the text's values and priorities?

Religious discourse strategies

In Chapters 2 and 3, I briefly discussed overlap between the study of religious language and language and ideology and collective identity. Work in these areas points us to patterns of meaning frequently used in the context of language and belief systems. If we start with an open definition of religion, we can refer to these patterns of meaning as religious discourse strategies, of which there are many (see van Dijk, 2006). In this section, I'll look at three of the most common strategies. Spotting these in a text helps us determine whether a text is functioning religiously.

The first strategy is **dichotomous worldview** (Francis and Knott, 2011). Some scholars call this an 'us vs. them' or 'good vs. evil' mentality. The dichotomous worldview strategy signals non-negotiable values and articulates the distinctiveness of what an individual or group holds sacred. In this way, this strategy serves the axiomatic function of religion. Perhaps more importantly, however, the dichotomous worldview strategy emphasizes social inclusion and exclusion. United around its distinctiveness, a sacred community uses this discourse strategy to reinforce group solidarity and group boundaries and may seek to encourage others to join the group or non-conforming members to leave. The general idea here is to emphasize what's good about being in the group and what's bad about being outside the group (see van Dijk, 2006). The dichotomous worldview strategy can also function emotively. Articulating sacred ideals and recommitting oneself to a sacred community can bring comfort and feelings of solidarity.

This discourse strategy has a variety of sub-strategies. And it can manifest in all sorts of ways lexically and grammatically. Linguistic choices to pay attention to include highlighting positive attributes, beliefs and actions of the sacred in-group or individual vs. negative ones of those outside of the group. For example, a text's use of pronouns (I/we/us/our vs. you/they/them/their) together with distinctive characteristics and actions of us vs. them is indicators that a text might be using this discourse strategy.

The billboard we looked at earlier implicitly relies on a dichotomous worldview, by suggesting that a politician claiming the name of Jesus Christ is best placed to heal 'our' land. And returning to the context of the UCU industrial action, tweets like the following, common among UCU strikers in early 2018, are likewise good examples of other ways this strategy might manifest itself.

1   KCL History picket, warmed by righteousness![2]
2   Sun shines on the righteous.[3]

The re-appropriation of religious language in the reference to 'righteousness' and the strategically incomplete reference to the words of Jesus in Matthew 5 of the Biblical text in the second example serve to differentiate not just one group from another but the sacred from the profane. Binkley and Hick (1962: 20) refer to this as a prescriptive usage of religious language. Language like this proclaims a policy of behaviour reinforcing a moral code. In this way, trade unions function at least for some as a sacred community and the strike as a sacred ritual, an assembly of righteous people affirming their transcendental values. By implication, those who are not striking are unrighteous at worst, common at best. The ritual visibly divides these two groups.

A second and related discourse strategy is the **push-pull strategy** (Chew, 2010). This strategy often appears in conversion narratives, where a religious community member recounts replacing one way of life with another. This exchange is often reported using the metaphor of a journey, which involves leaving behind (pushing away) an old, bad belief system and being pulled towards a new and positive belief system. In one conversion story, Jewish convert Elisa Hategan describes this dynamic as a feeling of being propelled towards her newfound faith (Hategan, 2015). She describes an abusive childhood, being 'friendless and desperate' and eventually joining a neo-Nazi hate group. After attempting suicide, she finally escaped but explains that 'something always clawed at the back of my consciousness, pushing me toward a Jewish path'. Upon finally claiming the Jewish faith, she 'burst into tears of joy' and felt a sense of empathy, recognition and understanding from the new community she now claimed. In this way, the push-pull strategy is facilitated by a dichotomous worldview strategy, the old life contrasted with the new. Scholars have also found this strategy among participants in Alcoholics Anonymous (AA), where attendees give testimonials about how bad things were before and how good life is now. According to some, this stems from the sacred belief system of AA, which encourages a redefinition and rejection of the old way of life and the adoption of a radically discontinuous new one (Greil and Rudy, 1983).

But the push-pull strategy might not always involve bad vs. good. Other contrasts might be present instead. Converts to Christianity among the Urapmin people in Papua New Guinea, for instance, distinguish not between bad and good but between hiddenness and openness when comparing their old traditional life with their present Christian one (Robbins, 2001). What matters is that a significant life transition has taken place that involves movement from one way of life to another.

A final religious discourse strategy is the use of a **sacred legitimating authority** to signal validity (Francis and Knott, 2011). Closed definitions of religion might require that this authority be a sacred text, an authoritative sacred person or a supernatural being. We saw this in the billboard example in the last chapter, and similar examples are quite easy to find. In spring 2018, for instance, over 1,000 people in San Francisco held a 'Beyoncé Mass', uniting around their icon Beyoncé's sacred music (Sigal, 2018). But a sacred legitimating authority need not be a person. For some, the authority could also be a set of traditions or even a set of values distinct from overtly religious sources. What is important is that the authority has the following qualities: the authority is **admired as an exemplar** of sacred ideals and practices, and the authority is **accepted to a level that it is difficult to question**. Appealing to authority works in affirming a way of thinking and living because of that authority's sacred status.

Reference and deference to a legitimating authority come in handy when meeting communal goals, regulating sacred boundaries and attempting to bring others into a sacred community. Although people don't seem to think well of hierarchy nowadays, it remains a fundamental structure for most communities. Sacred authority structures fulfil one of our deepest human longings for order and security. In appealing to authority, an individual or a community takes on some measure of that authority for themselves. They are no longer just an individual but an individual on good authority. This is the coercive potential of this discourse strategy, which is routinely exploited and used to enslave. In the billboard message at the start of Chapter 3, the name of Jesus Christ was used to support a political message about the current government. This appeal provided a platform for any politician to baptize their agenda with the name of Jesus.

But remember that a legitimating authority need not be overtly religious in nature. What matters is the nature of the authority and the way that it is used. Some have argued that, in fact, this transformation of intentionality and agency is the most powerful, important and widespread facet of religious language (Keane, 1997). Faced with a decision about what to buy, how to vote or what to think, the invocation of a legitimating authority provides guidance in living a life in keeping with one's beliefs. It can relieve our decision-making burdens in that if we do what the authority directs us to, we can deflect responsibility away from ourselves.[4]

Appeal to a sacred legitimating authority manifests itself in a variety of ways and can be as simple as naming the sacred authoritative ideal or person or directly quoting or paraphrasing their words, with or without naming them. We'll look at that more closely in Chapter 6. In the case of the UCU strike action in 2018 in the UK, strikers frequently appealed to a fundamental human right to fair pay in the form of pensions. Matthew Francis and Kim Knott use another example of Salman Rushdie's mention of the sacredness of freedom of expression, to which he appealed in the *Satanic Verses* controversy (Francis and Knott, 2011; see also Slaughter, 1993). More recently, in 2015, introducing Rushdie at a book fair, Frankfurt Book Fair director Juergen Boos expressed disappointment that Iranian publishers decided to boycott the fair. He nevertheless insisted that dialogue must continue saying,

> Freedom of speech is not a negotiable value. It is at the core of what we do. Publishers and booksellers are speaking up for freedom and it is the bedrock of a democratic society.
>
> (VoxEurop, 2015)

Like Rushdie, Boos used freedom of speech as a sacred legitimating authority to bolster the legitimacy of his event. Recall that when it comes to fundamental belief statements, we tend to argue from them, not for them. Their truth is assumed. So the use of a sacred legitimating authority in these instances gives more weight to our deeply held beliefs and is therefore a sign that our language to refer to this authority is functioning religiously.

This section has identified some of the common discourse strategies found in religious texts. A question to ask ourselves about a text's discourse strategies is:

> To what extent does the text rely on strategies commonly found in texts functioning religiously?

These strategies often primarily meet a social cohesive function, as they facilitate in-group and out-group dynamics. But this isn't all they do, as we'll see as we carry on.

Chapter summary

This chapter has covered larger-scale issues connected to the identification and analysis of religious language. I first drew a distinction between **explicit and implicit religious language** as a first step towards making sense of how religious language works:

1 explicit religious language: language that occurs more frequently in and is more obviously taken from world religion, whether that is a micro-feature like a word or phrase, a text type or a larger discourse strategy.

2 implicit religious language: language not directly associated with world religion but which nevertheless functions religiously. This kind of language may once have been explicitly religious.

This chapter also considered contexts where we are likely to find religious language, not only **moments connected to world religion** (worship, rituals, etc.) but also periods involving **conflict, crisis, high stakes** and **significant life transition**. Although I have presented these moments separately, they are closely interrelated. I next gave a brief overview of the concept of information structure and genre analysis. We can recognize texts taken from world religions by familiarizing ourselves with their structure. More than that, however, information structure gives us another window into considering what information is made more prominent and perhaps even more sacred. Finally, I considered common religious discourse strategies, including dichotomous worldview, push-pull and external legitimating authority. In the next chapter, I'll begin looking in more detail at individual religious language features, always keeping context at the forefront.

Further reading

Chew PG-L (2010) Metaphors of Change: Adolescent Singaporeans Switching Religion. In: Omoniyi T (ed.) *The Sociology of Language and Religion*. London: Palgrave Macmillan, pp. 156–89. DOI: 10.1057/9780230304710_8.

Francis M and Knott K (2011) Return? It Never Left. Exploring the 'Sacred' as a Resource for Bridging the Gap between the Religious and the Secular. In: C Kutz, H Riss, and O Roy (eds.) *Religious Norms in the Public Sphere: The Challenge*, pp. 44–8. European University Institute, Robert Schuman Centre for Advanced Studies, ReligioWes. Available at: http://igov.berkeley.edu/sites/default/files/francis-matthew.docx (accessed 29 November 2018).

Paltridge B (2006) *Discourse Analysis: An Introduction*. London: Continuum.

Pastor & Mrs V.P. Kariuki
and Major & Mrs John N. Wanjagi
request the honour of your presence
at the wedding of their children

Roni Mugure

A N D

Chris Wanjagi

as they exchange their marriage vows on
Saturday, the Twenty-Second of March, Two Thousand Fourteen
at Ten O'clock in the Morning, at Taji Gardens, Thika.

The reception will follow thereafter
at the same venue.

For the Christian, a wedding is a foretaste of the grand feast and
celebration that is to come when Jesus returns for his bride. Us, His church.

FIGURE 4.3 *Wedding Invitation, 2014.*

A & C

07.13.13

Mr. and Mrs. Daniel Vandewarker
request the honor of your presence
at the marriage of their daughter

Amanda Nicole Vandewarker
to
Cayman Keyes Gleason

Saturday, the thirteenth of July,
two thousand thirteen

five o'clock in the afternoon
Melrose Ranch
16757 Old Guejito Road
Escondido, Ca 92027

Reception to Follow

FIGURE 4.4 *Wedding Invitation Design, 2013.*

Discussion and exploration

1 The images above (Figures 4.3 and 4.4) are of invitations to a wedding in Central Kenya and in California. One invitation is more explicitly religious than the other. However, this does not mean that the other invitation is less religious per se. What differences in structure can you identify? And in what ways does the structure of each invitation encode religious beliefs?

2 What do you make of the claim that the transformation of intentionality and agency in an appeal to a sacred legitimating authority is the most powerful and important facet of religious language? Do you agree? Why or why not?

5

Investigating religious language: Vocabulary, archaism and parallelism

Foreword from Bishop John

There'll be a great deal going on during the period covered by this prayer diary. I mean 'a great deal' as in a lot happening, rather than in the Donald Trump sense of the phrase. That said, to use the term does, perhaps, remind us of Brexit and the need to pray earnestly for the coming together of our country following the huge divisions it continues to produce.

One of the best ways of overcoming upset and anger is to concentrate our prayerful attention on all the things for which we can be thankful. During this period we shall be celebrating harvest, an opportunity to give thanks for all the good gifts that God showers upon us. At Remembrance we can give thanks for the peace that this country has been able to enjoy since the conclusion of the Second World War. On Education Sunday we can give thanks for the education from which we all benefit in this country, free of charge.

Finally, our All Together as Kingdom People Day can serve as a reminder to give thanks for the redemption of the world by our Lord and Saviour and for the inauguration of the reign of God.

Prayer should be primarily about giving thanks and there is so much cause for gratitude.

September to November 2019

FIGURE 5.1 *Foreword from Bishop John, 2019.*

Figure 5.1 contains a text from the Diocese of Worcester in the Church of England, from their Prayer Diary from September to November 2019. As such, it's an overtly religious text about an overtly religious activity: prayer. But this text was also written during a time of unrest in Great Britain, following the popular vote to leave the European Union (EU) (Brexit) and the rhetoric on both sides of that significant issue. For some, leaving or remaining in the EU has become a core, even a sacred concern.

What is this text's sacred concern? In what ways is this sacred concern positioned in relation to Brexit? To what extent can you identify words and phrases that are doing the heavy lifting when it comes to the religious meaning in the text?

1 Identify the explicitly religious language (words and phrases) in the text.

2 Identify any additional language that may be involved in sacred-making in the text.

3 What is the religious language doing in this text? What concept/entity/belief is being made sacred?

Chapter 4 introduced contexts in which we are likely to find religious language, including overtly religious contexts and other key sites of sacred-making such as life transition and moments of conflict involving high stakes. I also differentiated between explicit and implicit religious language, moving on to introduce some of the macro features of texts functioning religiously, focusing on information structure and discourse strategies. In this chapter, as well as the next, I will provide an overview of common linguistic choices that an author makes at the micro level in order to do religion.

As I've mentioned elsewhere, all language systems are involved in sacred-making. I am unable to cover all of them in this book. These next two chapters will introduce religious language features largely connected to wording and word meaning. These include vocabulary, archaism, parallelism, metaphor and intertextuality. In this chapter, I'll discuss the first three. Along the way, I'll introduce methods for identifying and analysing each of these features. My focus here is of course on language, but we also need to keep our eyes on the worlds around that language. This includes all the contextual information I noted in the last chapter (who, what, where, when, why) but also any accompanying images and other non-linguistic elements, particularly since images, bodily posture, places, objects, music and so on, are significant in religion. Analysing religious language involves attending to these things as well, insofar as we can.

The main aim that we have in learning to identify religious language features is to understand what the religious language is doing in a text. What is it making sacred? In what ways and for what purpose? The questions that this chapter seeks to answer are:

1   What counts as religious vocabulary, archaism and parallelism?
2   What are their different types?
3   What steps can we take to identify these features?
4   Using what methods can we determine what these features are doing in a text?

Religious vocabulary and corpora

From our text at the start of this chapter, what words did you identify? Perhaps these words and phrases caught your eye:

bishop, prayer, prayerful, thankful, God, Lord, Saviour, giving thanks.

Aside from these, you might also have identified words like 'diocese' as overtly religious, though unless you are in the Church of England, this might not have been obvious. Bishop John also directs us to particular moments in the life of the Church of England, moments with formal names, like

Remembrance, Education Sunday, All Together as Kingdom People Day.

This text is a letter written by a church leader, intended for members of the Diocese of Worcester. So the language reflects the insider nature of the communication, to some extent. But ask someone from an English-speaking cultural context where Islam, Judaism or Christianity is prominent for an example of a religious word, and the answer is likely to be something like 'Allah', 'God' or 'Jesus'. Within the W_religion and S_sermon sections[1] of the British National Corpus (BNC),[2] three distinguishing words are 'parables', 'tabernacle' and 'Jesus' (The British National Corpus, 2007). The word 'Jesus', for example, appears around 114 times more frequently here than in other sections in the corpus. In Appendix 1 you can see the top 100 words that distinguish these two religion sections of the BNC from the rest of the corpus.

All of these words are explicit religious words almost every English speaker from a Christian-dominant culture knows and may even use but which are used with greater frequency in overtly religious contexts. For example, you may remember that in the last chapter, I discussed briefly the use of the word 'righteousness' to mark an industrial action in-group as positive and, by implication, the out-group as negative. Although the word 'righteousness' doesn't appear in this top 100 list, it is statistically more frequent in the overtly religious sections of the BNC than in the other sections (as are the words 'righteous' and 'righteously').

But not all of these explicit religious words are used outside of the religious in-group, however. What distinguishes the W_religion and S_ sermon sections of the BNC is mostly technical religious language, words like 'gentile', 'passover' and 'transcendent'. We saw some language like this in the Bishop John text as well. As an outsider to the Church of England, I don't know what 'Education Sunday' is, for example. These are words and phrases that the general public are less likely to recognize and use. This is because the texts from these sections were largely intended for an overtly religious audience or a subset of that audience.

Furthermore, many of these words are fairly formal, what we might refer to as academic. But not all specialized religious language is this way. A stream of viral videos have cropped up in recent years poking friendly fun at religious speak, like the 2012 viral video 'Things Muslims Say in Ramadan', which was re-booted in 2017 by British comedian Ali Official (Ali Official, 2017). And in 2013, Americans Tripp and Tyler posted a video on YouTube called 'Shoot [sic] Christians Say', which has since been viewed almost 2 million times and prompted comments like 'Came here as a Christian to laugh at myself' (Tripp and Tyler, 2013). The video contains clips of the two men repeating phrases that have become common among (particularly white) English-speaking Christians, particularly in the United States, like

> Bless his heart. It was a total God thing. I've been working on my testimony. I just pray you'd give him traveling mercies. You wanna be in our small group? Community group, access group, accountability group. He brought the Word. Don't they do seeker service there? I feel like that ruins my witness. I'm really trying to be intentional.

All of this language is insider language, but it isn't language you would expect to find in a sermon or another more formal religious text.

It's important to point out here that insider religious language isn't just confined to overtly religious groups. Any group that unites around sacred ideals will have particular words and phrases that outsiders are less likely to know and use. The global phenomenon known as the Burning Man movement has its own religious lexicon, including phrases like 'playa magic' and 'jackrabbit speaks' ('Glossary', n.d.). Specialized language like this is an important way of signalling and affirming sacred in-group identity and talking about sacred beliefs and practices. One thing all this tells us is that when it comes to religious vocabulary and indeed any kind of vocabulary, not all words and phrases are equal. Religious vocabulary can be inclusive in the sense that it is accessible to and used by outsiders, and it can be exclusive, used as a sacred in-group marker, for sacred in-group purposes.

We understand much more about the different types of vocabulary mainly because of the advent of corpora and corpus linguistics. Corpus linguistics is a method for studying language that involves building and analysing large collections of texts (both spoken and written) using sophisticated corpus tools. The BNC, which I have mentioned here and in other chapters, is one example of a publicly accessible corpus which has overtly religious sub-sections. And the American Brown Corpus and its British counterpart the Lancaster Oslo/Bergen Corpus likewise each have a religious sub-corpus, though each contains only seventeen texts (Francis and Kučera, 1964; Leech, Johansoon and Hofland et al., 1986).

Unfortunately, there are not many overtly religious corpora that are publicly accessible. Many scholars working on religious language have ended up building their own corpora in order to draw conclusions about how religious language works. But remember that religion as a category of meaning has most often been defined in a closed way. The religious texts in many of these specialized corpora tend to come from world religions, in other words.

In many of my own projects on religious language, I have built a corpus of texts, whether from overtly religious contexts or not, and compared it with larger, more general corpora. This has helped me identify both what is unique about the language of the texts I have chosen to study and also what is similar to more general language use. Let's pause for a minute in our discussion of religious language features and look further at the ways corpora can assist us both in investigating religious language and in building a theory around it. This will lay the foundation for what I will cover in the later chapters on religious language in prayer and at the time of death. In those later chapters, I'll illustrate the use of self-built and pre-existing corpora when analysing religious language. Here, these sections on corpora will also prepare us for a significant outcome of corpus-based studies of religious vocabulary: wordlists.

Corpus construction and analysis

One of the first issues to consider when constructing a corpus is of course whether or not you actually need one! Corpus-based studies start with a theory of or hypothesis about language and use a corpus to test that theory. But not all questions about language can be answered using corpora. Corpora are particularly helpful for determining what is most frequent, what is most prominent and what patterns are most common in a subset of language. They aren't as good for pointing to patterns of resistance in language. When building a corpus, a number of factors need to be considered. These include size, balance and representativeness.[3]

Size

There is no simple answer to how large a corpus should be. Some scholars argue that bigger is better, though 1 million words operate as a standard.

The important questions to ask include: How many words make up one text, how many total texts are in existence and how will the corpus be used? For instance, if we are interested in examining a particular genre, a smaller corpus could suit our purposes. One small study I worked on examined wedding exhortations that were only around 200 words long each, and the resulting corpus only included sixty-three texts. These were all of the texts in existence within the context I was looking at (V Hobbs and Miller, 2015).

Balance and representativeness

One of the reasons to design a corpus is so that you can generalize your findings and say something definitively about how religious language works. In order to do that, your corpus has to be balanced and representative.

Let's imagine that you wanted to build a corpus of Church of England Christian sermons during a ten-year period, with the aim of understanding what language is typical to those sermons. Your first instinct might be to collect all the sermons on the Church of England website within that time frame and get started. However, doing this raises questions of balance. The sermons may be of varying lengths, and the collection might contain ten sermons from one speaker and only one from another. This could lead you to think that the use of certain words or phrases is much more common in the corpus when actually one speaker has biased your sample. When designing a corpus, you need to make sure that the corpus is balanced in appropriate ways and represents the population you are trying to understand. Depending on your set of research questions, variables to consider might include: sex, class, age, ethnic background and belief system.

Existing corpora

Getting the size, balance and representativeness right in corpus design is not an exact science. There are many opinions on corpus design. But careful decisions must be made when building a corpus that suits the questions you want to ask and results in a principled design. The goal is to eliminate (at least some) bias so you can make reasonable claims about the ways language works. If you build a corpus to help you investigate patterns in religious language, you may wish to use an existing corpus as a model.

You may not have to build your own corpus, however, depending on what questions you want to answer about religious language. Pre-existing corpora can tell us how certain words and phrases are used in a wide range of contexts. If you come across a word or phrase and think it might be involved in doing religion, a corpus can help you build a case for that. Corpora can help us to determine whether particular words and phrases tend to have religious meaning and in which contexts. I've already mentioned some corpora in this chapter. Some others I have used in my own research include:

1 The BNC, XML Edition
   100 million-word collection of written and spoken samples of English representing a wide cross-section of British English in the late twentieth century ('The British National Corpus', 2007).

2 The Corpus of Global Web-based English (GloWbE)
   1.9 billion-word collection of texts from 1.8 million web pages from twenty different countries, collected in December 2012 (Davies, 2013).

3 The Corpus of Contemporary American English (COCA)
   560 million words of text (20 million words each year from 1990 to 2018), from a wide range of texts (Davies, 2008).

The BNC in particular is a favourite among linguists because of its size but also the care with which it was put together.

Corpus tools and tasks

Teams of linguists and software engineers have designed various online and offline interfaces to work with corpora. These tools allow us to perform various searches and run statistical tests in order to identify linguistic patterns. Some of these tools require a subscription fee. Others are free to use. Some of these interfaces have pre-existing corpora built into them. Others require that you upload your own corpora. AntConc is a popular, free and user-friendly corpus tool for self-built corpora (Anthony, 2014). #LancsBox is one of the most recent free software packages for the analysis of corpora (LancsBox: Lancaster University Corpus Toolbox, n.d.). One of its unique capacities is its data visualization tools.

Well-known, free interfaces for pre-existing corpora include English-Corpora.org (Davies, n.d.) and BNCWeb (Evert and Hoffmann, 2006), though registration is required. And for both pre-existing and self-built corpora, two popular interfaces that require a subscription are Sketch Engine (Sketch Engine, n.d.) and WMatrix (Rayson, 2009). I'll come back to WMatrix in the next section when I talk about religious vocabulary wordlists. Each of these tools has a wealth of how-to literature and manuals, many have videos to accompany them, and there are also many online videos created by users to guide you through the use of the tools.

There is some variation in what these different corpus tools can do, and a lot depends on how a particular corpus was annotated. Annotation is a process whereby a set of texts is tagged for morphological, phonological, syntactic, discoursal or stylistic features. The most common type of annotation is lexical, and this includes tagging individual words and phrases for part of speech (POS), lemmas (base word forms) and semantic fields. For instance, the CLAWS tagger is a POS tagger, which annotates each text with a grammatical category label (Rayson and Garside, 1998). Many of the corpus interfaces will annotate a corpus for you, using taggers developed by teams of researchers.

Some of the most common types of tests linguists perform using a corpus tool include frequency lists (or wordlists), collocations, keyness and concordancing.

1 Frequency
   These are a list of all of the items of a given type in a corpus (all the words, all the nouns, all the two-word phrases, for example), together with the number of times each occurs in a set of texts. If you are comparing texts or sets of texts of different lengths, frequencies will often be normalized (occurrences of a feature per thousand or million words, for instance). Often, looking at the most frequent content words in a corpus can tell you a great deal about the meaning being communicated.

2 Collocations
   These are words that occur together with statistically significant frequency. Collocations are identified using a statistical approach such as Mutual Information (MI) or t test. The higher the MI or t test score, the stronger the link is between the two items. However, it's good to look at both scores as evidence, since a t test accounts not only for statistical certainty but also for the size of the corpus. An MI score of 3 or higher (confidence level of 95 per cent) and a t test score of 2 or higher are usually taken as evidence that two items are collocates.

3 Keyness
   These are words, parts of speech and semantic concepts that are statistically more frequent in a text or set of texts compared to another set of texts (reference corpus).

4 Concordance lines
   These are a display of every instance of a particular word or other search term in a corpus, together with ten words or so on each side of every instance (co-text).

Religious vocabulary in the Bishop John text

To illustrate the use of these concepts, let's go back to the text at the start of the chapter. Looking at a word frequency profile of this text tells us something about the religious meanings that Bishop John is communicating. Setting aside common grammatical language (the, of, for), the most frequent content words are 'thanks' (5x), 'prayer(er)(ful)' (4x) and 'give' (4x). This gives us insight into what is being held sacred here in a time of intense political and social unrest: the need to give thanks through prayer.

Collocations are useful for telling us about the most common uses of words, phrases and other features of a text by calculating the kinds of language they tend to pair with. For example, the multi-word unit 'glass of' shows a semantic preference for words related to cold drinks, like 'water' or 'milk' (Baker, Gabrielatos and Khosravinik et al., 2008). Or, to return to our Bishop John text, the two-word phrase 'pray earnestly' is likewise a pair of word friends.[4] Put simply, language features have other features whose company they prefer due to frequent use and other factors.

Keyness, on the other hand, tells you the 'aboutness' of a text or set of texts. A corpus tool identifies key words, key parts of speech and key semantic concepts using two steps. First, it compares words, parts of speech and/or semantic concepts in one corpus with those in a (usually larger) reference corpus. The next step is identifying those words, parts of speech and/or semantic concepts that are statistically more frequent in one corpus as opposed to the other. Comparing the Bishop John text with the BNC reveals that the top 5 keywords and key phrases for our text are 'thanks', 'give', 'a great deal', 'prayer' and 'prayerful'. The text is consistent and in some ways unique in promoting a sacred ideal of thanks through prayer during unrest.

Explicit religious vocabulary: Wordlists

Research using corpora has given us important insight into vocabulary. It has allowed us to compile lists of words and multi-word expressions that are highly frequent in or unique to a particular set of texts. Such research enables us to classify different types of vocabulary (see Table 5.1).

In 2013, a group of scholars announced the creation of an updated list of core vocabulary, called the New General Service List (NGSL), containing 2,818 highly frequent words used in English across a wide range of written and spoken texts from the United States and Great Britain, comprising a 273,613,534 word corpus (Browne, Culligan and Phillips, 2013). The creators of this list claim that the list covers 92 per cent of the words in English texts in those contexts. For our purposes here, the NGSL contains at least thirty-six words with explicit religious meaning, for example,

church, convert, cross, pray, spirit, god.

While my estimate of thirty-six words may seem a small proportion of the entire list, this at least tells us that out of nearly 3 million words, explicit religious vocabulary is among the most commonly used vocabulary in the English language.

The NGSL gives us a starting point for identifying and making sense of the various kinds of explicit religious vocabulary in use in English. A problem we face, however, is that the words in these lists are not tagged for religious meaning. I identified thirty-six explicitly religious words in the NGSL based on intuition. I could check my intuition by looking at the use of these words in larger corpora (by examining concordance lines or collocation) or perhaps looking at the definitions of each word in a historical dictionary like the *Oxford English Dictionary* ('Oxford English Dictionary', 2007) or a dictionary based on corpora. But this is an extra step I'd have to take on

Table 5.1 Three Types of Vocabulary with Explicit Religious Examples

1 **General or core vocabulary:** words and phrases which most, even all, proficient users of a language know and use in general life contexts. Examples: pray, praise, spirit, god[5]
2 **Semi-technical vocabulary:** words and phrases which are used more frequently in specialized contexts than in everyday life but tend to be recognizable to and used on occasion by people outside of a particular community or discipline. Examples: holy, gospel, divine[6]
3 **Technical vocabulary:** words and phrases that have specialized and restricted meaning in certain contexts and so tend to be unrecognizable to (and rarely used by) people outside of a particular community or discipline. Some refer to this type of vocabulary as jargon. Examples: al-jumu'ah, catechism, heresy[7]

my own, and a rather lengthy one if I have a long text to work through. So these wordlists by themselves aren't particularly helpful for us when we're trying to identify more objectively the religious vocabulary in a text.

On the other hand, there have been a few attempts to create religious wordlists. One example is Michael Lessard-Clouston's *Complete Theological Word List* (Lessard-Clouston, 2009, 2010). It contains 100 frequent technical vocabulary words from lectures in a graduate school of Christian theology in central Canada. Lessard-Clouston published the complete list in 2010, which includes words such as 'apologetics', 'baptism' and 'doctrine' (Lessard-Clouston, 2010). The full wordlist can be found in Appendix 2. The Church of England text at the start of this chapter contains just one of these specialized words, 'redemption'. What we can reasonably conclude is that the intended audience of this overtly religious text is Christian but certainly not students on advanced theology degrees.

Before Lessard-Clouston, one of the more comprehensive attempts to identify and classify explicit religious vocabulary was by Thomas Chase (Chase, 1988). His work aimed to provide a detailed semantic classification of the religious vocabulary in English from Anglo-Saxon times to the present day. Using the bulk of the material from the *Oxford English Dictionary*, he organized 15,000 lexical items into 512 numbered categories, placed within five large sub-fields, which are:

1 belief, doctrine and spirituality
2 churches, sects and religious movement
3 the institutional church
4 worship, ritual and practice
5 artefacts

In 2009, Chase's work was included in *The Historical Thesaurus of English* ('03.08 (n.) Faith,' n.d.). The thesaurus is organized into three major sections and 377 sub-categories and further sub-categories. Chase's work on explicit religious vocabulary is found in the semantic category of 'Faith', which a user can browse for words with explicit religious meaning from the time of Old English to the present day. Another useful category is the semantic category of 'Morality' ('03.06 (n.) Morality', n.d.). For someone trying to determine whether a word or phrase carries religious connotations, this thesaurus' online search tool can be a good place to start ('Historical Thesaurus: Search', n.d.).

Another religious vocabulary list, developed from a broader set of contemporary contexts, is the 'religion and the supernatural' portion of the UCREL Semantic Analysis System (USAS). Designed by Paul Rayson and Scott Piao, USAS is a semantic tag set with twenty-one general discourse fields divided into 232 sub-categories. The tag set was designed using large representative corpora like the BNC (The British National Corpus, 2007) and large dictionaries like the *Collins English Dictionary*. The lexicon (wordlist) for the USAS tag set contains over 45,000 words and close to 19,000 multi-word units, and each entry in the lexicon is assigned one syntactic tag and one or more semantic tags.

The 'religion and the supernatural' semantic category is sub-category 9 of the *S* general discourse field (social actions, states and processes). S9 'religion and the supernatural' contains 1,167 single words, from 'abbess' to 'Zoroastrians', and 232 multi-word units. Table 5.2 contains prototypical examples of S9 listed in the USAS Guide (Archer, Wilson and Rayson, 2002), and the complete list can be found in Appendix 3.

There are two things to say at this point about this lexicon. First, the USAS lexicon acknowledges that formulaic language is frequent and important in language use. Formulaic language refers to the tendency of vocabulary to operate as multi-word units, like 'put a curse on'.

Second, as you can see from the examples in Table 5.2, like 'sixth sense' and 'Buddhism', the USAS semantic tagger doesn't just focus on explicit religious vocabulary from any one world religion. Instead, it reflects the

Table 5.2 Prototypical Examples of the USAS 'Religious and the Supernatural' Lexicon

afterlife	born again	Holy Spirit
Anglican	carol service	near death experience
apostolic	evil eye	non Christian
ark	God fearing	put a curse on
astrology	canonised	sixth sense
baptised	act of contrition	
Buddhism	bible studies	

language of several world religious. Still, the English version does reflect a bias towards language derived from Christianity, since the geographical context influencing the tag set, Great Britain, has strong historical and cultural ties to this particular faith. But the designers of USAS have extended it to cover many more languages, including Chinese, Malay, Dutch, Portuguese, Italian and Spanish. This makes it useful for investigating explicit religious vocabulary in these and other languages (and geographical contexts) in the near future.

USAS is more than just a tag set. The tag set serves as the basis for two online tools. Each of these tools allows you to run a text or set of texts through a semantic tagger. The free version, available online, lets you enter up to 10,000 words of English text (Rayson, n.d.).[8] It then tags each word with a general discourse field, a sub-field and other tags to indicate when the word is part of a multi-word unit or is part of a finer sub-field. This tool is another helpful step in locating religious vocabulary in a text.

The second online corpus tool USAS offers is WMatrix, which I mentioned earlier. There is a reasonably priced, yearly subscription fee for access to WMatrix, but you can also get a one-month trial for free. A strong advantage of this tool is that it accommodates texts written in a wide variety of languages (Rayson, 2009). Once uploaded, WMatrix annotates a corpus with POS and semantic labels. It then allows the user to choose among several options: calculating frequencies for single words, POS and semantic categories, identifying collocations and determining keyness. Just as you can do with the free semantic tagger online, you can upload a single text or a collection of texts to WMatrix and examine the extent to which words in USAS's 'religion and the supernatural' lexicon appear in your collection. For example, when I used WMatrix to compare a collection of Christian sermons on divorce with sermons on other topics (my reference corpus), I found that key categories of meaning include 'strong obligation and necessity' and 'cause and effect'. This told me something about the unique sets of meanings that accompany a conservative Christian concept of divorce (V Hobbs, 2019).

Using the 'Domain Tag Wizard', users can ask WMatrix to give preference to a particular semantic tag, like 'religion and the supernatural', when the tagger has to choose between possible tags for a particular word or phrase. Returning to the Church of England text at the start of the chapter, WMatrix initially identified only six words with explicit religious meaning:

God, diocese, pray, prayer, prayerful, redemption.

However, when I used the Domain Tag Wizard, it identified an additional three words:

celebrating, lord, saviour.

The tagger did not identify any multi-word expressions as being explicitly religious, though I suspect there are some it missed. These include:

pray earnestly, Church of England, give thanks, Lord and Saviour.

These may not be common multi-word phrases in English, but they do have explicit religious meaning. For example, the first four collocates for 'give thanks' in the GloWbE corpus are 'god', 'lord', 'let' and 'praise', pointing to the explicitly religious meaning that this phrase collocates with.

Implicit religious vocabulary

We've looked at how to get to grips with explicit religious vocabulary. But what about implicit religious vocabulary? Corpora can help us identify this kind of vocabulary as well, even in explicit religious texts. Let's look briefly at one example. Much of religious discourse relies on male images and metaphors, whether this is an overtly religious context or not. Many followers of world religions rely on such imagery to justify the subjugation of women in many contexts around the world, using it to construct a sacred quality attributed to being male.

Earlier in the chapter, I mentioned a project involving Christian sermons on divorce. As part of this project, I noticed that pastors rarely talked about or addressed women (V Hobbs, 2019). I wondered what evidence there might be that conservative Christian pastors are in fact largely directing their sermons at men, even when using seemingly inclusive audience-directed language. Does the Christian church's emphasis on male imagery and metaphors result in linguistic bias?

To answer these questions, I compiled a corpus of 101 sermons (743,693 words) from Sermon Audio ('SermonAudio.com', n.d.), an online conservative Christian sermon archive. This archive is international in scope but largely American-based. This corpus was made up of sermons by only male speakers (consistent with the archive), with no more than two sermons per speaker. The questions I asked were:

1 With what frequency are pastors referring to men and women in their sermons?

2 What patterns can be observed in the ways pastors talk to and about men and women?

3 What evidence exists that seemingly epicene (gender-neutral) pronouns are actually additional male references?

In order to answer these questions, I used #LancsBox and SketchEngine to identify collocational patterns and lemma frequencies along with close reading of concordance lines, where appropriate.

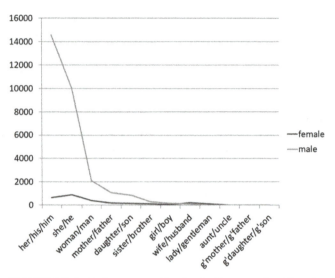

FIGURE 5.2 *References to Gender in Conservative Christian Sermons, 2018.*

Figure 5.2 contains the somewhat unsurprising results of this small study. Male references clearly dominate. I also counted the use of proper nouns in the corpus to consider the sex of named people, excluding Jesus (n=2,214). Pastors referred to named men 5,164 times, compared with 635 references to named women. From these sermons, I was able to get further information about the ways pastors represent gender by honing in on 'woman' and 'man' and examining their collocates. In the sermons, women were surrounded strongly by adjectives while men were to a greater extent surrounded with verbs. Men are doing, women are being.

Finally, I looked at epicene pronouns, including 'you', 'anyone', 'everyone' and 'whoever'. These were occasions where pastors were addressing or talking about the audience. In the sermons, the word 'you' occurred within five places of a male 2,814 times, compared to 156 times near a woman. The other words occurred close to a male fifty-five times, compared to ten times near a woman. I took it a step further and compared POS collocations of 'you' with 'man' and 'woman'. I found that 'you', like 'man', frequently collocates with verbs.

Findings from this corpus point to a strong discourse of **men talking about men**. This points to a notion of male as sacred within conservative Christian sermons and, as a key site of Discourse, conservative Christianity more widely. Considering collocational patterns of audience reference and explicitly gendered reference is a potential way to consider the extent to which **pastors are also talking to men**. We might consider that an audience is therefore, to some extent, primed in this way to consider the word 'you' as male, further cementing links between sacred and male.

This is one example of the study of implicit religious vocabulary, in an overtly religious context. In less obviously religious contexts, if we suspect there might be implicit religious vocabulary, we are better off starting with context, moving on to look at vocabulary patterns. We can then consider the ways that the vocabulary in that text is functioning religiously, even if implicitly so. I'll illustrate this in Chapter 8.

Religious vocabulary in summary

In summary, for those investigating explicit religious vocabulary, corpus linguistics has helped us in several significant areas. All of these areas tell us something about patterns in how religious language works. First, corpus linguistics helps us distinguish between the three different types of explicit religious vocabulary (core, semi-technical and technical) by looking at how these words behave in texts. Second, the analysis of large collections of texts has helped us begin to identify frequently used explicit religious words and multi-word phrases and formulate lists of words that tend to be used for religious purposes. Third, use of corpora can help us build a case for whether or not a particular word or phrase has religious meaning. This in turn means that we can more objectively analyse their use in any given text. We've seen that there are even a few online tools available to help us locate religious vocabulary. As these tools change and improve, our work gets easier, although remember that the usefulness of a tool depends greatly on the skill of the user.

In this section on religious vocabulary, I've sometimes referred to other linguistic systems like grammar. But when focusing on religious vocabulary specifically, wordlists and related tools give us a helpful first step to identifying this vocabulary. In a later chapter, I'll illustrate the use of USAS's two online tools, looking specifically at prayer. However, while wordlists can help us identify some religious vocabulary, they aren't fool-proof. Close reading of a selection of texts or your entire collection of texts (where possible) is an important step to check the use of words in context and to identify any additional words and phrases that might be religious in their function. You can verify your hunches by searching for these words and phrases in another corpus, reading them in context, considering the world around that context and using all of this to build a case that these words and phrases can and do carry religious meaning.

Once we've identified explicit vocabulary in a text, we can't stop there. Explicit religious vocabulary can and frequently does function as part of a larger discourse strategy like dichotomous worldview, push-pull or sacred legitimating authority. Using the name of an explicitly religious legitimating authority like Jesus, for instance, can be a powerful claim to legitimacy. Or, in conversion narratives, explicit religious vocabulary can be used to construct a semantic field of negativity around an old way of life and positivity around a new way. A **semantic field** is a group of words that share a particular property of meaning. In the case of religious language, a positive or negative field can establish boundaries, like old vs. new in a push-pull strategy or us vs. them and bad vs. good in a dichotomous worldview strategy. As we analyse the use of religious vocabulary in a text or set of texts, the aim is to explore what the use of that vocabulary is **doing** in that text. Tracking how individual words and phrases form a network of meanings in texts is an important aspect of that process. Questions to ask about religious vocabulary include:

1   To what extent does the text or texts contain explicit religious vocabulary from an existing wordlist?

2   What other words and phrases seem to carry religious meaning? To what extent does the context (and the use of these words in other texts) support your hypothesis?

3   Finally, what are the religious words and phrases doing in the text? Are they contributing to a set of religious discourse strategies? In what ways are they contributing to the three functions of religion?

Religious archaism

A second feature of religious language is archaism, language no longer in widespread use, 'a fossil of past linguistic usage' (Crystal, 1964: 152). Archaism is associated not just with religious language but also with the law and works of literature from writers like Shakespeare. Although not in widespread use, archaism also remains a feature of certain dialects that have resisted linguistic change. Archaism used for religious purposes is in some ways a sub-category of religious vocabulary, but it extends beyond to other systems of language like grammar and phonology.

Archaism is a hugely diverse set of elements, both linguistic and paralinguistic. Here, I'll discuss three common types: grammatical words, lexical words and syntactic structures.

1   **Archaic grammatical language:** words that don't carry content but instead connect the substantive, meaningful words in a stretch of text.
    Examples: ye, unto, O (in vocatives, which involve directly addressing a person or thing).

2   **Archaic functional language:** words that carry the meaning in a text. They are typically nouns, verbs and adjectives. They are sometimes called archaic lexis.
    Examples: hath, henceforth, thence, forthwith, whosoever, behold.

3   **Archaic syntactic structures:** unusual word order or syntactic structures that are out of place in most modern language usage. Archaic subjunctives that involve subject-auxiliary inversion are common, as in the first example below.[9]

Examples: so be it; God be with you; praise to the Lord, the Almighty; a treacherous foe and cruel.

These fossils of past language use do something important for us in contemporary sacred-making. In evoking the past, they offer a text a sense of tradition and history, giving an air of timelessness to whatever utterance we embed them into. They are therefore useful in meeting the three functions of religion by offering a sense of legitimacy through tradition. Many have argued, along these lines, for continued use of archaic language in overtly religious practice. But others are in favour of modernizing archaic texts on the grounds that archaism is too exclusive, especially when it is so out of use that few can make sense of it. Some have argued that in this way archaic language perpetuates unjustifiable boundaries between insiders and outsiders in a sacred community.

Still, archaic language use persists in many places as it remains useful for marking ideas, people, objects and traditions as timelessly sacred. Even the Beatles used it in their undeniably religious song 'Let it be', where 'Mother Mary' visits them in a time of trouble (see Figure 5.3).

FIGURE 5.3 *Let It Be, 2012.*

Here, as in other texts, we can recognize the religious significance of the archaic language by looking at the world around it, a world that draws on archaic language as one feature among many, to legitimize and emphasize the deep significance of its message.

Identifying archaism is not as straightforward as one might think, though sometimes it can stand out because of its less common usage. Looking at our Bishop John text at the start of the chapter, it is fairly clear that there is no use of archaism. This is likely to be because of the intended audience and current perceptions about the barriers that archaism can foster. But if we were to find archaism in a text, the question to ask is: What is it doing in the text? As always, we consider the world around the text and any other potentially religious stretches of texts and consider the extent to which the archaism is adding another layer of religious meaning. As we'll see in the chapter on prayer, the use of archaism can sometimes be parodic, for comic effect or ridicule.

Religious parallelism

If you have heard of the term 'parallelism', chances are it's because of the work of Robert Lowth, a Bishop of the Church of England and Oxford Professor of Poetry in the eighteenth century. In 1753, Lowth used the term to refer to a tendency in Hebrew poetry to pair words and phrases, which he defined as a 'correspondence of one verse, or line, with another' (Lowth, 1825: 14). In short, parallelism refers to the repetition of sounds, images, words, concepts, grammatical structures, phrases or sentences.

Like archaism, parallelism is frequent in a wide range of contexts, from poetry and art to law and astronomy. Its use dates back to some of the earliest-known texts, including sacred texts like the Bible and the Qur'an. Largely because of its links to these sacred texts, but also because of its poetic and rhetorical power, parallelism is still common in contemporary religious contexts (whether explicitly or implicitly religious). It adds emphasis, significance and authority as well as a certain poetic quality that comforts, stirs our emotions and arouses a sense of mystery. But just as we've seen with other linguistic features that can be used to communicate religious meaning, not all parallelism is used in this way. Determining what parallelism is doing in a text requires, as always, considering context.

There are many, many kinds of linguistic parallelism. There is parallelism in sound (phonological parallelism), in text structure (parallel structure), in syntax and in meaning. Let's look in particular at parallelism of syntax and meaning, as these are particularly common in religious language.

Parallelism can involve repetition of the first part of a sentence (sometimes called **anaphora**) or repetition of the last part of the first sentence (**epistophe**). One of the most famous examples of anaphorous parallelism in English occurs in Winston Churchill's speech during the Second World War.

We shall fight in France, we shall fight on the seas and oceans, we shall fight with growing confidence and growing strength in the air, we shall defend our island, whatever the cost may be. We shall fight on the beaches, we shall fight on the landing grounds, we shall fight in the fields and in the streets, we shall fight in the hills; we shall never surrender. ('We Shall Fight on the Beaches', 1940)

Most who heard this speech or who reads it now will have felt the impact of the repetition of 'We shall fight ... We shall fight ... We shall fight'. Churchill's use of the phrase over and over emphasizes to the audience that no matter the context, Great Britain will take the same action. It gives an air of simplicity to it all. What shall we do? We shall fight.

Here is another example of anaphora from the 'Ten Principles' of Burning Man, a growing community which meets in Nevada's Black Rock Desert every year to perform rituals connected to community, art, self-expression and self-reliance.

We achieve being through doing. Everyone is invited to work. Everyone is invited to play. (Burning Man, n.d.c.)

There isn't as much use of parallelism here, but perhaps even here you can feel the effect of the anaphoric repetition of 'everyone is invited'. It adds emphasis to a core concern of Burning Man, to build community, to involve everyone.

Former President of the United States Barack Obama often used epistophe in his speeches. One prominent example occurs in his speech to a church congregation in Charleston whose members a gunman killed. Here, the parallelism is working alongside other explicit religious language like 'amazing grace' and the direct quote from the hymn by that name. Together, they evoke sacred beliefs, uniting the congregation in an act of social cohesion and stirring their emotions at a significant life-transition moment.

If we can find that grace, anything is possible.
If we can tap that grace, everything can change.
Amazing grace. Amazing grace.
Amazing grace, how sweet the sound, that saved a wretch like me;
I once was lost, but now I'm found; was blind but now I see.
Clementa Pinckney found that grace.
Cynthia Hurd found that grace.
Susie Jackson found that grace. (Obama, 2015)

The listing of names here connects with every individual death and, as in Churchill's speech, brings calm and peace in suffering through the simplicity that repetition offers. Each victim has 'found that grace'.

Parallelism can also involve verbatim or near-verbatim repetition, like 'forever and ever'. Or it can manifest as **syntactic repetition,** where the grammatical structure stays the same but the words change. In the Bishop John text at the start of the chapter, there is an instance of syntactic repetition in these two sentences:

> At Remembrance we can give thanks for the peace ...
> On Education Sunday we can give thanks for the education ...

And James Matisoff gives this example of syntactic parallelism in his work on Lahu religious poetry, which also contains epistophe:

> Ah! for male and female pigs we beg and beseech thee
> for barking-deer male and female we beg and beseech thee. (Matisoff, 1991: 5)

We see here that part of the first utterance is repeated verbatim, while at the start of each utterance the structure stays the same and the words change. We can see another example of syntactic repetition in Psalm 114.1-2 from the Bible, shown in Table 5.3.

The first two lines (verse 1) involve syntactic repetition, followed by the last two, with some minor ellipsis (omission of a word).

Parallelism can also be **contrastive** (antithesis), which is where the meaning in the first utterance or sentence contrasts with an opposite meaning in the second utterance or sentence. Here is an example of contrastive parallelism from the Book of Mormon (Smith, 1921):

> For I say unto you that whatsoever is good cometh from God,
> and whatsoever is evil cometh from the devil (Alma 5.40).

This excerpt might look like an instance of epistophe or syntactic parallelism, and there is certainly some of that as well, but the contrast between good and evil also makes this an instance of contrastive parallelism.

One final type of parallelism I will mention is **synonymous parallelism**, where the same thought is repeated using words with similar meaning, as in Isaiah 2.4 in the Hebrew Bible:

> They will beat their swords into plowshares
> and their spears into pruning hooks.

Table 5.3 Syntactic Parallelism in Psalm 114.1-2

When Israel came out of Egypt, Jacob from a people of foreign tongue,	(When) V (came out) of W
Judah became God's sanctuary, Israel his dominion.	X (became) Y's Z.

In this type, the second line is an echo of the first, using near synonyms.

Just as with archaism, not all parallelism is used for religious purposes. As always, we consider the use of parallelism in light of the world around the text, its context and macro strategies, as well as any other explicit and implicit religious language features. This allows us to build a case that a stretch of parallelism is functioning religiously. Questions to consider include: Is the instance of parallelism taking place in a key site of sacred-making, such as conflict or life transition? Is the use of parallelism in the context of an overtly or implicitly religious group? All of these will help us build a case that the parallelism is functioning religiously. We'll look in more detail at an example of this in the chapter on prayer.

Chapter summary

This chapter has presented the first three of five religious language features I will cover in this book: vocabulary, archaism and parallelism. It has explored the usefulness of corpora in differentiating between types of vocabulary and more objectively identifying religious vocabulary and building a case for its role in doing religion.

In this chapter, I identified three types of religious vocabulary:

1 **general or core religious vocabulary**: words and phrases which all proficient users of a language know and use in general life contexts to do religion

2 **semi-technical religious vocabulary**: words and phrases which are used more frequently in religious contexts than in everyday life but tend to be recognizable to and used on occasion by people outside of that particular religious community

3 **technical or specialized religious vocabulary**: words and phrases that have specialized and restricted meaning in religious contexts and so tend to be unrecognizable to (and rarely used by) people outside of a religious community. Some refer to this type of vocabulary as jargon.

In the second, shorter part of the chapter I looked at **archaism,** which is words and syntactic structures out of common use which evoke a sense of tradition and therefore legitimacy to an utterance. Archaism is often fairly easy to identify, and some of its common types include:

1 **archaic grammatical language**: words that don't carry content but instead connect the substantive, meaningful words in a stretch of text

2 **archaic functional language**: words that carry the meaning in a text

3 **archaic syntactic structures**: unusual word order or syntactic structures that are out of place in most modern language usage.

Finally, the chapter gave an overview of parallelism. Parallelism is a common feature of religious language which refers to the repetition of sounds, images, words, concepts, grammatical structures, phrases or sentences. It comes in many types, some of which are:

1 **anaphora**: repetition of the first part of an utterance

2 **epistophe**: repetition of the last part of an utterance

3 **syntactic**: repetition of a grammatical structure of an utterance, using different words

4 **contrastive**: the meaning in the first utterance contrasts with an opposite meaning in the second utterance.

5 **synonymous**: the repetition of ideas across two or more utterances, using different words. This is closely related to synthetic parallelism, where the first utterance is completed or expanded in the second part.

In all, it's important to keep beating the drum of context. Any feature of language can be involved in doing religion. And various linguistic features work together to do religion. Any discussion of a particular linguistic feature must always be included in a larger question asking what religious ways the text is functioning and using what other linguistic means does it accomplish these purposes.

Further reading

Crystal D (1964) A Liturgical Language in a Linguistic Perspective. *New Blackfriars* 46(534): 148–56. DOI: 10.1111/j.1741-2005.1964.tb07472.x.

Fox J (2014) *Explorations in Semantic Parallelism*. Canberra: ANU Press.

González-Fernández B and Schmitt N (2017) Vocabulary Acquisition. In: Loewen S and Sato M (eds.) *The Routledge Handbook of Instructed Second Language Acquisition*. New York: Routledge, pp. 280–98.

Lessard-Clouston MA (2010) Theology Lectures as Lexical Environments: A Case Study of Technical Vocabulary Use. *Journal of English for Academic Purposes* 9(4) 308–21. DOI: 10.1016/J.JEAP.2010.09.001.

Corpora and corpus tools

Anthony L (2014) *AntConc (Windows, Macintosh OS X, and Linux) Build 3.4.1.* Tokyo, Japan.

English-Corpora.org (n.d.) English Corpora: Most Widely Used Online Corpora. Available at: https://www.english-corpora.org/ (accessed 8 November 2019).

NOTE: This allows access to corpora such as GloWbE, COCA, COHA, as well as the BNC.

Kilgarriff A, Baisa V, Bušta J et al. (2014) The Sketch Engine: Ten Years On. *Lexicography* 1(1): 7–36. DOI: 10.1007/s40607-014-0009-9. (see https://www.sketchengine.eu/)

Rayson P (2009) WMatrix. Lancaster: Computing Department, Lancaster University. Available at: http://ucrel.lancs.ac.uk/wmatrix3.html.

SermonAudio.com (n.d.). Available at: https://www.sermonaudio.com/main.asp (accessed 8 August 2018).
(an online archive of conservative Christian sermons).

The British National Corpus (2007) 3 (BNC XML Edition). Oxford University Computing Services. Available at: http://www.natcorp.ox.ac.uk/ (accessed 14 January 2019).

Discussion and exploration

1   If a text uses mostly core or mostly technical religious vocabulary, what might that tell us about the text's function?

2   There is other language in the Church of England text that is communicating explicit religious meaning. What other words and phrases did you identify?

    a   Go to https://www.english-corpora.org/glowbe/. In order to use this corpora interface, you will need to register as a user. This is free of charge.

    b   Click on 'Collocates' on the search bar and input the word 'kingdom'. The range below the search bar may automatically specify ± 4 words on either side of the search word, but you can also click on those numbers to indicate range. Click on 'find collocates'.

    c   Look at the first ten results. What does this suggest about the meanings associated with this word? Depending on where you are in the world, you can click on a collocate in that column (GB/Great Britain, for example) and examine the concordance lines for further context.

    d   For any other words or phrases you suspect have religious meaning in the text, perform a similar search.

6

Investigating religious language: Metaphor and intertextuality

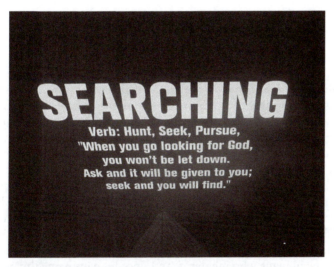

FIGURE 6.1 *Kanye West's 'Yeezus' Tour, 2013.*

This image in Figure 6.1 is from Kanye West's 2013 'Yeezus' Tour, at a performance at the Verizon Center in Washington, DC, on 21 November. The album and tour contained prominent religious language and imagery. In this image, you can see the top of what some called Mount Yeezus, a 50-foot high mountain that could turn into a volcano (Lopez-Sanchez, 2013).

His tour had a theme of redemption, and each performance contained five parts: fighting, rising, falling, searching and finding. Twelve female dancers whom some called disciples participated throughout, sometimes even carrying incense and crucifixes.

The text in this image has explicit religious vocabulary, such as the reference to God. The title is not explicitly religious, but its prominence in the text gives it a sacred quality, which the context surrounding the text affirms. However, there are other religious language features that are more prominent here. Can you identify these? Why do you think Kanye relies more on these religious language features and less on explicitly religious vocabulary?

Having talked about religious vocabulary and archaism, this chapter discusses two final more linguistic features which are commonly used to communicate religious meaning. These are metaphor and intertextuality.

Religious metaphor

More than any other feature of religious language, metaphor has received overwhelming attention by scholars, whether they are philosophers, historians, theologians or linguists. Much of the debate has come from a closed definition of religion and the limitations of human language in capturing a world-transcendent being. In other words, if religion involves a belief in supernatural beings, how can we talk about beings we cannot see?

Some, like the Protestant Christian reformer Martin Luther, felt the need to make language about God and other divine beings as precise as possible to reflect reverence. In this way of thinking, misrepresentation of the divine is the greatest danger. Others have sought to use analogy, with the assumption that the divine shares attributes with the material world. Thomas Aquinas proposed, for example, that if a divine being is the cause of the world, including the humans who inhabit it, and since humans name things as they experience them, we can attribute properties of worldly (created) things to the divine. For example, we may experience a quality of 'goodness' in people. If we believe that God made people, then surely we can apply this quality to God and say that 'God is good'. As some have pointed out, however, what of the differences between humans and the divine? And what about those who don't believe that a divine being created the world? The question remains: How can we speak about things that we don't completely grasp with our minds? Rejecting this divine-human causation, more recent theories have looked to metaphor to describe the ways we speak about things we can't fully articulate literally.

Metaphor is just one of many types of figurative representation. A symbol, for example, is a non-linguistic type of figurative representation, like Kanye's use of the Christian crucifix. Within language, figurative representation can take place through Aquinas's preferred method of analogy, which is a type of relation without tension, a connection between two concepts that seems appropriate. Other types of figurative language include allegory and satire as well as synecdoche and metonymy. In these last two, one word or phrase is used to stand in for the whole. We can find a complex mixture of synecdoche, metonymy and metaphor in this verse from the Gospel of Mark 16.19 in the Bible:

After the Lord Jesus had spoken to them, he was taken up into heaven and he sat at the **right hand of God.** (emphasis mine)

The hand of God is a synecdoche in the sense that a part is used to represent the whole, but there is also a layer of metonymy and metaphor. God is represented as having a physical body (metaphor) and Christ's throne figures his reign over the heavens and earth (metonymy). What results is 'a metaphorically and metonymically complex anthropomorphic image of power and status, which is mapped onto the divine' (Barcelona, 2003: 10).

Figurative language is found anywhere and everywhere we communicate, from politics, science and the law to everyday conversation on all manner of topics. Metaphor's main function is to help us talk about things that we can't fully make sense of cognitively. Metaphor in particular taps into the limitations we experience with a purely rationalist approach to knowledge and experience. As embodied humans, we encounter and experience things in our environment through our senses, our emotions, our minds, all aspects of our bodies. The language that we use to describe our embodied human lives reflects that reality. So metaphor and also metonymy are rooted in human bodily experience and interaction with the world around us. As Janet Martin Soskice puts it, a metaphor's virtue is in its vagueness (Soskice, 2007). It extends our limited cognitive understanding of what we experience by viewing that experience through the lens of things we **can** more fully understand, things we can touch, taste, see and locate in the world. But metaphors also shape our experience of the world, as I'll explain in a moment.

In terms of meaning, a metaphor has two components: the target domain and the vehicle domain.

The **target domain** is what we are trying to explain or understand. Think of it as the notion we are trying to aim for.
The **vehicle domain** (sometimes called the source) is what we use in order to reach a better understanding of the target domain.

So in metaphor, the vehicle is what we take to get to the target. Between these two domains is a kind of tension, an incompatibility in the sense that there

FIGURE 6.2 *Jesus Light of the World, 1974.*

is no complete overlap in meaning. This tension is crucial to metaphor and what makes it distinct from analogy, though these two categories are often difficult to differentiate. When a metaphor is new, that tension is noticeable and helps us see the target in a new way. But when a metaphor has been used many times over, the tension becomes less noticeable. In Figure 6.2, for example, the vehicle domain of light helps us understand the target domain of Jesus more fully. As humans, we experience light through various senses. It helps us see things, and it provides warmth.

Linking the concept of light with something good is something we do all the time. In other words, it's an **enduring metaphor**. Enduring metaphors are so typical that they pass for fact. They have become a kind of literal truth and are difficult to question. Furthermore, we use these enduring metaphors as filters for our experience, often unconsciously. In Chapter 9, I'll discuss the ways that the enduring metaphors we use to talk about cancer privilege hegemonic masculinity and shape the ways we view our bodies.

Another example of enduring metaphor is metaphor used to talk about divorce within conservative Christianity. Within this context, the concepts of marriage and divorce are constructed largely using a dichotomous worldview strategy. Marriage is good; divorce is evil. Metaphor is one means by which divorce is associated with evil, and one of the most common metaphors portrays divorce as an act of violence (V Hobbs, 2018b). Repetition of this metaphor affects the way that we think about the act of divorce and the ways we initiate, experience and respond to it. We can contrast enduring metaphors with **novel or new metaphors**, which push us to think about things we encounter in new ways. Because novel metaphors are more visible, we are sometimes suspicious of them, particularly if they seem to contradict enduring metaphors. The final type are **dead metaphors**, which have fallen out of use.

Table 6.1 Common Explicit Religious Metaphors

Bible	animals, conflict, plants, light, building/shelter, food and drink, body, journeys, weather, fishing and hunting, fire, treasure/money, direct and cleanliness, clothes
Qur'an	journeys, weather, fire and light, plants

Source: Charteris-Black (2004).

As an earlier chapter mentioned, linguist Jean-Pierre van Noppen was one of the first to conduct a systematic analysis of religious metaphor, cataloguing the wide variety of linguistic metaphors used to answer the question, where is God (van Noppen, 1980). As we seek to articulate and understand our relationship with an invisible deity, metaphor allows us to position that deity in places both close and far away. The metaphors we choose reveal what we believe about that deity's character and nature. But of course, not all metaphor is used for religious purposes. It'll probably come as no surprise that deciding whether a metaphor is religious is by no means straightforward. As Edward Bailey aptly put it, not everything is religious, but anything can be religious (Bailey, 2010). Still, just as we've done with other features of religious language, we can start by differentiating between explicit and implicit religious metaphor.

Explicit religious metaphor is metaphor more frequently used in an overtly religious context. In his book *Corpus Approaches to Critical Metaphor Analysis*, Jonathan Charteris-Black documents some of the most commonly used metaphors in the Christian Bible and in Islam's holy book, the Qur'an (Charteris-Black, 2004). Some of the ones he identifies are in Table 6.1.

Note in particular the light metaphor, which appeared in the image in Figure 6.2. The image from Kanye's 'Yeezus' tour at the start of the chapter also contains another metaphor common to religious texts. This metaphor, appearing in the wider context in Mark's Gospel, portrays spiritual knowledge as treasure and life as a treasure hunt, a journey towards spiritual knowledge. The use of the word 'verb' gives this journey a strong dynamism. More than a journey, says Kanye, life is a hunt for God. And it appears that as a recent convert to Christianity, Kanye has found what he was looking for, though some remain cautious about what exactly that is (Corry, 2019).

So explicit religious metaphor can draw on enduring metaphors taken from sacred texts and traditions. But explicit religious metaphor can also often draw on an explicitly religious person or concept or even religion itself. For example, let's look closely at this extract from an article on climate change 'deniers' that appeared in *The Independent* in January 2007.

Denier's Myth Number Five: Global warming is a religion. People have always had an innate psychological need to believe in a looming apocalypse – this is just the latest version.

Precisely the opposite is the truth. Global warming is based on very close empirical observation of the real world, and deductions based on reason. If its conclusions fall into one particular niche in intellectual history, that doesn't change the fact they are true. It is you, the deniers clinging to myths, who resemble the faithful. Far from being Galileos, you have been siding with the fossil fuel Vatican. (Hari, 2007)

In this extract, the author challenges figurative comparisons between climate change and religion and global warming and end times, or as he colourfully puts it, a 'looming apocalypse'. The author draws on two significant Discourses: the idea that science and organized religion are at odds and the idea that religious people are unintelligent and irrational (see Figure 6.3).

The author's technique is, then, to turn the metaphor around on people who downplay global warming and connect **them** with religion. They are 'deniers clinging to myths', they are 'the faithful', they are followers of the 'Vatican', not the 'Galileos' they think they are. Each of these is explicit uses of religious metaphor, articulating sacred boundaries and legitimizing sacred beliefs.

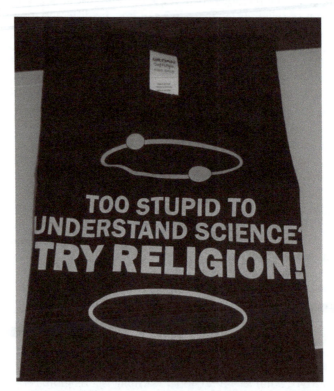

FIGURE 6.3 *Too Stupid to Understand Science? Try Religion!* 2016.

Metaphor has also been used to make sense of religion itself. On a post for *Patheos*, Yvonne Aburrow documents some of the many ways we've grappled with the complexity of religion itself through metaphor (Aburrow, 2016). Among the vehicle groups she mentions that we use to make sense of religion are: religion as languages, as software, as people, as landscapes, as light, colour and energy, and as art-forms. One example she gives is from an online comment comparing religion to dance (Rathbone, 2009).

Contemporary, Jazz, Ballroom, Hawaiian, Crump, Latin, Hip-hop. To get really good at one, you have to focus on it and do it a lot. You can admire someone who is really good at another type of dance without feeling it takes away from your own dancing. And you are, of course, completely welcome to learn as many dances as you like, doing one or another depending on your mood. Except that, in a way, religion as dance isn't a metaphor but a tautology.

Are these metaphors used religiously? I'd say so. As the commenter says, this is more than just a set of metaphors. They constitute a set of axiomatic statements about the purpose and function of religion itself. In the case of the dance metaphor, they say something about how religions should relate to one another. They are statements about how we are to interact as human beings in community. These are not explicit religious metaphors but they are indeed functioning religiously.

An **implicit religious metaphor,** therefore, is one that may not have its origins in an overtly religious context but which is nevertheless used in sacred-making. It helps make sense of the cosmos, validates a particular sacred notion, arouses a sense of the mystery of being, assists in establishing sacred social boundaries and enables us to cope with the various stages of life (Campbell, 2001). Like all implicit religious language, an argument that a metaphor is functioning religiously must arise from the context. Darren Kelsey, for example, analysed articles on right-wing news website Mail Online and found that two articles in particular on the British politician Nigel Farage[1] used metaphor, together with narrative and interdiscursivity, to portray Farage as a missionary. Kelsey writes:

Farage says that his dedication is not 'wholly rational' and that he 'can't explain' his feelings but he 'just knows' he is right. This takes the political and ideologically informed opinion to a deeper, spiritual level of metaphor that suggests there is something naturally, eternally, and instinctively right about his feelings, which he cannot ignore. His heroic instincts inform his dedication to 'spread his message'.

(Kelsey, 2017: 58)

The metaphor isn't obviously religious, but it is constructed through archetypal language that constructs powerful religious imagery.

The form of religious metaphor

I've talked about the two meaning units in metaphor: vehicle and target. Let's talk about form now. Metaphor can take many forms linguistically, but these fall into two categories: **grammatical and lexical**. Grammatical metaphors involve the transfer of meaning from one grammatical form to another, embedding figurative meaning into the form of the language itself.[2] For example, a grammatical metaphor can be formed via nominalization, the process by which an adjective or a verb is converted to a noun. In order to recover the full meaning, we have to unpack all of the grammatical structures. Consider this pair, as an example:

1   The Session wrote the Smiths, asking them to forgive them. At that time they forgave them.

2   The Session wrote the Smiths, asking forgiveness, which at that time was granted (V Hobbs, 2018a: 147).

In Extract 2 above, taken from a religious higher education employment document, the text abstracts the act 'to forgive' by turning it into a noun. You can see the underlying form in Extract 1 (which did not appear in the document). The action 'to forgive' is now an entity that one party transfers to another. The grammatical metaphor 'forgiveness', working together with the passive voice in 'was granted', distances the Smiths from the act of forgiving. This is a linguistic manoeuvre with significant religious meaning, an act of unmistakable sacred meaning. It places the Smiths dangerously close to, even outside of, sacred group boundaries, given the importance of forgiveness within Christianity.

For our purposes here, let's set aside grammatical metaphor for now and focus on **lexical religious metaphors**. These involve the use of one particular word or phrase, which has a literal meaning, to express a new abstract meaning. In Extract 3 below, from the Qur'an, a man's actions (target: human behaviour) are visualized as plants (vehicle: natural world/plants) farmed by men and which produce fruit (vehicle: natural world/fruit). This metaphor and the one in the biblical extract below it (4) tap into a common comparison between the spiritual and the natural world. The metaphor is useful here in capturing the extent to which deeds are evaluated in terms of their fertility and strength.

3   Every man shall **reap the fruits** of his own deeds (Dawood, 1990: Cattle 6: 164).

4   **The root of the righteous** endures (Proverbs 12.12).

A few paragraphs ago, I mentioned Jonathan Charteris-Black's work on the more common explicit religious metaphor vehicle groups, including plants, found in Christianity and Islam. These vehicle groups tend to be used for religious purposes in contemporary contexts since they are commonly used in and associated with sacred religious texts. However, again, it's important to make a case from the context that a metaphor is meeting religious goals: functioning axiomatically, social cohesively and emotively religious.

Religious metaphor identification

After we've identified a text that seems to be functioning religiously, one approach to analysis of religious metaphor in a text or set of texts involves identifying vehicles and tracking their development. This means carefully and systematically documenting religious vehicle terms across a text, noting patterns and changes in their use as well as related words and phrases (Cameron, 2008). One way of doing this involves the following steps:

1 Insert line numbers into the text and underline all explicit religious vehicle terms. These may be words or whole phrases.
2 Note any additional metaphors that may be functioning religiously.
3 Sort and label vehicles into thematic groups (and sub-groups).
4 Track the development of thematic groups across the text.
5 Note any other religious language features and the extent to which they contribute to these thematic groups. These can be used to strengthen a case that the metaphor is functioning religiously.

Often, a scholar writing about metaphor vehicles will put the name of the vehicle in all capital letters. In Chapter 7, I will illustrate the analysis of metaphor using two prayers. In summary, metaphor is a significant means by which we perform religion using language. It fulfils the axiomatic functions of religion, enabling us to speak about things which we can't fully grasp cognitively. Functioning emotively, it helps us cope with moments of crisis, wonder, mystery and doubt. Shared religious metaphor forms the fabric of a sacred community's thought and existence. But metaphor also has radical consequences for embodied experience. Through metaphor we understand the world, and it forms the fabric of our lives.

Religious intertextuality

In order for a text to be comprehensible to its audience, it must contain words and phrases found elsewhere. The start of Chapter 3 introduced a billboard containing the words, 'Jesus Saves. He will heal our land'. In my discussion of the billboard, I noted that the phrase 'Jesus Saves' is a phrase often repeated among Christians around the world and re-appropriated by the billboard's authors for religious-political purposes. The image from Kanye's tour that appeared at the beginning of this chapter likewise has language taken from elsewhere, from Kanye's album but also from the biblical text. This is what is known as **intertextuality**, the property texts have of being composed of other texts. The term was first used by Julie Kristeva to capture the extent to which 'any text is the absorption and transformation of another' (Kristeva, 1986: 37).

Intertextuality is closely linked to the construction of Discourse (see Chapter 3). Any stretch of language, when repeatedly used in similar situations many times over, becomes associated with those situations and so shapes our thinking and our experience of the world. Religious intertextuality is, put simply, the invocation of a sacred legitimating authority. One example I have looked at in my own research is the expression 'God hates divorce', a reference to Malachi 2.16 in the Bible, often used out of its original context when the topic of divorce comes up in Christian circles (V Hobbs, 2019). As I mentioned in the section on metaphor, this and other similar ways of talking about divorce stem from and foster a view of divorce as taboo, an enemy. This process is sometimes called interdiscursivity, the ways in which a text contributes to and props up one or more Discourses.

Functions of religious intertextuality

Instances of religious intertextuality fulfil all three functions of religious language. First, they often articulate axiomatic statements. Second, they also serve an emotive function (like comforting someone at a time of loss). Finally, of course, they facilitate social cohesion. Indeed, frequent repetition of a particular piece of text like 'Jesus saves' or 'God hates divorce' marks us out as members of a particular community doing particular actions and thinking in particular ways.

Most importantly, however, religious intertextuality can make sacred the person who invokes that authority as well as their set of beliefs and their actions. In her work on Christian missions in Yorùbáland, West Africa, Sandra Nickel describes the functions of intertextuality in missionary correspondence like this:

> Quotations from and allusions to these texts in the missionaries' correspondence are often used in the context of setbacks in the mission or sad news, such as the death of a missionary or a convert. Agents also used quotations and allusions in contexts where they wished to express a point emphatically or to indicate a biblical precedent for their current situation, thus giving them guidance on how to respond to the situation or highlighting that they stood in the tradition of the Christian narrative. In all of these instances quoting from the scriptures or other Christian texts creates an intertextual bond between the original text and the missionaries' writing. (Nickel, 2015: 124)

So intertextuality can bind together a sacred source and a person or community who invokes it. But sacred people and beliefs can also be made illegitimate through intertextuality. As one of my students recently pointed out, some music reviewers have used excessive and over-the-top religious intertextual reference to critique Kanye West's latest album, to position him as a kind of extremist, in comparison to musicians they see as more reasonably religious, like Kendrick Lamar.[3] Citing that famous passage from the book of Genesis, one reviewer writes,

> In the beginning, Christianity rippled through the music of Kanye West ... But *Jesus Is King* is too slight a record, too lacking in substance, to offer any sense of purification or real insights into West's mind. (Van Nguyen, 2019)

The author's connection of Kanye's music with the creation account in Genesis 1 isn't a positive one. As we saw in the last section on metaphor, remarks like these tap into an existing Discourse, where to be too religious is to be irrational and absurd, even extremist. So we see again that the use of religious language, including intertextuality, is a double-edged sword. By it we both bless and curse.

In short, whether it legitimizes or de-legitimizes, religious intertextuality helps meet the axiomatic, social cohesive and emotive functions of religious language, facilitating the construction of in- and out-groups. The more a text, a person, an entity, an idea is cited, the more sacred (or taboo) it can become, as it achieves a level of authority (or disdain) many recognize and can call upon at key moments. However, the more sacred a text is, the more difficult it can be to interpret, to critique or even to cite. Indeed, some people consider these actions off-limits except for people with certain credentials.

Identifying and analysing manifest intertextuality

All texts contain snatches of other texts. Even the use of a single word can be considered an instance of intertextuality. The use of religious metaphor is also itself a kind of intertextuality. This means that identifying and analysing intertextuality can be like opening a can of worms. One way of finding our way through the complexities of intertextuality is to focus on a series of questions related to source of authority, intertextual method and linguistic context.

The authoritative source

By way of reminder, religious intertextuality is the invocation of a sacred legitimating authority. This authority can be a supernatural being, a person, some other living entity, a text, a place or even a sacred concept. The authority can even be an invention of the author. For example, in some of my own work on sermons, I found that Christian pastors on occasion use invented reported speech from hypothetical people to give substance to their arguments (V Hobbs, 2018b). Here is one example of this, where the preacher positions divine authority against an invented quote from a would-be counsellor of domestic violence.

> But when we give counsel, we must give 'Thus saith the Lord', not 'I feel really bad, oh, you should really, you know, oh, you have a right to, oh, you really could'. (V Hobbs, 2018b: 97)

The archaic language used here, 'Thus saith the Lord', further distances the Lord's words from the invented quote and reinforces the preacher's point of view with significant authority.

Work on language and ideology offers us additional help when looking at how intertextual sources are depicted as legitimate or illegitimate. Van Leeuwen's framework for the representation of social actors in particular assists us in looking at the ways that texts demonstrate the following:

1   selectivity: what is excluded or included
2   role allocation: the roles that social actors are given in representations
3   indetermination and differentiation: when social actors are represented as anonymous or unspecified (indetermination) or if their identity is made clear (differentiation)
4   collectivisation and specification: refers to the extent to which social actors are represented as groups (collectivization) or as individuals (specification) and to what end (van Leeuwen, 2008).

Analysing intertextuality involves looking not only at what sources are cited but also at what sources are noticeably absent. It involves looking at the ways that those sources are portrayed, the roles they are given. Are the sources anonymous or specified and what effect does that have? Are the intertextual sources portrayed as groups or as individuals? Later in this section I'll demonstrate how these categories help us consider religious intertextuality specifically.

Methods of citing: Manifest intertextuality

A second way to cope with the complexities of religious intertextuality is to consider intertextuality on a continuum, from explicit to implicit. Quite a few scholars have taken this approach, one of the most well-known models being Fairclough's typology, with irony on one end (implicit) and direct quote on the other (explicit) (Fairclough, 2003). However, models like these neglect a certain feature of intertextuality which is highly significant, particularly for religious language: **networks of intertext**. As I mentioned in the last paragraph, the more a text is cited, the more sacred it can become and the more individuals call on its authority to accomplish sacred-making. Many existing models also neglect to account for the **absence of intertextuality**, which is something we must attend to as well (Farrelly, 2019). As I alluded to in the previous section on the authoritative source, a text's exclusion of intertextuality or its source often says something significant. Excluding the source can blur the boundaries between speaker and source, for instance, attributing greater sacred power to the speaker. Intertextual absence can also mean excluding certain voices (e.g. women), suggesting they do not have authority. I'll look at this in more detail as we go on.

Following Michael Farrelly's recent work in intertextuality, in this book I'll focus on the explicit end of the intertextuality scale, what is frequently called **manifest intertextuality** (Farrelly, 2019). This type of intertextuality occurs when a text overtly draws on another sacred text. The most explicit form of manifest intertextuality is when the source text is expressly cited, either in whole or in part, as a **direct quote**. Quotation marks are likely but may not be used, especially if the quote is well-known or if the entire text is re-used.

Manifest intertextuality also includes **paraphrase** (where the source may or may not be mentioned, depending in part on audience's familiarity) and **reference,** where a text is referred to but not directly quoted or paraphrased in the text. Crucially, as well, we must also consider what Farrelly calls **conceptual absence** (Farrelly, 2019). A final form of manifest intertextuality that is particularly significant in doing religion is parody. Parody can involve a specific text, a particular style of writing or a genre. When it comes to religious intertextuality, parody involves re-appropriating an often well-known overtly religious phrase or quote for another use, such as mocking or otherwise critiquing.

Here are examples of some of these types, taken from Christian, Mormon and Jewish sermons, respectively. Later, I'll provide an example which shows what role the absence of intertextual reference might have in doing religion:

1 **direct quote:** in similar fashion, great saints and mystics throughout the centuries have described God this way. St. Anselm of Canterbury prayed: 'Jesus, as a mother you gather your people to you; you are gentle with us as a mother with her children' (Glover, 2015).

2 **paraphrase:** as I gave the talk, a depressing feeling of failure troubled me. Afterwards, when I was alone, I knelt down and asked the Lord why I had failed after trying so hard (Bachman, 1991).

3 **reference:** but we each must wrestle like Jacob did with the angel, even to the point that it hurts or wounds us to do so, until our relationship with God, with Torah and with Israel becomes uniquely ours (Resnicoff, 2014).

4 **parody:** 'We three kings of Orient are, one in a taxi, one in a car, one in a scooter blowing his hooter. Following yonder star' (Opie and Opie, 2001: 88).

Often, we can find religious parody in advertising. Here, overtly religious language, symbols and imagery are placed in an unexpected context in a humorous or even shocking way, giving a brand sacred value. Three Lithuanian commercials, for example, presented Jesus and Mary as style icons, re-appropriating the interjection 'Jesus, Mary!', which many Catholics use to express admiration, in images of the clothes of fashion designer Robert Kalinkin ('Jesus, Mary! What a style!', 2012). But religious parody can also be used by one religious community to establish clear lines between themselves and another religious community, as we'll see in the next chapter when we look at prayer.

Figure 6.4 contains two levels of parody, which creates a network of intertexts. At the deepest layer, we encounter the phrase 'In God We Trust', which has a long history in the United States, in use since the Reverend Mark Watkinson petitioned the National Treasury for its use in 1861. 'In God We Trust' is also the motto of the Republic of Nicaragua (in Spanish) and of the city of Brighton, England (in Latin). Because of its cultural familiarity, it is a phrase that has been parodied all around the world, used to do such things as venerate football coaches in the UK ('In Arsene we trust') and comment on the gold standard in Canada ('In gold we trust') (Davies, 2013). Likewise, as we see in our text in Figure 6.4, fish and chips patrons in various countries have parodied this phrase when talking about the sacred institution of the chippy ('In Cod We Trust – The Codmother Fish & Chips – San Francisco Traveller Reviews,' n.d.). This parody, in turn, has been parodied again in the image in Figure 6.4 as a commentary on the overharvesting of cod, particularly in the Atlantic Ocean. This final layer, with the addition of past tense 'trusted' functions as a critique of the

FIGURE 6.4 *In Cod We Trusted, 2007.*

FIGURE 6.5 *God's Billboard, 2005.*

devastation of the cod population, both in Canada and elsewhere (Watkins, Schoch and Webb et al., 2015).

The source that one cites, the method one chooses (direct quote, paraphrase etc.) to cite another text and the language that one uses around that citation tell us a great deal about what intertextuality is doing in a text. With regard to the method of intertextuality, generally speaking, the more explicit the religious intertextuality, the more the author is affirming a hierarchy of authority that exists between the source and the quoting author. **In direct quote, for instance, the boundaries between sacred authority source and the person citing it are clearly drawn.** 'The original context shines through in the quotation so that the new context cannot totally be read separately from the old context' (Nickel, 2015: 131). Certainly, the person using intertextuality is still claiming the authority of the text, but the distinct authority of the source is more clearly articulated.

It's important to say, however, that direct quotes can be misleading in their acknowledgement of the boundaries between the person quoting and the text they are quoting. For example, invented quotes can have the appearance of being a faithful representation of a sacred authority when, instead, they are merging a speaker and the sacred legitimating authority into one. So-called quotes by God on American billboards and church signage are obvious examples, like in the image in Figure 6.5. As in the 'Jesus Saves' billboard I discussed in Chapter 2, here we have a mixing of American politics and Christianity into civil religion.

The blurring of authority lines between the person quoting and the quoted text is a feature of paraphrase as well. Paraphrase by necessity involves a re-working and rewriting of the original source. In a study analysing speeches by former Egyptian President Anwar Sadat, the scholar Emad Abdul-Latif shows how skilled Sadat was at framing and altering the Qur'anic text in ways that blurred the lines between his own authority and that of the sacred text (Abdul-Latif, 2011). In one speech, Sadat strategically quoted the middle of a Qur'anic verse to suit his political purposes, leaving out the start and the end. Sadat combined these intertextual references to the Qur'an with non-linguistic signs of authority, like a prayer mark on his forehead, a religious garment known as an abaya and a rosary, presenting himself as lord-like. All of these efforts combined allowed Sadat to strengthen his sacred authority and his discourse. In using a less explicit form of manifest intertextuality, he took on more of the Qur'an's authority.

Finally, within manifest religious intertextuality, certain sacred texts and people are often named without being quoted. It is simply enough to refer to the sacred person, concept or text to invoke its authority. We might say that by naming a legitimating authority, an author is affirming the boundaries between himself or herself and that authority. However, the lack of direct quote means that the author can use the sacred entity any way that author pleases. To use an explicitly religious metaphor, the name of the legitimating authority baptizes whatever a speaker or writer says with authority.

In summary, any intertextual reference involves some kind of subjective commentary on the original text and some claim to authority. As you move down the continuum from explicit to implicit, the intertextual reference tends to take on a greater degree of subjectivity, blurring the lines of authority between speaker and sacred source.

Verbs of saying

Now we turn to the language that surrounds intertextual reference. In their book *How to Do Critical Discourse Analysis*, David Machin and Andrew Mayr discuss how different reporting verbs or 'verbs of saying' can make the words of certain participants either legitimate or illegitimate, authoritative or deferential (Machin and Mayr, 2012). These can help us determine the extent to which a text, person or concept is being made sacred. I'll focus here on three of the most common reporting verbs:

1   **neutral structuring verbs:** these introduce manifest intertextuality without overt evaluation. These kinds of verbs draw our eye to the intertextual reference itself and away from the author's reporting of it. They can be used to make a speaker appear more factual, more authoritative.
    Examples: say, tell, ask, enquire, reply, answer

2   **meta-propositional verbs:** these are verbs that reveal the author's evaluation of what has been said. They often invoke power relations. They declare a source to be more or less legitimate, in a more explicit way.
    Examples: declare, remark, explain, agree, urge, order, accuse, complain, assert, claim, point out

3   **descriptive verbs:** these verbs mark the manner and attitude of the speaker in what has been said. Descriptive verbs are often highly gendered. These too can mark legitimacy.
    Examples: whisper, murmur, mutter, laugh, giggle, moan, gasp, shout

It's important to say that these categories are not absolute. For example, what might seem like a neutral reporting verb can make a speaker seem quite cold, if another speaker is portrayed as speaking 'warmly' for instance, nearby in the text. We can bring sources of intertextuality closer or push them further away using the language we introduce and surround them with. Much can be learned by comparing the different ways that different intertextual references within one text are introduced. Let's now look at an example of how we can use these various tools within work on intertextuality to approach religious intertextuality.

Religious intertextuality: An example

For a project I completed in 2018, I focused on a 5,668-word text written by the president of Greenville Presbyterian Theological Seminary in the United States in January 2013 (V Hobbs, 2018a). This text's main purpose was to explain and justify the Christian seminary board's decision not to renew a professor's contract. Some of the contextual features surrounding this document include:

1   As a religious employer, the Christian seminary has freedom regarding wages, hours and terms of employment, granted by the Supreme Court of the United States.

2   One of the terms of employment of the seminary is that staff maintain a 'good family' ideal, which is not explicitly defined in their staff handbook but tends to refer to the Apostle Paul's requirement that Christian leaders 'manage their own household well' (GPTS, 2000).

3   The seminary terminated a professor's (Dr Smith) contract on the ground that his wife wasn't attending church frequently enough. They interpreted this as evidence that he was failing to meet the seminary's terms of employment, specifically that his was not a 'good family'. Their action to terminate Dr Smith was inherently a religious one.

4   Dr Smith's wife is officially classed as disabled under the American Disabilities Act and has been diagnosed with multiple chronic illnesses.

For my analysis, I looked in particular at the seminary board report's use of intertextuality and the ways that the board characterized Dr Smith's wife Laura (pseudonyms). In this chapter, I'll only be focusing on intertextuality, including some excerpts from the text along the way.

In institutional contexts, witness accounts are a powerful instrument. When an employer fires an employee, they frequently call on witnesses to justify what is essentially a legal action involving contract termination.

In order to examine the treatment of witness statements in the report, I first identified every instance of manifest intertextuality (of various types), considering amount and type of witness statements as well as whether witnesses were named and the amount of space given to their accounts. I also considered any noteworthy absence of intertextuality as well as the language around each witness account, considering factors like choice of reporting verb. Greenville Seminary's board report cited numerous pre-existing texts, incorporated them as witness statements and treated the various sources differently. Overall, the board report contained over 200 instances of manifest intertextuality. Of these, the president of the seminary attributed 126 to members of the seminary board and to named and unnamed sources and 82 to the Smiths. This in itself points to imbalance.

The manifest intertextuality took various forms. Some of these were the use of whole texts, like letters written by Dr Smith or members of the board. There were also many instances of paraphrase, also known as projection or reported speech. This is where the message is presented in a separate reported clause. For example,

> I told [Dr Smith] that I thought **there were spiritual and emotional issues underlying some of [Mrs Smith]'s illness.**

In this example, we have a paraphrase of what 'I' (the seminary president) told Dr Smith. In the board report there were also three extended direct quotations, one brief quote and two full letters. All this demonstrates that witness accounts of varying length and type were important and highly frequent in this document.

I next turned to the question of which authority the board report cited. In other words, I looked at the type and naming of witnesses. First, the board report contained a much larger amount of negative reports about the Smiths than it contained the Smiths' own reports. But the president who wrote the report showed bias in other ways. A witness statement from a South African church, for instance, was solicited 'because he had heard that the organizers in South Africa were very concerned about [Laura Smith]'s behavior' (GPTS, 2013). The board report included no outside witness reports supporting the Smiths and gave no evidence that the president attempted to find any such witnesses. In this sense, the absence of intertextuality was also highly significant in meeting the report's overall aim.

The board report also contained no witness statements from Laura Smith herself. This was despite the fact that the president frequently mentioned Laura and her actions. Instead, the president reported her statements and actions as witnessed by (mostly nameless) others. Hiding the names of witnesses testifying against Laura Smith demonstrates bias towards protecting these witnesses. Van Leeuwen (2008: 40) writes that the use of anonymous witnesses 'endows social actors with a kind of impersonal authority, a sense of unseen, yet powerfully felt coercive force'. Anonymous witnesses can be anyone around us, including people we might think are friends. Worse still,

<u>Procedures</u>

At the Nov, 2011meeting of the Trustees, they reviewed the material and appointed the committee. At that meeting and the May 2012, the Trustees also received other information: Dr. [Smith] was forbidden to preach at a Mission Church of the Presbytery because of the behavior of his wife; there are other examples of congregations offended by Mrs. [Smith]'s behavior and demands, some of which have asked that Dr. [Smith] not return (see below letter from South Africa; [President] suggested he not take her when he did conferences); new students had been counseled not to accept work in the [Smith] household; Mrs. [Smith] made a very unseemly remark to a student's wife who was cleaning her house; Dr. [Smith] had accepted a long term preaching assignment out of town leaving his wife without a car on the Lord's Day; Mrs. [Smith] would feel good enough to shop, but not make services on the Lord's Day; on one occasion [President] asked Dr. [Smith] if he thought his wife was converted to which in [President]s opinion, he received a non-committal answer (this is not the way Dr. [Smith] remembers the conversation) ; the Deacons of Covenant Community OPC passed a unanimous motion recommending that ladies in the church who were uncomfortable assisting in the [Smith]' home because of a pattern of manipulation and taking advantage of those who helped, were under no obligation to help.

FIGURE 6.6 *Extract from Greenville Presbyterian Theological Seminary Board Report, 2012.*

we can't confront these witnesses. They are used authoritatively, but they cannot be challenged. In this way, they are highly sacred.

The board report also used a collectivization strategy. For example, the excerpt in Figure 6.6 contains a pre-emptively conclusive statement of fact, that 'there are other examples of congregations offended by [Laura Smith]'s behavior and demands'. The plural 'congregations' functions as collectivization. It signals agreement by many that the Smiths have a bad reputation. The audience is drawn in, the implication being that the reader will also be offended by what follows.

This strategy of collectivization, like the anonymization of witnesses, gives the impression of a powerful, even sacred force standing against the Smiths. This occurred several other times, as in the following:

1   'elders and ministers have raise [*sic*] a unanimous voice of concern'
2   'Deacons of Covenant Community OPC passed a unanimous motion'.

When considering who speaks and with what weight, it isn't merely that individual witnesses are privileged but also that they speak with one voice. Together, they constitute substantial sacred legitimating authority.

I next looked at the kinds of language surrounding the instances of manifest intertextuality. Throughout, the board report framed the witness reports in different ways. For example, the choice of reporting verb in the board report revealed favouritism for negative witness reports about the Smiths' actions and statements. Compare, for instance, the following pair, involving meta-propositional verbs of saying:

3   It **was pointed out** to [Dr Smith] that his statement was not true …
4   [Mrs Smith's] calling a friend while the presbytery was meeting and **claiming** that the session was after her husband's job.

In the first in the pair above, the verb 'point out' shows the reader just how certain the president is that Dr Smith said something untrue. It simply draws the receiver's attention to its existence. By way of contrast, the word 'claim' introduces doubt. In fact, the president of Greenville Seminary used reporting verbs with negative or undermining connotations twice as many times for the Smiths' reported speech as he did for both the seminary board and witnesses combined. And in every occasion except for one, the president used passive voice or 'no one' as the subject. In these ways, he distanced the witnesses from their negative statements. You can see this in the following examples:

5 In addition, the Board was informed that Dr [Smith] **had been accused of** speaking intemperately at that meeting.
6 Session responded by pointing out that no one **was denying** that Mrs Smith was ill.

The board report treated the Smiths' words quite differently. The president used active voice every time the reporting verbs had negative connotations. Here is one example, where the president directly connects Laura Smith and Dr Smith to their 'demands' and 'boasts':

7 [Mrs Smith] **demanding** that a friend who was babysitting three boys come to her house to help her.
8 Dr Smith's selective memory: at times **boasting** in his perfect recall ...

The language that surrounded these instances of manifest intertextuality points to a dichotomous worldview strategy (us vs. them) by painting the Smiths in a negative light and the witnesses in a positive light. This facilitated the creation and enforcement of sacred social boundaries, which make it clear that the Smiths are outside of the group.

The board report used other strategies to accomplish the same goal, though I won't go into much detail about those here. One example is the amount of space in the text given to witnesses. Overall, the president of Greenville Seminary used manifest intertextuality extensively but unevenly. In contrast to the framing of the Smiths' reports, the president introduced critical witness statements in a way that directed readers to accept and even commend them without scrutiny. In his choice of reporting verb and in his discursive framing of these statements, the president of the seminary made clear that these critical voices are the ones that carry weight. Given that this is an overtly religious context, where the employment criteria derive from a sacred text (the Bible), the seminary board's actions have deeply significant religious meaning.

In summary, intertextuality is a powerful feature of religious language in its claiming of sacred external legitimating authority and its rejection of voices it declares untrustworthy or taboo. This plays an important role in maintaining sacred group boundaries. Since religious intertextuality is often used as an external legitimating authority, questions to ask when identifying and seeking to understand manifest religious intertextuality in a text include:

1 Which authority is cited? To what extent is it a sacred authority? (admired, difficult to question)

2 In what wider context(s) does the manifest intertextuality appear?

3 What form does the manifest intertextuality take? (whole text, direct quote, paraphrase, reference, parody)

4 Is the source text modified? If so, how?

5 What language surrounds the manifest intertextuality that might indicate the speaker's evaluation of the source? (verbs of saying, for instance)?

6 To what extent is the absence of intertextual reference playing a role in meeting the goals of the text?

7 For what purposes is the manifest intertextuality included? Is it contributing to any religious discourse strategies?

Chapter summary

This is the last of three chapters covering macro and micro features that are common to texts involved in doing religion. This chapter gave an overview of religious metaphor and religious intertextuality. Each of these fosters the building of a sacred community, instils an emotive quality and gives legitimacy to a sacred belief system.

First, I gave an overview of religious metaphor. Religious metaphor is a form of figurative language which extends our limited cognitive understanding of what we experience by viewing that experience through the lens of things we **can** more fully understand. In this way, it can comfort and communicate mystery and wonder. Because of metaphor's connection to lived experience, it powerfully shapes the ways that we think and live our lives. Shared metaphor unites a community and enforces borders.

What distinguishes metaphor from analogy is the tension between the two metaphorical concepts. Some points to remember about metaphor's form and identification are:

1 A metaphor has two components: target domain (what we are trying to understand) and the vehicle domain (what we use to understand the target).

2 Metaphor can be novel, dead or enduring.

3 Metaphor is typically grammatical or lexical. Lexical metaphor involves the use of one particular word or phrase, which has a literal meaning, to express a new abstract meaning.

4   Religious metaphor can be explicitly or implicitly religious.

5   Religious metaphor identification and analysis involve systematically tracking metaphor vehicles across the text, grouping them thematically and considering their function in relationship to other metaphors and religious language.

This chapter also covered religious manifest intertextuality. This feature involves an overt reference to a sacred person's words, a sacred text or a sacred concept.

1   Religious manifest intertextuality is commonly used as an external legitimating authority. The absence of religious intertextuality can be as important as its presence.

2   The sacred authority can be real (an entity or concept) or invented.

3   Manifest religious intertextuality can be a direct quote, a paraphrase, a reference or a parody.

4   The language that surrounds an instance of manifest religious intertextuality can tell us a great deal about the way the author views that person, text, or concept and how they (consciously or unconsciously) intend us to view it, and by extension, the author themself.

In the next chapter, I'll move on from discussing religious language features to look closely at prayer.

Further reading

Charteris-Black J (2004) *Corpus Approaches to Critical Metaphor Analysis. Corpus Approaches to Critical Metaphor Analysis.* London: Palgrave Macmillan. DOI: 10.1057/9780230000612.

Farrelly M (2019) Rethinking Intertextuality in CDA. *Critical Discourse Studies*: 1–18. DOI: 10.1080/17405904.2019.1609538.

Soskice J M (2007) *The Kindness of God: Metaphor, Gender, and Religious Language.* Oxford: Oxford University Press. DOI: 10.1111/j.1468-0025.2009.01546.x.

Discussion and exploration

1   One context where we can expect to find religious language is at moments of crisis. It is no surprise, then, that discussion around climate change is often religious in nature. In a speech in 2003, science-fiction writer and climate change sceptic Michael Crichton argued that environmentalism is a new religion, which 'remaps' basic tenets of

the Christian faith.[4] Roger Gottlieb's introduction to his edited book *This Sacred Earth* is also a useful source for examining the extent to which religious language appears in discussions about climate change (Gottlieb, 1995).

a Choose a newspaper and find an article within the past year on climate change that, on first reading, appears to be connecting climate change with religion. If you have access to these, here are a few from *The Times* and *The Independent*:

- Baker, G. (2006, 15 September). When it comes to climate change, I'll take a small bet that Pascal was right. *The Times*. Retrieved from https://advance.lexis.com/api/permalink/aa57e156-5c04-48ad-b1e8-3efbb37a29c8/?context=1519360
- Hari, J. (2007, 25 January). The last gasp of the global warming deniers. *The Independent*. Retrieved from https://advance.lexis.com/api/permalink/1d1d2eb7-258e-4222-b9f5-232a60d0f749/?context=1519360
- Hume, M. (2007, 27 April). Thou shalt not go religiously green. *The Times*. Retrieved from https://advance.lexis.com/api/permalink/5b979286-4128-4e97-ac0c-49126a8e140f/?context=1519360

b Write down the main thesis or a brief summary of the author's argument.

c Identify and group any religious metaphors

- Underline all metaphor vehicles in the text. For each, what is the target (i.e. what is the metaphor intended to illuminate)? You may wish to start with the explicitly religious metaphor.
- Sort the list of linguistic metaphors into vehicle groupings.
- Examine multiple metaphors across each text and determine if systematic metaphor(s) is at work.

d What function(s) are the religious metaphors accomplishing in the text? What is being made sacred or taboo?

e What other religious features of these texts, if any, strike you as being important for the construction of a Discourse around climate change? How might you investigate these further?

2 In 2018, Ariane Grande released 'God Is a Woman', the third track in her album *Sweetener*. At around minute 2.23, pop singer Madonna's disembodied voice makes a cameo appearance. She recites (sort of) a

passage from the Bible, Ezekiel 25.17, taking on the voice of God in the passage. She says,

I will strike down upon thee, with great vengeance and furious anger, those who attempt to poison and destroy my sisters, and you will know my name is the Lord, when I lay my vengeance upon you.

You may want to watch the video to see the overall effect (https://youtu. be/kHLHSlExFis).

a   What kind of manifest intertextuality is this? (You can find the original text here: https://www.kingjamesbibleonline.org/ Ezekiel-25-17/).

b   What visual and linguistic features, if any, frame this instance of intertextuality?

c   What do you make of Madonna taking on the voice of God? What implications does this have in terms of boundaries between Madonna, Ariana, the sacred text and the God of the Bible?

7

Religious language and prayer

Table 7.1 'The Lord's Prayer' from Matthew 6.9-13 and 'The Atheist's Prayer'

The Lord's Prayer	The Atheist's Prayer
Our Father which art in heaven,	Our brains, which art in our heads,
Hallowed be thy name.	treasured be thy name. Thy reasoning
Thy kingdom come.	come. Thy best you can do be done on
Thy will be done	earth as it is. Give us this day new
in earth, as it is in heaven.	insight to help us resolve conflicts and ease
Give us this day our daily bread.	pain. And lead us not into supernatural
And forgive us our debts,	explanations;
as we forgive our debtors.	deliver us from denial of logic.
And lead us not into temptation,	For thine is the kingdom of reason,
but deliver us from evil:	and even though thy powers are limited,
For thine is the kingdom,	and you're not always glorious,
the power, and the glory,	you are the best evolutionary adaptation
for ever.	we have for helping this earth now and
Amen.[1]	forever and ever. So be it.

Source: The Bible: Authorized King James Version (2012) and Author Unknown

---

Read the two prayers above. Then consider the following questions:

1 For what purposes do people pray?
2 What features of these texts first signal to you that they are prayers? What other features of religious language (both macro and micro) can you identify in each of the prayers?

> 3   What sacred beliefs does the religious language in each text reveal?
> 4   What would you say are the functions of each of the two texts? In other words, what do you think these prayers intend to accomplish?

In this chapter, we look at prayer. Prayer is an act that many people are familiar with, even though perhaps most would associate it with organized religion and people of faith. In the sections that follow, I hope to begin to problematize this closed view of prayer. The two prayers that this chapter focuses on, taken together, constitute a site of conflict. Comparing sacred sets of belief at a site of conflict allows us to delve more deeply into what makes these two sets of beliefs distinct from one another.

The overall aim here is to use concrete examples of prayer, an act that many are familiar with, to exemplify the analysis of religious language. I will look first at what is prayer and who does it, moving on to look closely at one of the most well-known prayers in the world, the Lord's Prayer, and a parody of that prayer, the Atheist's Prayer. In so doing, we keep our main question in mind: In what ways are these prayers functioning religiously?

What is prayer and who does it?

The philosopher William James once described prayer as 'the very soul and essence of religion' (James, 1987: 416). The English word comes from the Latin precari, meaning 'to entreat'. Prayer gives a person a sense of security, communicates their deepest thoughts and wishes and enables them to reach beyond themselves to a larger community and/or to something or someone else. Some believe prayer prompts God's intervention in the world.

Do you pray? In 2016, the European Social Survey released new religious data as part of a cross-national survey carried out every two years since 2002. They looked at four religious indicators: religious affiliation, attendance, prayer and personal religiosity. They found that across the 2,286 adults aged fifteen and over that they surveyed, 29 per cent prayed once a week or more ('European Social Survey (ESS)', 2016). A similar study in 2017 found that over 50 per cent of the UK population pray, including as many as one in five people who consider themselves non-religious ('Half of adults in the UK say that they pray', 2018). Studies in other countries report similar frequencies. Three in ten Australians pray or meditate at least once a week (Powell and Pepper, 2017), 20 per cent of non-religious Americans pray daily (Pew Research Center, 2014), and 96 per cent of Afghans and 87 per cent of Iranians report praying daily (Pew Research Center, 2018). In fact, on average, across 105 countries surveyed by the Pew Research Center in 2018, about half of adults (49 per cent) say they pray every day.

Prayer as a human activity stretches back as far as historians have kept records. A prayer from the time of the ancient Babylonians appears on a tablet dating from the mid-seventh century BC. The writer entreats all gods and goddesses known and unknown, to forgive all sins known and unknown (Harper, 1901). The noted philosopher Friedrich Nietzsche is also known for his prayers to a deity seemingly beyond his reach, which he published starting from the age of eighteen or nineteen. His last book, published in 1888, contains a prayer entitled 'Ariadne's Lament' which ends,

No!
Come back!
With all your afflictions!
All my tears gush forth
To you they stream
And the last flames of my heart
Glow for you.
Oh, come back,
My unknown god! my pain!
My ultimate happiness!

(Nietzsche, 2001)

More recently, in 2012, comedian Junior Simpson hosted a short video for the British Broadcasting Corporation on his own prayer and the prayer of people around Britain, from all walks of life (BBC, 2003). What he found is that people pray in times of trouble, at crisis points in their lives, when they need a source of strength, while jumping up and down and listening to music, anywhere, at any time. People pray in order to give them some sense of security, to communicate their deep, innermost feelings, to call on God or some sort of help.

A common way of categorizing prayer is to consider its aims. These include petition, praise, thanksgiving and confession. Some scholars add lament, accusation, blessing and cursing. Prayer can involve one or any combination of these, in any order. Many scholars of religious language rely on speech act theory to understand language as a means of performing a religious act. In the case of prayer, this theory captures not just what we say when we pray (locutionary act) but also our intention in saying it (illocutionary act) as well as the consequences of what we pray (perlocutionary act). This is particularly relevant for prayer since, in many overtly religious traditions, it is believed that the act of prayer can influence the mind of a deity and affect the material world. This is beyond the scope of this book but worth considering. Even if one dismisses any effects prayer has on the material world external to the one praying, psychologists have documented the positive effects of prayer on health, even the health of people who don't consider themselves religious.

To simplify the complexity of models like these, some scholars identify two layers of factors in prayer: directionality and intentionality (see Table 7.2).

Directionality refers to prayer's orientation, whether upward, outward or inward. **In upward directionality, a person prays towards an immaterial or supernatural power.** This is sometimes called vertical self-transcendence (Schnell and Becker, 2006). Sometimes this power or presence is something or someone unknown. Atheist J. D. Moyer puts it like this,

> When I pray, I don't believe any sort of conscious entity is hearing my thoughts. So who am I addressing? I like to think of it as the 'externality construct.' I might give it a name, like 'The Universe,' or 'All-That-Is-Not-Me,' or 'Layer Zero,' or even 'God,' but the name doesn't matter. The entity I'm addressing exists in my mind – a construct. But it *feels* like I'm addressing someone outside of myself – an externality.
>
> (Moyer, n.d.)

In prayers like these, the focus is on building a human-divine (or otherwise external, felt or otherwise) connection, often in pursuit of comfort, stillness or healing. In this way, prayer meets the emotive and social cohesive functions of religion. But prayer also involves making axiomatic commitments about who we are, what life means and where we are going. **What we pray reveals what we believe.**

The next type of directionality of prayer is outward. Prayer can strengthen a connection between humans or with some other part of the material world.

Table 7.2 The Intentionality and Directionality of Prayer

Intentionality	Type of Prayer	Directionality
highlights internal conditions of others and oneself	intercession	outward on behalf of someone's difficulty
	joy or suffering	outward to share someone's joy or pain
	examination	inward to evaluate one's spiritual health
connection through prayer brings both peace and pain	rest	upward or outward to search for stillness
	sacrament	upward or outward to encounter tradition and truth
	joy or tears	inward experiencing personal happiness or turmoil
bold use of prayer, placing one's desires at the centre	radical invocation	outward to assert
	petitionary invocation	outward to make material requests

Source: Based on Ladd and Spilka's (2006) Model of Cognitive Aspects of Prayer.

This fulfils the social cohesive and emotive functions of religious language. This orientation is sometimes called horizontal self-transcendence. Prayer oriented outwards involves taking responsibility for affairs beyond one's immediate concerns, like other people's pain and difficulty. But it could also involve feeling close to nature or even someone a person doesn't know personally. People have even been known to pray to pop stars, like this prayer to Saint Rihanna, which appears on an online shop offering a Rihanna prayer candle.

> Saint Rihanna, we pray. May we all be as bold as you in the sheer, Swarovski-crystal-encrusted Adam Selman gown that you wore to the 2014 CFDA Fashion Awards – with a crystal do-rag, no less – and yet also as effortlessly charming as you were in the bubblegum pink Giambattista Valli Couture dress that you wore to the 2015 Grammys. Amen.
> ('12 Weird and Wonderful Gifts for Pop-Culture Fanatics,' n.d.)

For some, prayer like this represents genuine devotion. For others, it's just a bit of fun. Then again, a person might still spend hard-earned cash on a celebrity prayer candle. This not only demonstrates a commitment to Rihanna's sacred status but also points to the commodification of prayer by a capitalist economy, which is certainly no new thing.

The last type of orientation is inward orientation. Prayer can emphasize self-examination and self-improvement. In this sense, practices like yoga, meditation or mindfulness-based relaxation techniques are also instances of prayer. Prayer can explore feelings of grief, sadness, regret, longing or loneliness. But for many, prayer is also prompted by joy and thankfulness or simply self-awareness.

A prayer's intentionality is its purpose. Prayer declares what we believe to be true, draws attention to our own and others' internal state, forges connections, and aims to bring about change in ourselves and others. Some prayer seeks a sense of peace or well-being. Other prayer seeks to bring about a more visible change in the world around us, a prayer for healing from disease, for instance. We can link this to the functions of religion and religious language: to articulate deeply held truths, to build a sacred community, to intercede (by invoking a deity, for example) on behalf of other members of the community and oneself and to meet emotional needs.

This model of the different layers of prayer is a helpful way to think about prayer's potential, but it's important to remember that any typology cannot fully capture prayer. Prayer is extraordinarily complex. It can be free and unstructured or standardized. It can be sung, spoken, thought or written down. Prayer can be constructed individually or communally. It can be public or it can be private. It can be obligatory like the Salat prayer in Islam or non-obligatory. It can involve any number of linguistic features or none at all. It can be as simple and spontaneous as a single thought, sound or word, or it can be as complex and lengthy as a Navajo prayer for healing lasting an entire night. Prayer is sometimes accompanied by physical objects (prayer beads, for instance) and frequently involves a change in posture like a bowing of the head, kneeling or even lying face down in a posture of humility. In the Muslim tradition, repetition in prayer occurs both in its internal structure and in one's bodily posture and time of prayer (Baquedano-López, 1999). Prayer is a hugely diverse set of practices carried out all over the world.

Most of the scholarly work on prayer by linguists looks at prayer among overtly religious people and often focuses on grammatical features. Navajo prayer has received special attention over the years. Scholars have pointed to the emphasis these prayers place on a standardized information structure and the significance of commanding and compelling a deity. One of the more recent studies on Navajo prayer focuses on metonymy, a kind of parallelism involving a series of semantically related items that move upward and outward (Field and Blackhorse, 2002). Gladys Reichard offers the following translated example, which begins with the feet and moves upward to the legs:

> With your strong feet rise up to protect me,
> With your sturdy legs rise up to protect me.
>
> (Reichard, 1944: 73)

In another context, prayers by the Urapmin people in Papua New Guinea exhibit formulaic, ritualized qualities with discrete beginnings and patterned closings (Robbins, 2001).

Aside from this, much of the linguistic scholarship written in English focuses on Christian prayer. One of the only studies on a large collection of prayers is Thomas Kohnen's research on early modern Christian prayers (Kohnen, 2012). Kohnen focuses on a variety of features, including pronouns and explicit performatives like 'I thank thee' or 'I entreat thee'. Among his findings is that contemporary Protestant prayer has a much more communal orientation. In linguistic terms, this means a shift away from the use of 'I' in Christian prayer (common in the early modern period) towards use of 'we', a feature some have argued typifies the Protestant Reformation.

We can contrast this with the findings of Jean-Pierre van Noppen's study comparing two Christian prayers by the Rt. Rev. V. Gene Robinson and the conservative evangelist Rev. Rick Warren, at the inauguration of American President Barack Obama (van Noppen, 2009). Van Noppen looked at differences in terms of genre, inclusiveness, lexical differences (who is invoked and how), pronouns and verbal groups. He concludes that Warren's prayer more strongly emphasizes individuals and behaviour evaluations, where Robinson's prayer is more collectivist, relying on inclusive pronouns (we, us, our) and abstract nouns. While the use of 'we' may be more common now overall in Protestant Christian prayer, this study shows that the picture is slightly more complex. Context still matters.

Other work on prayer includes Robin Shoaps's study of Pentecostal Christian prayer which also looked at categories of vocabulary and grammar like performatives and pronouns as well as intertextuality (Shoaps, 2002). Her findings locate core beliefs embedded in Pentecostal prayer, which are personal involvement, spontaneity rather than rote prayer and the importance of being earnest. There is certainly other scholarly work on prayer. But we have still only scratched the surface when it comes to our knowledge of what prayer looks like linguistically, despite the rich variety and frequency of prayer around the world. In the sections that follow, I'll return to the two prayers at the start of the chapter, illustrating the analytical methods I proposed in the last two chapters. The questions that the next sections will answer are:

1   Where do the two prayers originate? What does the context of each reveal about their purpose and meaning?

2   What is the structure of each prayer? What might this reveal about their intentionality and directionality?

3   What religious language features appear in each prayer, both explicit and implicit?

4   What are the functions of each prayer? What are they making sacred?

The Lord's Prayer and the Atheist's Prayer

Although there are numerous examples of prayer in all kinds of contexts, the Lord's Prayer is one of the most well-known prayers in the world, first uttered by Jesus Christ and recorded in the biblical text as a model for his followers. Scholars have dated it to sometime during the period of AD 27–9, later written down by Jesus's apostles. The author is highly significant, as you'll no doubt know already. Jesus Christ, as God in human form, is a source of infallible authority for Christians. The Lord's Prayer appears in two places in the Bible: Matthew 6.9-13 and Luke 11.2-4. The version in Matthew 6 is longer than the one that appears in the book of Luke and tends to be cited more frequently.

The Lord's Prayer, a highly poetic text, follows in the tradition of ancient Jewish liturgical prayer (Martin, 2015). Some of these striking features are lost in translation from the original Koine Greek to other languages like English, particularly the strong parallelism in the original text that draws on poetic devices of Hebrew poetry. The version I have used here is from the *Authorized King James Bible* (The Bible: Authorized King James Version, 2012). This is the translation on which the parodic Atheist's Prayer models itself. But it is also one of the most recognizable and influential translations of the Bible. The publication of the King James Bible in 1611 influenced the history of England and America and was indeed a landmark event that would forever change English and American literature and beyond

(Ryken, 2011). When we study the Lord's Prayer in this version of the Bible, therefore, we are not just studying an old translation of an even older text. We are studying a text and a translation of a text that has had and continues to have a powerful influence on the world and on the English language.

The language of the Lord's Prayer reveals core components of the Christian belief system, including references to God's holiness, authority, parental relationship with Christians and Christians' need for forgiveness. Central to the prayer, as we will see shortly, are the person and work of Jesus Christ. Although prayer can function as a means to communicate beyond oneself, some prayers portray a deity as distant, so far removed as to be incapable of interacting with humans. The Lord's Prayer reveals that the Christian God is a deity who hears, in a way comparable to how humans hear. The title of the prayer doesn't appear in the biblical text. Given to the text by Christians, it signals an important sacred value: prayer belongs to the Christian God. It is not a prayer of the Christian. It is the Lord's Prayer.

Uttered many times over since then, in many contexts and treated with much reverence as well as disdain, the Lord's Prayer is immediately recognizable worldwide. These attributes (recognizable, sacred) make the Lord's Prayer a particularly useful text for parody. In 2001, for instance, British newspaper *The Telegraph* drew attention to a 'Lord's Prayer Parody for Drinkers' (Petre and Capon, 2001). In this text, the opening lines of the Lord's Prayer 'Our Father, which art in heaven, hallowed be thy name', become 'Our beer, which art in barrels, hallowed be thy drink'. Although these changes dismayed some Christians, the authors responded that they wished to draw attention to the reality that for some the pub functions as a place of worship and drinking with friends as ritual.

Now we come to our second text. Another parody, with a seemingly different aim, 'the Atheist's Prayer' (author unknown), was featured on 16 March 2008 on *The Friendly Atheist*, a site on Patheos.com,

> the premier online destination to engage in the global dialogue about religion and spirituality, and to explore and experience the world's beliefs.
>
> (About Patheos, n.d..)

The author of the site, Hemant Mehta, aims to create 'positive ongoing dialogue between atheists and believers' ('Books – Friendly Atheist,' n.d.). The name of the site is particularly noteworthy and in some ways countercultural. Atheism has become associated with dogmatism, even vitriol, largely due to the rhetorical style of prominent new atheists like Richard Dawkins and Bill Maher. As Stephen Pihlaja points out, atheists often represent themselves in terms of response to Christian belief as progressive, where Christians are regressive and irrelevant (Pihlaja, 2018). Posting a parody of the Lord's

Prayer on this site is unsurprising in some ways, then. But it is still somewhat provocative, as it positions atheism as a foe rather than a critical friend. In this way, we can approach the context around this prayer as a **site of conflict**, a key site for the use of religious language.

There are many published prayers by atheists, of a wide range of directionality and intentionality types. Although atheism is a broad church, as is Christianity, it is often associated with a physicalist and rationalist worldview (Draper, 2017). In this way of thinking, matter is the most fundamental substance and all things, including our mental consciousness, are a result of material interactions. The practice of prayer among atheists may come from an affirmation of things greater than the individual, such as nature, science, music, art and human cooperation. The author of the 'Friendly Atheist' site, Hemant Mehta, wrote in *The New York Times* that atheist prayer is purely outward and inward, never upward. He goes on to say,

> Prayers benefit only those believers who say or hear them. Prayer gives them comfort. It lets them think they have some control over a situation that may be out of their hands. It's the last resort of people who have run out of ideas, and the first resort of people who never bothered to think about how they could actually fix the problem at hand.
>
> (Mehta, 2013)

We can see this reflected in the Atheist's Prayer, which contains key substitutions reflecting a notion of the material world, the importance of our involvement in fixing problems and perhaps most importantly, the human mind as sacred. Note the title of the prayer and its distinctiveness: prayer belongs to the atheist.

These contextual details provide us with a lens through which to view the linguistic choices in the two prayers at the start of the chapter. The Lord's Prayer comes from an overtly religious context and the Atheist's Prayer from a site devoted to religion, the two contexts presenting convincing evidence that both texts are functioning religiously.

Religious language features in the two prayers

Given that we are here studying two prayers, we can reasonably assume that all of the contents of each text have some religious meaning, even if the Atheist's Prayer is functioning as a parody and may not have been intended as a prayer in the same sense. Still, some of the two prayers' content has more overtly religious meaning than other content. In other words, there are certain key aspects to the two prayers that carry most of the religious meaning. Identifying these features of both texts can help us to:

Table 7.3 *Analysis of the Lord's Prayer and the Atheist's Prayer*

Prayer Structure	The Lord's Prayer	Linguistic Features	Notes on Differences	The Atheist's Prayer	Linguistic Features
Opening Address	Our Father,	archaism: vocative metaphor: *father* VEHICLE GROUP: FAMILY	• The Atheist's Prayer directionality is primarily inward and outward rather than primarily upward. • removal of metaphor (or possibly not?)	Our brains,	metonymy: brain for intelligence archaism: vocative implicit religious vocabulary: *brains*
	which art in heaven,	archaism: *art* (lexical word) explicit religious vocabulary: *heaven* metaphor: *in* VEHICLE GROUP: SPATIAL	heaven vs. heads • head takes on religious meaning • supernatural vs. materialist	which art in our heads	archaism: *art* (lexical word) implicit religious vocabulary: *heads*
Section 1: Invocation A in relation to God/brains	Hallowed be thy name.	archaism: *hallowed* (lexical word); *thy* (grammatical word); syntactic structure	hallowed vs. treasured	Treasured be thy name.	archaism: *thy* (grammatical word); syntactic structure

Prayer Structure	The Lord's Prayer	Linguistic Features	Notes on Differences	The Atheist's Prayer	Linguistic Features
Section 1: Invocation B in relation to God/brains	Thy kingdom come.	archaism: *thy* (grammatical word); syntactic structure syntactic and symmetric parallelism with next line metaphor: *kingdom* VEHICLE GROUP: RULER; metaphor: *come* VEHICLE GROUP: MOTION	kingdom vs. reasoning • removal of metaphor, replaced with materialist element	Thy reasoning come.	archaism: *thy* (grammatical word); syntactic structure syntactic parallelism with next line metaphor: *come* VEHICLE GROUP: MOTION
Section 1: Invocation C in relation to God/brains with second clause	Thy will be done in earth, as it is in heaven.	archaism: *thy* (grammatical words); syntactic structure syntactic and symmetric parallelism with previous line explicit religious vocabulary: *heaven* metaphor: *in* VEHICLE GROUP: SPATIAL	will vs. your best • authority/power vs. limitations removal of 'heaven' • supernatural vs. materialist	Thy best you can do be done On earth as it is.	archaism: *thy* (grammatical words); syntactic structure syntactic parallelism with previous line implicit religious vocabulary: *earth*

(continued)

Prayer Structure	The Lord's Prayer	Linguistic Features	Notes on Differences	The Atheist's Prayer	Linguistic Features
Section 2: Invocation for our needs	Give us this day our daily bread.	archaism: syntactic structure explicit religious vocabulary: *daily bread* VEHICLE GROUP: FOOD metaphor: *daily bread* syntactic parallelism	• removal of physical need • emphasis on conflict resolution and care for those in pain	Give us this day new insights to help us resolve conflicts and ease pain.	archaism: syntactic structure implicit religious vocabulary: *insight; resolve conflict; ease pain* metaphor: *give* VEHICLE GROUP: IDEAS ARE OBJECTS
Section 3: Invocation C in relation to ourselves with second clause	And forgive us our debts, as we forgive our debtors.	explicit religious vocabulary: *forgive* (2x) metaphor: *debt* VEHICLE GROUP: MONEY syntactic and symmetric parallelism	• removal of agency of problems and pain • removal of need for forgiveness;		
Section 3: Invocation B in relation to ourselves	And lead us not into temptation,	archaism syntactic structures explicit religious vocabulary: *supernatural* metaphor: *lead into* VEHICLE GROUP: CAPTIVITY	temptation vs. the supernatural • evil is the supernatural	And lead us not into supernatural explanations	archaism: syntactic structures explicit religious vocabulary: *temptation* metaphor: *lead into* VEHICLE GROUP: CAPTIVITY

Prayer Structure	The Lord's Prayer	Linguistic Features	Notes on Differences	The Atheist's Prayer	Linguistic Features
Section 3: Invocation A in relation to ourselves	but deliver us from evil:	syntactic and contrastive parallelism with next line explicit religious vocabulary: *evil* metaphor: *deliver*, VEHICLE GROUP: CAPTIVITY syntactic and contrastive with previous line	evil *vs.* denial of logic • evil is denial of logic	Deliver us from the denial of logic	implicit religious vocabulary: denial of logic metaphor: *deliver* VEHICLE GROUP: CAPTIVITY contrastive parallelism with previous line
Doxology (not present in all translations of the Lord's Prayer)	For thine is the kingdom,	archaism: *thine* (grammatical word), syntactic structure metaphor: *kingdom* VEHICLE GROUP: RULER	kingdom *vs.* kingdom of reason supernatural *vs.* materialist	For thine is the kingdom of reason,	archaism: *thine* (grammatical word); syntactic structure metaphor: *kingdom* VEHICLE GROUP: RULER
	the power,	implicit religious vocabulary: *power*	limitless *vs.* limited power	and even though thy powers are limited,	archaism: *thy* (grammatical word)
	and the glory,	explicit religious vocabulary: *glory*	limitless *vs.* limited glory	and you're not always glorious,	explicit religious vocabulary: *glorious*

(*continued*)

Prayer Structure	The Lord's Prayer	Linguistic Features	Notes on Differences	The Atheist's Prayer	Linguistic Features
			added emphasis on physicalist/materialist philosophy	you are the best evolutionary adaptation	implicit religious vocabulary: *best evolutionary adaptation*
			added emphasis on environmental preservation	we have for helping this earth now and	implicit religious vocabulary: *helping this earth*
	for ever.	implicit religious vocabulary: *for ever*	added repetition	forever and ever.	implicit religious vocabulary: *forever and ever* repetition
Closing (not present in all translations of the Lord's Prayer)	Amen.	explicit religious vocabulary: *amen*	Amen vs. So be it • Similar meaning but perhaps 'Amen' is seen as too explicitly religious	So be it.	archaism: syntactic structure

1   understand the meaning and function of each text more fully and
2   equip us to understand better the use of this language to do religion
    in other texts.

I've inserted both texts into Table 7.3 and analysed them line by line. In the
next sections, I'll discuss my analysis in more detail.

The structure of the two prayers

I turn now to the structure of these prayers. The titles of course tell us
explicitly that these texts are prayers. But the Lord's Prayer and the Atheist's
Prayer are also easily recognizable as prayers because of how they are
framed, with a form of address at the start of the prayer ('Our Father … '
vs. 'Our brains … ') and a closing ('Amen' vs. 'So be it'). Let's look at this in
more detail now.

Although prayers take many forms in many contexts, these two prayers
follow a common prayer structure, which begins with a vocative. A vocative
is an expression used to address or invoke a person or thing. Scholarship on
prayer frequently reports this pattern, but we can verify this by looking at
online archives of Christian prayer. The website of the Church of Scotland,
for instance, has a regularly updated collection of prayers. Recent additions
include a section on 'Brexit prayers', nearly all of which begin with some
sort of vocative, from 'God of all time' to 'Gathering God' (The Church
of Scotland, 2019). This points to prayer which is primarily upwardly
directional, spoken to a deity. On the other hand, the Atheist's Prayer
addresses 'Our brains', which suggests both an inward directionality (one's
own brain) and an outward one, towards all human minds.

The structure of the two prayers also reveals something about the
sacred belief system underlying each prayer. In Christian prayer, following
the Lord's Prayer, the one praying often starts with God and who God
is, moving on to who humans are, in relation to God. In his work on the
Lord's Prayer, David Wenham points to Jesus's structuring of the prayer
as a poem, divided into three main parts (Wenham, 2010). The first asks
for the Father's glory, the second asks the Father to supply earthly needs
and the third asks for help in our struggle with evil. This structure is not
new and patterns itself after the Ten Commandments in Exodus 20, which
begin with recognition of God (first four commandments) and end with
how humans are to relate to one another (final six). The version of the
Lord's Prayer from Matthew 6 ends in the King James Version of the Bible
with a doxology (see Table 7.3), which isn't included in all translations. We
can find many echoes of Jesus's model prayer in contemporary Christian
prayer. For example, in his analysis of an inaugural prayer by the Rev. Rick
Warren, Jean-Pierre van Noppen writes, 'Warren's prayer starts with the

declarative statement that everything exists through and thanks to God' (van Noppen, 2009).

In the Atheist's Prayer, the replacement of 'God' with 'brain' makes a similar statement about the origin of meaning, in this case the human mind. After this, the Atheist's Prayer continues to follow the structure of the Lord's Prayer with two notable exceptions. First, it removes the first invocation in relation to ourselves, which in the Lord's Prayer is about forgiveness. The Atheist's Prayer seems to suggest a reluctance to attribute wrongdoing to anyone and to repair that wrong. Second, there is an extended doxology in the Atheist's Prayer, which emphasizes a physicalist worldview and a sacred goal to help the earth.

Discourse strategies in the two prayers

We have seen already that both prayers have adopted the information structure of an overtly religious text. The Atheist's Prayer mimics the Lord's Prayer but with significant semantic differences, modelling itself on its distinctiveness from Christianity. We've looked at some of these differences already. However, we can't assume immediately that this is a critique. Remember, for example, 'The Lord's Prayer Parody for Drinkers', which was written to draw attention to and even critique the idea of the pub as a place of worship.

Given the context, however, it's clear that the author of the Atheist's Prayer (or at least the site that published the prayer) is pro-atheist, positioning atheism as an alternative or even solution to Christianity. This is a clear signal of an overall us vs. them, dichotomous worldview strategy, giving us a starting point for analysis. We can then move on to consider the linguistic choices within the text, like word choice and grammatical structure, and consider how these contribute to an overall set of discourse strategies.

Religious vocabulary in the two prayers

Our goal in identifying and analysing religious vocabulary in a text is to account for the lexis that carries the religious content of the text. We want to identify language that is central to the task of doing religion in the text. Recall that the Lord's Prayer is a very old text, but its language is still recognizable and used by many, even today. Returning to the task at the start of the chapter, what words and phrases did you identify in each prayer as explicitly religious? In the Lord's Prayer perhaps you marked words like

kingdom, daily bread, forgive, temptation, evil, glory, Amen.

Perhaps you went a step further and marked certain seemingly out-of-date words, phrases and grammatical structures as religious, like

art, thy, hallowed be.

We'll return to this archaic language in the next section. In the Atheist's Prayer, on the other hand, examples of explicit religious vocabulary are the words 'supernatural' and potentially 'glorious'. So far, my analysis is mostly intuitive, and I need to test these intuitions at certain points in order to build a stronger case. In the last chapter, I introduced religious wordlists and tools, which tag texts and identify words with religious meaning. Let's try some of these tools out on our texts here.

Comparing our texts against Michael Lessard-Clouston's *Complete Theological Wordlist* (Appendix 2), we find that 'evil' and 'glory/glorious' (head word: glorify) occur more frequently in overtly religious contexts. These are likely to be carrying concentrated religious meaning here. Let's turn next to the USAS free online semantic tagger. So you can see what this process looks like, Table 7.4 contains the results of putting the Lord's Prayer into the USAS tagger. According to USAS, the only words and phrases in the Lord's Prayer that indicate religious meaning are 'Our Father' and two instances of 'heaven'. As for the Atheist's Prayer, the tagger identified only one word, 'supernatural', as having religious meaning. So far, this doesn't mark these texts as particularly religious, which isn't particularly helpful.

Let's see if WMatrix can expand our analysis. WMatrix allows users to access something called a 'Domain Tag Wizard' to give the semantic tagger extra information about the text or set of texts they want to analyse. In

Table 7.4 *The Lord's Prayer, Tagged by USAS Free Semantic Tagger*

Our_S9/Q2.2[i1.2.1 Father_S9/Q2.2[i1.2.2 **which**_Z5 **art**_C1 **in**_Z5 heaven_S9

,_PUNC **Hallowed**_S7.2+ **be**_A3+ **thy**_Z8 **name**_Q2.2._PUNC

Thy_Z8 **kingdom**_G1.1 **come**_M1._PUNC

Thy_Z8 **will**_X7+ **be**_Z5 **done**_A1.1.1 **in**_Z5 **earth**_W3,_PUNC **as**_Z4[i2.3.1

it_Z4[i2.3.2 **is**_Z4[i2.3.3 **in**_Z5 heaven_S9._PUNC

Give_A9- **us**_Z8 **this**_M6 **day**_T1.3 **our**_Z8 **daily**_T1.1.2 **bread**_F1._PUNC

And_Z5 **forgive**_G2.2+ **us**_Z8 **our**_Z8 **debts**_I1.2,_PUNC **as**_Z5 **we**_Z8 **forgive**_
    G2.2+

our_Z8 **debtors**_I1.2/S2mf._PUNC

And_Z5 **lead**_S7.1+ **us**_Z8 **not**_E2-[i3.2.1 **into**_E2-[i3.2.2 **temptation**_O4.2+,_
    PUNC

but_Z5 **deliver**_M2 **us**_Z8 **from**_Z5 **evil**_G2.2-:_PUNC **For**_Z5 **thine**_Z99
    is_A3+

the_Z5 **kingdom**_G1.1,_PUNC **the**_Z5 **power**_S7.1+,_PUNC **and**_Z5 **the**_Z5
    glory_X2.2+

,_PUNC **for**_T1.3+[i4.2.1 **ever**_T1.3+[i4.2.2._PUNC

Amen_Z4._PUNC

Note: I have modified the results to make them easier to make sense of. The text of the prayer is in bold, and the 'religious and the supernatural' portions which USAS identified are underlined.

this case, for the Lord's Prayer, I entered the preferred semantic field as S9, which is 'religion and the supernatural'. However, despite this additional step, the tagger only identified one additional word, 'hallowed', as religious. So far, the tools have identified the following words and phrases as explicitly religious in our two prayers

evil, glory/glorious, our father, heaven, supernatural, hallowed.

But there remain other words and phrases that may also be carrying explicit religious meaning.

In order to test my intuitions about the religious meaning that other parts of the text carry, I turned to the Corpus of Global Web-Based English (GloWbE) (Davies, 2013). Leaving the metaphorical language for a later section, the words and phrases that I suspect have explicit religious meaning are:

will (noun form), daily bread, forgive, temptation, Amen.

I won't take you through all of these, but let's look at 'daily bread' as an example. I've chosen this phrase in particular since it doesn't appear in the *Historical Thesaurus of English* ('The Historical Thesaurus of English,' n.d.).

In GloWbE, I have the option of searching for all uses of 'daily bread', and this search reveals 940 instances, across twenty countries. Looking at the first page of results in the United States, Canada and Great Britain, it's clear that this phrase is still repeated in prayer but also has become a common name for a food bank.[2] Rather than looking at the concordance lines of all 940 instances, I used the corpus tool's collocation function to calculate the words that most strongly associate with 'daily bread'. The top 10 collocations that appeared within five spaces to the left and to the right of the phrase include language from the Lord's Prayer (see Table 7.5).

We can confirm this further by looking at the concordance lines for each collocate. For example, I looked at the first 100 instances of 'our' within five spaces to the left and the right of the phrase 'daily bread' in the UK and in the United States (see Table 7.6). These preliminary findings indicate that the multi-word unit 'daily bread' remains in use to communicate primarily explicit religious meaning. This might seem an obvious conclusion, but it's nevertheless important to make a solid case as far as we can rather than rest solely on assumption.

Table 7.5 Top 10 Collocates of 'Daily Bread' in GloWbE

our, their, us, day, earn, give, today, earning, order, provide	daily bread	us, our, forgive, food, bank, sins, butter, trespasses, 6.11, prayer

Table 7.6 First 10 Concordance Lines of 'Our' as a Collocate of 'Daily Bread' in GloWbE

	United Kingdom	United States
1	done, on earth as it is in heaven Give **daily bread**. And forgive us **our** debts	Pr 31:27, but the bread honestly gotten. We ask for **our daily bread**; which teaches us constantly to depend upon Divine Providence. We beg of God
2	your will be done, on earth as in heaven Give today **our daily bread**. Forgive us **our** sins, as we forgive those who sin against us	we wish many blessings for you! # To God who gives **our daily bread** A thankful song we raise, And pray that he who sends us food May
3	earth, as it is in heaven. **daily bread**. And forgive us **our** trespasses, As we forgive them that trespass against us	done on heaven. Give us this day **our daily bread**, and forgive, as we forgive those who trespass against us
4	of the poor: # The words ' Give us this day **our daily bread** ' have not much meaning to us; do we ever think what they mean	for all When there's trouble for one! While we're earning **our daily bread** She's the one with her hands in the butter You must send the slut
5	will be done, on earth as in today **our daily bread**. Forgive us **our** sins as we forgive those who sin against us. Lead	done on heaven. Give us this day **our daily bread**; and forgive trespasses as we forgive those who trespass against us;
6	**our daily bread**. And forgive trespasses as against us	on earth heaven. Give us this day **our daily bread**, and forgive, as we forgive those who trespass against us
7	on **daily bread**. And forgive against us	Earth as it is in Heaven. # Give us this day **our daily bread**. # And forgive as we forgive those who trespass against
8	the country pays it's [sic] bills and finances itself, do we earn **our daily bread** or do we keep on borrowing until the bailiffs call. # For society to	earth **daily bread**. And forgive us **our** trespasses, As we us
9	dinner at the new inn, and had earned that portion of **our daily bread** by admiring the Abbey all the morning. So we pitied the poor workmen doubly	the bread platter etched with the words 'Give Us This Day **Our Daily Bread**'. # Of course MacBride died and his daughter had taken over the writing

(continued)

	United Kingdom	**United States**
10	will be done, on earth as in today **our daily bread.** Forgive us **our** sins as we forgive those who sin against us. Lead	works to reap life, victimize and give us this day to make **our daily bread** Cause if I'm broke, I'm serving cavvy in Bethlehem Or selling my

We've already seen that the Atheist's Prayer contains limited explicit religious vocabulary. Instead, this prayer uses mostly implicit religious vocabulary, imbued with religious meaning because of the nature of the text (prayer) and the way it is positioned against the Lord's Prayer. For example, replacing the word 'Father' with 'brains' signals that this word has sacred significance in this prayer and within an atheist belief system. Other implicit religious vocabulary includes:

heads, earth, insight, resolve conflict, ease pain, denial of logic.

These words don't carry explicitly religious meaning in all or even most contexts, but here the context (prayer and site of conflict) reveals their religious function. If I expanded this study, I could look for the extent to which words and phrases like these function as keywords within atheist discourse more broadly.

At this point, we can draw two conclusions from this look at religious vocabulary. First, we see an emerging picture for each prayer. The Lord's Prayer prioritizes a parental human-divine relationship yet still differentiating between an all-powerful God and a created world. There is a strong sense of good vs. evil in this prayer and a belief in a need for forgiveness. The religious vocabulary in the Atheist's Prayer looks within the human body for truth, and evil arises from any violation of the brain's sacred status as a centre of reason. The goal is insight and resolving of conflict, and the path to these is human reason.

Second, we can conclude that explicit religious language wordlists and tools like USAS and large corpora interfaces can be a useful first step to systematically identifying religious vocabulary in a text. They help us remove some elements of bias and account for the different types of religious vocabulary in a text. However, they are only a start and, in many cases, we will need to test our intuitions about the religious meaning of a word or phrase using a larger corpus. We also need to look closely at context to identify words and phrases that are doing religion and what this language means, even though it might not typically carry religious meaning.

Archaism in the two prayers

Both prayers use archaic language throughout, of various types, including,

archaic grammatical language: thy, thine
archaic functional language: art, trespass, trespasses, hallowed
archaic syntactic structures: Treasured be thy name, Thy reasoning
come, Thy best you can do be done, hallowed be thy name, thy kingdom
come, thy will be done, Lead us not, For thine is the kingdom.

The use of archaism in the King James translation of the Lord's Prayer isn't
that surprising since it was compiled in 1611. But this translation is still
in common use today, and the Atheist's Prayer's replication of its archaic
language shows that this language is still relevant and recognizable, even to
people outside of organized religion.

As a previous chapter discussed, archaic language evokes tradition, a past
time and a sense of authority. Perhaps the author of the Atheist's Prayer is
poking fun at an old-fashioned way of talking and, by extension, critiquing
its belief system and distancing its author from the prayer. After all, the
author doesn't consistently use archaism, sometimes using archaic pronouns
and structures and sometimes not. Either way, the use of archaic language
in both is a prominent feature that contributes to their religious meaning.

Parallelism in the two prayers

As I mentioned before, the Lord's Prayer is modelled on Hebrew poetry,
containing parallelisms. These add emphasis, beauty, significance and
authority. The prayer's parallelism echoes the Ten Commandments, situating
the prayer firmly within the larger biblical narrative (see Clowney and
Clowney Jones, 2007). As for the prayer's internal parallelism, it is based not
so much on rhyme as it is on the balance of ideas. In the Authorized King
James version of this biblical passage, we encounter mostly symmetrical
parallelism, which provides emphasis and clarity. At each main point, the
prayer gives one concept or thought, then provides additional meaning with
a second thought. Consider this pair, for example:

Your kingdom come;
Your will be done.

Here, we encounter a parallelism that indicates that the coming of the
Father's reign is connected to the doing of his will. In fact, in the original
Greek, the first three petitions parallel each other not only symmetrically but
also in form and grammar, as do the last three petitions. And as you can see

in Table 7.3, the first three petitions balance the last three, with the fourth sandwiched in between. According to biblical scholar David Wenham, these parallelisms reflect a priority on God's kingdom and God's righteousness without neglecting material needs, which have a central place (Wenham, 2010).

Table 7.7 Contrastive Parallelism in the Atheist's Prayer

Treasured be thy name	→ Deliver us from the denial of logic
Thy reasoning come	→ And lead us not into supernatural explanations
Thy best you can do be done on earth as it is	→ N/A

The Atheist's Prayer mimics some of the parallelism in the Lord's Prayer, for example in the use of syntactic parallelism in sections 2 and 3 of the prayer (see Table 7.3). And interestingly, the Atheist's Prayer maintains some of the internal balance between sections 1 and 3 of the prayer, as in Tables 7.3 and 7.7.

In the first two pairs, one can see a sort of contrastive parallelism, between the human brain and the denial of logic, between reasoning and supernatural explanations. In these ways, the use of parallelism not only lends a poetic (and emotive) appeal to the prayers but reinforces the belief system inherent in both prayers.

Metaphor

In the last chapter, I presented Lynne Cameron's approach to metaphor analysis (Cameron, 2008). Using this method, I identified and tracked the metaphors in both prayers. Unsurprisingly, the Lord's Prayer uses metaphor vehicles common to Christianity including:

- representations of God (FAMILY, RULER, SPATIAL)
- sin (CAPTIVITY, MONEY)
- MOTION
- Jesus (FOOD).

The reference to 'daily bread', which is both literal and metaphorical, may be less visible to those unfamiliar with the Bible and the meaningfulness it places on bread, beginning with the Israelite's freedom from Egyptian captivity. Exodus 16.4-5 lays the foundations for Jesus's meaning here, when the Israelites were given enough bread on Saturday for that day and the next.

Then the lord said to Moses, 'I will rain down bread from heaven for you. The people are to go out each day and gather enough for that day. In this way I will test them and see whether they will follow my instructions. On the sixth day they are to prepare what they bring in, and that is to be twice as much as they gather on the other days.

In other words, in the wilderness, God gave His people their bread for Sabbath rest a day early. And by surpassing their earthly need that day, by calling their minds to the day of rest that was coming, God was teaching His people of a need and a rest far greater. The Lord's Prayer, therefore, offers Christians a taste of the heaven God promises by giving His people Jesus Christ today, the Bread of Life that they will one day taste in all its fullness (John 6.35). In fact, a closer translation from Greek to English of this line of the Lord's Prayer might be 'Give us tomorrow's bread, today'.

Likewise complex is the combination of God as RULER and the vehicle of MOTION in the phrase 'Thy kingdom come'. The notion of kingdom in the Bible encapsulates not only a physical space but also a relational and ideological space. The vehicle of MOTION in the Lord's Prayer refers both to a literal second coming of a resurrected Jesus Christ, which the Bible frequently refers to, and to a more abstract kind of motion as people accept Jesus into their hearts (Harkness, n.d.). As for the combination of sin as CAPTIVITY and sin as MONEY, these evoke the notion of a debtor's prison. Both are images Jesus uses elsewhere, for example, in a parable in Matthew 18.

When considering the metaphors for God, a modern reader might see discontinuity (or at least an additional layer of meaning) between God as FATHER and God as RULER. But as biblical scholar Aída Besançon Spencer (Spencer, 1996) points out, the image of father in the ancient world is unique and must be understood through the lens of that context. In the ancient Jewish, Greco-Roman world in which Jesus uttered the Lord's Prayer, a father could also be a judge or a ruler. Women, on the other hand, could not adopt and could rarely inherit. Besançon Spencer gives the example of Emperor Claudius, known as 'father of the fatherland' (pater patridos). What is unique about the biblical text's use of this metaphor for God is that the father-son metaphor communicated not only power but also intimacy, love, care and guaranteed inheritance.

In the Atheist's Prayer, we find some overlap in use of metaphor and also some removal of metaphor worth our attention. At the start of the prayer, we have what might seem to be a literal use of the word 'brains'. Here it functions as an instance of metonymy, the physical brain used to represent related concepts such as thinking and intelligence. The difference between metaphor and metonymy is in the tension or lack thereof between the two concepts. The reference to a physical brain and the removal of metaphor to refer to it are consistent with atheism's axioms, the focus it places on rationality and physicality. Also in the opening of the prayer, we find another significant removal of metaphor in the phrase 'which art in our heads'. This creates a contrast between a physical space and the abstract idea of God existing spatially. This happens again in the removal of 'in heaven' in the phrase 'on earth as it is'. These again reflect a physicalist philosophy.

The Atheist's Prayer does contain some metaphor, however. For instance, in 'Thy reasoning come', we encounter metaphor vehicles that portray ideas as OBJECTS with MOTION. This is an enduring metaphor, so perhaps it's expected, unintentional. However, this metaphor is nevertheless imbued with religious meaning here since it parallels the reference in the Lord's Prayer to the literal and metaphorical second coming of the Christian Saviour of the world, Jesus Christ. Come save us, reasoning, prays the atheist. This same vehicle pair is echoed in section 2 of the prayer (see Table 7.3), where the prayer directs, 'Give us this day new insights'.

The last two metaphors in this prayer are the same as those in the Lord's Prayer. Denial of logic is seen through the lens of CAPTIVITY and the brain is portrayed as RULER over the kingdom of reason in the doxology. Again, the substituted language is consistent with the belief system in atheism, where the material world and human rationalism are the source of truth and meaning.

Intertextuality in the two prayers

In the last chapter, I noted that the more a text is cited, the more sacred (or taboo) it can become. As a parody, the Atheist's Prayer is an example of manifest intertextuality, an immediately recognizable commentary on the Lord's Prayer. An overt reference to the Lord's Prayer itself isn't necessary precisely because the prayer is so well-known. The Lord's Prayer is one of the most frequently repeated stretches of religious text in the world. It is embedded in the collective consciousness not only because of its sacred status but also by its frequent repetition. Even short excerpts from the prayer are highly familiar to many. Mimicking and unsettling it with key substitutions are powerful and even risky moves.

As we've already seen, the Atheist's Prayer has a similar structure and uses similar archaisms (though fewer). There are also some similar uses of metaphor and religious lexis. The ways that the Atheist's Prayer modifies the source text are significant in revealing the functions of the Atheist's Prayer. First, the substitutions reveal a shift in focus to a materialist/physicalist worldview. We can see this first in the pattern of address ('Our brains, which art in our heads') but also later in the sacred marking of 'logic'. The power and glory of God in the Lord's Prayer are substituted for qualified praise of 'our brains', brains which are 'limited', 'not always glorious' and capable of 'Thy best you can do'. Despite these limitations, the message is that materialism is the best option available to us to accomplish the sacred aim of helping the earth. The act of constructing a prayer to communicate this message points to a form of sacred-making that disrupts and critiques Christianity. We might ask the extent to which this is tongue-in-cheek, but this would require looking at other texts and particularly in more detail at the Discourses that accompany atheism.

Chapter summary

Prayer is a highly complex set of human activities, which many people carry out, not just people who think of themselves as religious. Indeed, prayer is a deeply human activity, a reaching beyond or within oneself to connect with and articulate one's deepest held truths about the world, often to reach emotive or even material ends. A useful model of prayer presents two layers of factors: directionality and intentionality:

1   **directionality:** upward, outward, inward.
2   **intentionality:** articulate deeply held truths, build and strengthen a sacred community, to intercede in the world (by invocation) and to meet emotional need.

Prayer can involve all of these factors and sub-factors or emphasize a few.

This chapter looked at religious language features in two prayers: the Lord's Prayer and the Atheist's Prayer. The Atheist's Prayer, as a parody of the Lord's Prayer, creates a site of conflict. This gives us points of comparison by which we can more clearly see the sacred beliefs at the heart of each prayer. It also helps us to see the Atheist's Prayer as perhaps primarily aimed to strengthen sacred group boundaries by establishing a point of difference.

Where the Lord's Prayer is primarily upward in its directionality, the Atheist's Prayer is inward and outward. The two prayers are similar structurally, but at the heart of each is distinct difference: 'daily bread' vs. 'new insights'. In its vocabulary and metaphor, the Lord's Prayer emphasizes the familial relationship between God and humankind as well as the distinct natures of each. It also presses a need for forgiveness and freedom from captivity (evil) through Jesus Christ as a means to participate in that relationship. The Atheist's Prayer draws on similar metaphors. But here the human mind is the source of freedom, denial of the mind is the source of evil and the goal is not a relationship with a deity but with the earth. There is scope for much more work on prayer, particularly what we might call unconventional prayer. Prayer is indeed a deeply sacred and highly complex activity.

Further reading

Field C D (2017) Britain on Its Knees: Prayer and the Public since the Second World War. *Social Compass* 64(1): 92–112. DOI: 10.1177/0037768616685014.

Field M and Blackhorse T (2002) The Dual Role of Metonymy in Navajo Prayer. *Anthropological Linguistics* 44(3): 217–30. DOI: 10.2307/30028848.

Katz M H (2013) *Prayer in Islamic Thought and Practice*. Cambridge, UK: Cambridge University Press. DOI: 10.1017/CBO9781139034333.

Martin M W (2015) The Poetry of the Lord's Prayer: A Study in Poetic Device. *Journal of Biblical Literature* 134(2) : 347–72. DOI: 10.15699/jbl.1342.2015.2804.

Discussion and exploration

1   Figure 7.1 contains a food prayer, which the photographer says she keeps on her dining room table.

   a   What religious language, both explicit and implicit, appears in this prayer?

   b   What sacred values is this prayer communicating through that language?

   c   What are the directionality and intentionality of this prayer and what do these tell you about the prayer's function?

FIGURE 7.1 *Food Prayer, 2013.*

2   The Christian Parish of Bengeo in Hertfordshire, UK, describes itself as 'A family, together in faith with God our Father'. In their online prayer archive, select either one recent prayer or a larger selection of prayers (the twenty-five most recent, perhaps): https://www.parishofbengeo.com/church/prayer-archive.html

a Write down the main topic(s) of each prayer. What does this tell you about what might be typical content of prayer on this site?

b What is the information structure of the prayer(s)? Can you identify any patterning? Is it similar to or different from the prayers in this chapter?

c For at least one prayer, complete a full comparison between the religious language features in the Lord's Prayer and the prayer you have chosen.

d What can you conclude about the extent to which these prayers communicate a similar set of sacred beliefs, compared to the Lord's Prayer?

8

Religious language at the time of human death

FIGURE 8.1 *A Life Well Lived, 2017.*

What does the phrase 'a life well lived' mean to you? What constitutes such a life?

What does this inscription on a park bench in Figure 8.1 contribute to the idea of such a life?

The last chapter considered prayer, in particular the Lord's Prayer and the Atheist's Prayer. Viewed together, the two prayers form a site of conflict between different notions of the sacred. In this chapter, we turn to another place where religious language is likely to occur: a moment or period of significant life transition. This chapter focuses on religious language at the time of human death, examining the phrase a 'life well lived'. In the last chapter I presented and analysed two short texts. In this chapter, I'll expand to a larger collection of texts, illustrating the use of a wider range of analytical tools and focusing in particular on implicit religious language. Specifically, this chapter will focus on the discursive construction of a 'life well lived' in two collections of texts: the Corpus of Global Web-Based English (GloWbE) (Davies, 2013) and recent obituaries from the UK on Legacy.com ('Legacy.com – Where Life Stories Live On,' n.d.).

A life well lived

Not long ago, I was in a pub with a friend, and we started talking about how her young son was worried about the inevitability of her death. Any parent will likely be able to pinpoint a time when their kids have expressed this concern, and I asked her what her response was. She explained that she'd said something along the lines of 'Well, at least I've lived a life better than most'. This struck me as particularly axiomatic, pointing to fundamental beliefs my friend holds about herself and life itself.

As it happened, I was also talking to my religious language students about the condolences that members of the public had posted online after the death of Stephen Hawking ('Stephen Hawking Obituary,' 2018). We noticed several things about the online guest book entries, including the frequency of archaic language. But we also encountered repeated mention of the phrase 'life well lived'. One anonymous member of the public put it like this,

> May your hearts soon be filled with wonderful memories of joyful times together as you celebrate a life well lived.

A closer look at Legacy.com pointed me to the following quote, which reveals how central the concept of a life well lived is on the site.

> Legacy.com is the place where the world pauses to embrace the power of a life well-lived. We believe that a single story can provide extraordinary inspiration, even after that person has died. So we champion every life, knowing it can connect us in unexpected, powerful ways. ('About Us,' n.d.)

Various cultures at various times throughout history have responded to and coped with the reality of death in many different ways. However, one impulse we all seem to share is a compulsion to measure the human life. For centuries, philosophers have attempted to explore and explain what makes life worthwhile, from Plato to Aquinas, from Kant to Sartre. What constitutes a life that matters? For Epicurus, it was all about pleasure. For Socrates, a good life was about virtue. For Aristotle, living a good life was more complex, involving virtue, prosperity, health, friendship, good luck, rational thought and so on (Ostenfeld, 1994). More recently, psychologists, accountants, sociologists and religious scholars have explored links between mental health, forgiveness, finances, autonomy, curiosity and personal spirituality and a sense of a life well lived (Fairman, Knapp and Martin, 2005; Irving, 2012; Kashdan and Steger, 2007; Niemiec and Ryan, 2013; Piferi and Lawler-Row, 2006; van Dierendonck and Mohan, 2006). Indeed, when we attempt to measure a life, our measuring stick can involve any number of things. Debates about which of these things matter when it comes to declaring a life well lived ultimately involve decisions about the nature of value and, of course, the existence and source of truth.

For many, measuring life comes alongside grappling with moments of crisis or conflict as well as suffering and death. According to the stoic philosopher Seneca, for example,

> while death is inevitable, how we die is highly dependent on the virtues, skills, planning and attention we bring to it, and ... the best deaths are well-prepared ones.
>
> (Scarre, 2012: 1082)

Similar views can be found in world religion. In Islam, for instance, death is seen as 'a reward for those pious and virtuous individuals who have led exemplary lives' (Al-Kharabsheh, 2011: 39). And beyond death, the deceased enter the afterlife where they may be rewarded for their virtue and righteousness during their time on earth or punished for lack thereof (Al-Kharabsheh, 2011: 44). In some religious communities, those whose lives embody the qualities of a good citizen receive the posthumous honour of achieving ancestor status (Bonsu, 2007).

So it is that, for some, a good life leads to a good death and good life after death. Those who survive also receive honour through their connection to someone with revered post-mortem status. So measuring life can also be about considering the meaningfulness of our life to our descendants. Some argue, for example, that making environmental-friendly choices is primarily about the legacy of a healthier planet we leave behind after death. So attempts to measure and achieve a life well lived can function as a means to achieve honour in death and to improve the everyday lives of those we leave behind.

On the other hand, for some, measuring human life has little to do with reward for oneself or anyone else and more to do with the finality of death. As the saying goes, 'You only get one life'. Faced with the possibility of wasting that one life, of missing chances quickly lost, we construct and justify various scales as proof that our existence has been wisely spent. For those left behind, death can be an occasion to reflect on the deceased's life, to celebrate it and in so doing to consider the extent to which their own lives are meaningful.

The way we describe death is a particularly visible way we articulate our measure of life. More specifically, obituaries can point us to society's attitudes towards life and death. Most obituaries, which are death notices often published in local newspapers, contain the name of the deceased, the cause of death, positive attributes of the deceased and relevant details about the place and time of the funeral. However, different obituary writers place differing amounts of emphasis on these types of information. Some obituaries are more informative and others more sentimental (Hernando, 2001). Cultural factors play a significant role in these choices. One recent study carried out on Dutch and German obituaries, for instance, found that the Dutch share more personal information about the character of the deceased in obituaries than their German counterparts (Barth, van Hoof and Beldad, 2014). This sharing of positive attributes is often not so much about the dead as it is about the living. Victorian obituaries used a

> wide range of euphemistic, consolatory and eulogistic strategies to mark the social status of the deceased and signal the social standing of the grieving family in their community.
>
> (Fernández, 2007: 8)

In this way, Victorian references to a 'well-spent life', as they put it, were a form of impression management. These were intended to compliment those who had died by means of overstatements. And in contemporary Ghana, obituaries often publish and promote favoured aspects of the deceased's identity in order to create ideal images of the bereaved family and boost their social status (Bonsu, 2007). Obituaries serve the dual purpose of measuring the lives both of the living and of the dead (Moore, 2002), with the ultimate aim of comforting or otherwise benefiting the living. Of course, as I've already mentioned, the criterion for a 'life well lived' differs from place to place and from time to time. However, what remains the same is the tendency to show preference in death for those lives deemed worthy.

If some lives are worthy, then of course some lives are unworthy. In her book *Obituaries in American Culture,* Janie Hume points to the many deaths mainstream newspapers in the United States overlook (Hume, 2000). These especially include deaths of Black Americans as well as children, the poor, the disabled and the socially outcast, whose failure to fit social ideals prevents them from being acknowledged in the public memory. And then there is the favour that men tend to receive over women at the time of death. Obituaries in Malaysia, for example, signal the importance assigned to the male figure not only in terms of number of obituaries about men versus women but also in the discourse of obituaries more generally (David and Yong, 2000). We see also, in Stephen Moore's analysis of the obituary column in *The Economist* from 1995 to 1997 that the typical subject profiled is an influential, white, English-speaking male from a western industrialized country, who dies in old age.

(Moore, 2002: 524)

In the rest of this chapter, I will consider this phrase 'a life well lived', prominent in the world's largest provider of online memorials, obituaries and death notices. It is a phrase that occurs regularly in a wide variety of online texts, both overtly religious and not. And it is a phrase with a long tradition, going back centuries, which speaks to our human impulse to measure a life. In order to get to grips with the phrase 'life well lived', I will look at the use of this phrase in two large collections of texts, as I will now explain.

The texts and methods of analysis

For this chapter, I use two sources of data. The first is the GloWbE, which contains 1.9 billion words of text from twenty different countries (Davies, 2013). This allowed me to look at the ways in which the phrase 'life well lived' is used in contexts beyond obituaries. This corpus is unique in that it allows for comparison among different varieties of English as well as analysis of one or more varieties.

I used several analytical methods on this corpus. In the first instance, I examined the collocational profile of the phrase 'life well-lived/well lived' (216 instances total)[1] across the entirety of the corpus. You may remember that collocations are words that occur frequently in combination to a statistically frequent degree. I identified the top 20 collocations (occurring within four places either side of the phrase) and grouped them thematically, a procedure consistent with content analysis (Hsieh and Shannon, 2005).

Next, and in order to consider the phrase 'life well lived' in its broader contexts, I collected every text from the UK sub-corpus of GloWbE (GloWbE-UK) containing the same phrase 'life well-lived/well lived'. This resulted in a sub-corpus of twenty-nine texts (39, 901 words). The texts come from newspapers and other news sites like *The Guardian, The Telegraph, Daily Mail* and *The BBC* (13), personal blogs (6), magazines like *Big Issue* (4), sites linked to academia (3), Christian websites linked to cathedrals or churches like *Durham Cathedral* (2) and official celebrity sites (1) (see Appendix 4). I scrutinized the discursive construction of the phrase within each text, focusing on:

1 demographic features, such as age and gender, of any person whose life was marked as 'well lived'
2 whether or not the phrase was explicitly defined and if so, in what terms

3   whether or not the phrase was contrasted with another kind of life
    and if so, what features and actions mark such a life and
4   the extent to which rationale, means and reward are articulated.

The second source of data was obituaries from Legacy.com. Legacy.com is
an American-owned company based in Evanston, Illinois. It was founded in
1998 and is now the world's largest provider of online memorials, obituaries
and death notices ('About Us,' n.d.). In fact, according to worldwide
newspaper database *Nexis*, many newspapers no longer publish obituaries
('Finding Obituaries,' n.d.). Instead, over 1500 newspaper affiliates in North
America, Europe and Australia now use Legacy.com, to which they direct
the bereaved in order to create an online obituary and publicly accessible
guestbook.

As of 17 April 2019, a Google site search reveals that Legacy.com
contains nearly 500,000 uses of the phrase 'life well lived'. Clearly, this
is an important way of talking about death on this site. I selected forty-
four obituaries for this chapter because they comprise all of the obituaries
(out of 1,000+) which contain the phrase 'life well lived' during a twelve-
month period (March 2018–March 2019). The hope is that these obituaries
provide a window into the uses of the phrase in question on this site. I'll call
this corpus Legacy Life Well Lived or LegLWL. Finally, I also collected the
top 220 results in a search for all obituaries in England over a one-month
period. None of these obituaries contain the phrase in question (8 February
2019–8 March 2019). This resulted in another corpus of 13,654 words. I'll
call this corpus Legacy Reference or LegRef.

I used the corpus tool SketchEngine to compile a list of keywords and key
multi-words for the LegLWL corpus (Kilgarriff, Baisa and Bušta et al., 2014),
using the LegRef as a reference corpus. You may remember that keywords
and key multi-words tell us the 'aboutness' of a text (see Chapter 4). They are
identified by compiling wordlists for both a corpus and a reference corpus
and then identifying words and phrases that are statistically more frequent
in one corpus as opposed to the other. In this case, keywords allowed me to
identify words or phrases that might be contributing to the discourse of a
'life well lived'. I'll explain this more as I go along.

In summary, here are the various corpora I used for this chapter:

1   GloWbE: 1.9 billion words of text from twenty different countries
2   GloWbE-UK: twenty-nine texts (39, 901 words), which include
    every text from the UK sub-corpus of GloWbE that contains the
    phrase 'life well lived'
3   LegLWL: all of the obituaries on Legacy.com (forty-four texts) which
    contain the phrase 'life well lived' during a twelve-month period
    (March 2018–March 2019)
4   LegRef: 220 obituaries from Legacy.com during a one-month period
    in England (13,654 words).

Constructing sacred lives

In these next sections, I will discuss the ways that the phrase 'life well lived' encodes a set of beliefs about life and death. I will explore how it creates and on occasions enforces sacred boundaries. And finally, I will consider the extent to which the phrase both comforts and devastates people encountering one of life's most vulnerable events.

The axiomatic function of a 'life well lived'

Although we can find examples of axiomatic religious statements in many different contexts, remember that we are particularly likely to make religious statements in times of conflict or crisis, high stakes and key life transition. Here, it becomes particularly important to rearticulate and reassess what we hold sacred. Sacred-making at times like death is often more about emotional support and social cohesiveness than it is about articulating statements of belief. Still, language at the time of death reveals what a person believes about the value of life (human or otherwise), what it is to be a human being, whether or not there is an afterlife and so on.

Within the GloWbE corpus, collocates of a 'life well lived' reveal this human impulse to measure life, the significance and nature of a life well lived and the various rationale for that measurement (see Table 8.1). The language of measurement is immediately obvious in the frequency of words like 'measure', 'components' and 'key'.

Each of these signals that the process of appraising a life's sacred value is taking place. This process involves deciding what a life well lived 'looks' like, which 'components' are necessary, which of these are 'key' or 'fair' and which are 'actually' accurate. We can see these things in the concordance lines below (1–4, emphasis mine):

1   the first thing is to decide what a life well-lived **looks** like
2   a range of other essential **components** of a life well-lived

Table 8.1 Top 20 Collocates of a 'Life Well-lived/Well Lived' in GloWbE

celebrate	fair
full	looks
dazzling	key
glow	human
legacy	joyfully
death	mourn
yes	shadows
times	gift
components	actually
measure	God

3   agree, seems to be the **key** of a life well-lived. A **fair measure** of what makes life worthwhile for us would then be
4   it seems to me that a life well-lived is **actually** one

In concordance lines 5–8 below, showing other collocates in context, we see some clues about what comprises a life well lived. It is a human life (5), not one of animals or other living things (see McKay, 2015). It is a 'very full life' (6). But perhaps more significant is the value placed on a life well lived as well as its attractive nature. It is something of 'wonder', 'dazzling' with 'glow'. A life well lived is a 'gift'. The rationale for a life well lived is its appeal, the benefits it promises to the person who lives it (6–9) and, indirectly, those who survive (10):

5   **human** life well-lived
6   acknowledging the wonder of a very **full** life well lived
7   the warm **glow** of a life well lived. This **dazzling glow**
8   A life well lived is a precious **gift**
9   Life Well Lived gives **Death** the uppercut
10 A life well lived is a **legacy,** of **joy** and pride and pleasure

We can see the significance of metaphor in these extracts, linking a life well lived with the explicitly religious vehicles of LIGHT and WAR, and the notion of a GIFT.

But there is one further rationale that appears in these collocates. Remember, the use of an **external legitimating authority** to signal legitimacy often points to deeply held beliefs. In the GloWbE corpora, we find this kind of appeal to an external authority, framed as a rationale for measuring and aiming for a life well lived (11).

11 we owe **God** a **life well-lived;**

In this text, a life well lived is an obligation. This wasn't typical, however. In most of the texts, the reason given for measuring a human life is that this kind of life offers some reward. So looking at collocates in context points to the rationale for measuring and the reward of a life well lived. But so far, this hasn't revealed much about what exactly constitutes a life well lived nor by what means we can achieve it. So I next examined the smaller collection of texts from the GloWbE-UK. This not only produced a similar pattern in terms of the attraction that a life well lived offers but also offers a richer and more complex account.

First, the texts in the GloWbE-UK corpus reveal that, once again, the rationale for a life well lived is mostly about reward. The texts assure us that, consistent with Seneca, a well lived life is 'rewarding', giving us 'hope' of 'a good death', a 'painless death'. It promises 'satisfaction', allows us to feel 'pleasant' and 'comfortable' while we are still alive, ensures we will be 'missed by many who we have never met but whose lives we have touched' and, in so doing, 'leave a legacy'. This points to an underlying selfish ethic, though the texts also point us to altruistic reward as well. In living life well, we benefit and inspire our relatives through a life they can 'look back on with directness' and not shame. A minority of the GloWbE-UK texts point to some of the ways we can achieve a life well lived. For example, we can attain a good life by looking after our health. We should 'exercise', 'don't drink', 'enjoy sex', 'get medical attention'. For some, it is a matter beyond our control, as in 'God has been good to me and so has this country'.[2]

The GloWbE-UK texts also offer more detail about what comprises a life well lived. Although there are only twenty-nine texts in this sub-corpus, there are both major and minor themes which also appeared in the Legacy.com obituaries. First, a well lived life is primarily **a male life**. Seventeen of the twenty-nine texts discussed specific lives, and of these twelve were male. Following this pattern, twenty-seven of the forty-four LegLWL obituaries were about men who had died. Key multi-words for this corpus (compared to LegRef) also linked a 'life well lived' with being male. People whose lives were well lived included a 'much-loved husband' and various other male figures like a 'husband' and 'father'. This confirms findings from other research on obituaries more generally but adds an additional layer of privilege to the lives of men.

Second, the texts in GloWbE-UK point to a well-lived life as **full**, both in length and in terms of level of activity. A well-lived life is someone with a 'very full' life with 'big dreams' who 'contribute[s] so vastly', who 'lived to the full' 'however long it takes'. One text mentioned old age several times and contrasted it with the lives of 'premature babies whose lives will never be viable' and a 'wife and mother [who died] at such a young age'.

Likewise, in LegLWL, a life well lived was sometimes 'long', though more often these obituaries mentioned the old age (mid-seventies or older) of the deceased. The phrase 'grand age' was also more frequent in LegLWL than in the reference corpus. There were two exceptions that bucked this trend, however. One woman was described as dying 'peacefully at home, aged 59 years … a short life well lived'. In this case, the grieving person prioritized criteria other than age. Likewise, in one of the GLoWbE-UK texts, the comments section of a personal blog argues for

12 A life well lived, however short, which ends as painlessly as possible is probably what we should be aiming for.[3]

I'll come back to the significance of health later.

In the GloWbE-UK corpus, a life well lived was linked to the act of **doing**. Such a life involves accomplishments. This will come as no surprise considering the grammatical construction of the phrase itself. A life well lived is a life that involves the **action of living and living well**. But it is a specific type of living which counts in the measurement of value. A life well lived requires specific 'goals' as well as 'shape and direction' towards becoming an 'expert', work which involves primarily doing notable things for oneself,

> pursuing, doing, enjoy[ing] work, [being a] perfect drummer, pursuing a modest activity and perfecting it, [being able to refer to] things he had done, achievements [like being] the first black mayor, [receiving] an MBE from the queen, action, learning a craft and doing it well.

On Legacy.com, obituaries containing the phrase 'life well lived' were more likely to mention expert professions than those obituaries that didn't contain the phrase. Reference to jobs like 'chief engineer' and 'civil engineer' were common. In the GloWbE-UK corpus, an active and therefore meaningful life contrasted with an attitude of:

13 I always wanted to do X but never got around to it. I wish I didn't have X holding me back.[4]

One text made this point explicit, distinguishing a life well lived from the life of a woman unable to work, in this case,

14 a woman whose entire adulthood has been dominated by an eating disorder and who has never been strong enough to do more than occasional menial work, despite her obvious intelligence.[5]

A well-lived life is also one that benefits others. A few texts in GloWbE-UK emphasized acts of service, like 'wartime service' as well as sharing 'truth' and 'alleviating human suffering'. Some texts praised being an inspiration for others to **do** similar notable things. A life well lived is one that 'inspire[s] enterprise'. As we've seen already, Legacy.com has this sacred value at the forefront of their ethos. On their homepage, 'where life stories live on' and where we can 'learn how to preserve [our] loved one's life story', we see that some lives are more enduring than others. This is mostly related to how inspirational, how public they are. Near the top of the page, the site points us to 'notable deaths', 'celebrity deaths' and 'inspirational lives' ('Legacy. com – Where Life Stories Live On,' n.d.).

In addition to accomplishments, GloWbE-UK contained many references to personal qualities and attributes that mark a life well lived. These were fairly diverse. People who achieve a life well lived are privileged in these ways:

15 physically: 'strong', 'powerful'
16 emotionally/psychologically: 'joyful', 'modest', people who are 'happy'
17 morally/spiritually: 'holy', 'holiness', 'transparency to God', 'meekness', 'mercy', 'poverty of spirit', 'purity', 'integrity', 'salt of the earth'

18 intellectually/mentally: 'courage', 'brilliant'
19 economically/socially: 'middle class', have 'true love'

In one *Daily Mail* text, the author identified the specific qualities that a female life well lived possesses. These are qualities that she retains despite old age, a woman's clothing (sensible 'slacks and flats'), her 'hair', 'etoliated neck' and 'high cheekbones'. She is 'bright', 'lively', 'vital', 'beautiful', even 'sexy'. For men and women both, old age is a significant marker of a life well lived, but in this text we see an additional requirement for women to remain youthful and sexually appealing in their old age. Such a woman is contrasted, rather shockingly, with a woman

20 depicted in a care home, or suffering from dementia, sitting mute in her Marks & Spencer cardi.[6]

This excerpt and the previous one referring to an eating disorder suggest that mental health seems a particularly crucial attribute for women specifically.

In summary, opinions vary regarding which personal qualities matter. But what is consistent is the belief that people who live their lives well are 'distinguished' and 'incredible', 'great' people who possess 'talent' and a 'dynamic personality', who are a 'legend' because of these traits. They are contrasted with people who have 'guilt' and 'regret', whose lives are 'unconsidered'. So far, then, **depictions of a life well lived privilege a human life that is long and full, primarily male, and involves accomplishment and a range of personal attributes and qualities.** This is an act of sacred-making as it speaks to fundamental anthropological and axiological questions. But what of the people who didn't achieve a life well lived? These are lives of people who 'never got around to it', lives of babies and young mothers whose lives ended tragically, 'when the circumstances of death have been so hideous'. They are lives of women with mental illness or dementia. These depictions signal, with only one exception, an assumption that everyone has both equal access to these kinds of accomplishment and a desire to mark their lives in this way.

The social cohesive function of a life well lived

Religion and religious language foster community united around common sacred ideals, sacred places, sacred people and/or sacred things, living or otherwise. In fact, the act of writing an obituary is itself an act of social cohesion. It places the life of the individual into the public memory. Times of crisis and significant life transitions, like death, are times for a community and its members to reflect on what unites and distinguishes them.

But besides this, as I mentioned in the last section, some of the GloWbE-UK texts pointed to service of others and to God as the substance of a life well lived. Here is another example of that, in the Archbishop of Canterbury's speech on the Papal visit in 2010:

21 our ministry together as bishops across the still-surviving boundaries
   of our confessions is not only a search for how we best act
   together in the public arena; it is a quest together for holiness and
   transparency to God, a search for ways in which we may help each
   other to grow in the life of the Holy Spirit.[7]

There is strong emphasis on social cohesion here, across 'still-surviving
boundaries'. It seems that the Archbishop is attempting to resolve conflict.
Note language like:

together (3x), our (2x), we (2x), across the still-surviving boundaries,
public arena, each other.

The Archbishop's articulations of sacred ideals work to unite a divided
community around a common goal: a life well lived marked by 'holiness
and transparency to God' and help of others.

The Archbishop may be casting his net widely within the Christian
community, but remember that sacred communities always have boundaries.
These dividing lines are constructed in multiple ways, including using
axiomatic statements like those in the Archbishop's speech. The phrase 'life
well lived' is socially cohesive in that it differentiates between good (lived)
and bad (unlived) lives, makes explicit the means to achieve them and offers
a rationale. Setting aside the Archbishop's words, we can see a good life
contrasted with a bad life particularly in the counter-examples in excerpts
14 and 20 above. In the larger context surrounding excerpt 14, the writer is
actually correcting the woman with anorexia, who expresses willingness to
die on the grounds that she'd lived well. She says,

22 I've done everything I wanted to do, I am quite happy to die now.[8]

The writer responds,

23 For a moment, she sounds like an elderly person, looking back at a
   life well lived. This is difficult to reconcile with the life experience of
   a woman whose entire adulthood has been dominated by an eating
   disorder.

This correction acts as a kind of sacred border protection. Still, as we've
also seen, other texts in the corpus transgressed these boundaries, referring
to shorter lives as well lived, for example.

Finally, when it comes to policing sacred boundaries, reference to an
external legitimating authority comes in handy. Remember that in appealing
to authority, an individual or a community takes on that authority for
themselves, 'expanding the presumptive speaker above the level of the
individual' (Keane, 2008: S122). The 'life well lived' corpus contained a few
references to God as an external authority (see excerpt 11), but this was

not common practice. But Legacy.com does point us to 'notable deaths', 'celebrity deaths' and 'inspirational lives'. Holding up high-profile lives is a powerful sacred legitimating tool. The implicit message here is that these particular lives are models. Legacy.com prompts us to compare our lives against these authoritative ones, and this use of celebrity amplifies the sacred power of the life well lived.

The emotive function of a life well lived

Life-course transition rituals like birth, marriage and death are sites where emotive religious language is highly important and particularly likely to occur. At the beginning of the chapter, I cited studies which refer to the comfort that articulating positive attributes about the deceased brings to those who survive them (Bonsu, 2007). But this chapter's work on the two sets of data reframes that discussion to consider this as a process of sacred-making. It is ultimately religious in nature, no matter who does it.

To declare a life well lived is to make a statement of value with emotive force. It reassures both the dying and the bereaved that life has meaning, even beyond the grave. It comforts us with a promise rooted in a belief that those who achieve a life well lived will receive immediate benefits and will inspire others to live meaningful lives. A life well lived is 'rewarding', 'pleasant' and 'comfortable'. Such lives prompt 'celebration' and are a source of 'hope' in the face of suffering and death. For these kinds of lives, says one author, we offer 'heartfelt thanks'.

Such declarations give us a feeling of control over death. In the GloWbE-UK corpus, we see that a good life secures a 'good death' which 'ends as painlessly as possible' and the chance to 'die contentedly'. As in excerpt 9, a 'Life Well Lived gives Death the uppercut', giving death a capital 'd' (death personified) and embedding it in a battle metaphor to further underscore the significance of the 'life well lived' as a tool of empowerment. **A life well lived is, for many, humanity's ultimate triumph.**

A life well lived, a life of privilege

This chapter has looked at the phrase 'a life well lived' in order to illustrate the potential of a functional model of religious language. This approach allows us to consider not just overtly religious contexts but also implicitly religious ones. It is an opportunity to move beyond the constraints of what we **expect** religious language to look like to consideration of how people use language, sometimes in unexpected ways, to accomplish sacred-making.

The phrase 'a life well lived' does not immediately sound religious to most ears. It doesn't involve linguistic features that carry religious connotation as typically understood. There is no reference to a deity, to a religious text nor to other words or phrases that are either distinctly religious or likely to be imbued with institutionalized religious meaning (see Coe and Chenoweth, 2013). A 'life well lived' doesn't appear on the wordlists some scholars and educators have compiled to attempt to document religious vocabulary, such as the *Religion, Spiritual Inspiration Vocabulary Word List* ('Religion, spiritual inspiration word list,' n.d.), the 'religion and the supernatural' portion of the University Centre for Corpus Research on Language (UCREL) Semantic Analysis System (Rayson, 2009) or the *Catholic Religious Vocabulary* wordlist (Jordan, 2019). And yet, the phrase is deeply religious in meaning insofar as it points to deeply held assumptions about what it is to be human and the nature of value. People unite around assumptions like these and even on occasion defend them. They provide comfort at moments of suffering, crisis and life transition.

The phrase 'life well lived' is both deeply religious and part of a wider Discourse around death. It is prominent in the world's largest provider of online memorials, obituaries and death notices. It regularly appears in obituaries and in a wide variety of online texts, both overtly religious and not. It is a phrase with a long tradition, going back centuries, which speaks to our human impulse to measure a life. Focusing on the use of the phrase in a global corpus and in online obituaries, I've discovered that a life well lived is primarily a human life, more specifically a male life. It is a full life, a life of accomplishments and elite qualities such as intelligence, happiness and dynamism. It is no surprise then that a life well lived is often that of a celebrity or other notable person who is 'inspirational'. It is a long life, free from illness, that promises rewards both to the one facing death and to those they leave behind.

Certain texts, particularly those taking an overtly religious perspective, frame accomplishment in terms of acts of service. But this way of measuring life fails to acknowledge the lives of those who most need that service. Is the act of asking for and receiving help of less value? Are lives such as these not well lived? For those who wish to mark their lives as well lived, the answer seems to be a resounding yes. Articulating the phrase 'life well lived' marks a life of privilege, a person who is born with or has subsequently been able to access opportunity and quality healthcare. This raises fundamental ethical questions about the use of the phrase.

In 2019, I presented my work for this chapter at an academic conference. While there, I met a hospice chaplain, who recounted the conversations he has with people who are coming to the end of their lives. In many cases, he said, people close to death express anxiety and fear that their lives were not full enough, not meaningful enough, not world-changing enough. What he witnessed was the consequence of Discourses of privilege like a 'life well lived', their impact on people at their most vulnerable moments. We might argue in favour or against the measuring of life in the ways I've explored in this chapter as well as other ways. But let's be clear that in essence what we are doing here is an act of sacred-making, based on deeply held and subjectively formed assumptions. Language such as this points to the valuing of certain lives over others and the pressures on possessing such a life often without acknowledgement of the privileges required.

Although there are quite a few studies on obituaries, few scholars have specifically examined religious language, defined in an open sense, and especially its role in constructing and perpetuating ideas about life and death. Considering the case of funerals, linguists Guy Cook and Tony Walter lament the scholarly neglect of language's ritual function, despite its significance and power in society. They conclude that whether 'secular' or traditionally religious, funerals 'still bring mourners together and bind them together ... This is the essence of ritual' (Cook and Walter, 2005: 386). The work in this chapter could be expanded to examine other phrases that work in tandem with 'a life well lived', phrases like 'waste my life', 'waste of life' and 'living my best life'. The latter has become more frequent in recent years, appearing only 17 times in the first ten years (1990–9) in the Corpus of Contemporary American English and then 111 times between 2000 and 2017 (Davies, 2008). In GloWbE, it appears 650 times (Davies, 2013).

Funerals and other rituals around death, such as the measuring of a life and the writing of an obituary, are simultaneously axiomatic, social cohesive and emotive acts. In coming together to talk about a life, we reaffirm Discourses about the value and meaning of life and death and share the burden of death collectively, whether we identify as religious or not. Such work prompts self-reflection about our own values. What criteria determine the worth of a life? To what extent can we justify such criteria? But it also affirms a need for greater open-mindedness going forward regarding what counts as religious language.

Chapter summary

In this chapter, I investigated religious language at the time of human death, focusing on the common phrase 'life well lived'. I used two sources of data, the GloWbE and online obituaries from Legacy.com. Whereas in the last chapter I organized my findings according to linguistic feature, in this chapter I grouped my findings according to the ways that the phrase 'life well lived' encodes fundamental beliefs, binds a community together and functions emotively. Among my findings were the following:

- A life well lived is primarily a human life, more specifically a male life.
- It is a full life, a life of accomplishments, service and elite qualities such as intelligence, happiness and dynamism.
- A life well lived is often that of a celebrity or other notable person who is 'inspirational'.

- It is a long life, free from illness, that promises rewards both to the one facing death and to those they leave behind.

Most importantly, however, language like 'life well lived' points to the valuing of certain lives over others and the pressures of possessing such a life often without acknowledgement of the privileges required. In the next chapter, I will give an overview of several other contexts where we are likely to find religious language.

Further reading

Cook G and Walter T (2005) Rewritten Rites: Language and Social Relations in Traditional and Contemporary Funerals. *Discourse & Society* 16(3) : 365–91. DOI: 10.1177/0957926505051171.

Hume J and Bressers B (2010) Obituaries Online: New Connections with the Living - and the Dead. *OMEGA – Journal of Death and Dying* 60(3) : 255–71. DOI: 10.2190/OM.60.3.d.

Pantti M and Sumiala J (2009) Till Death Do Us Join: Media, Mourning Rituals and the Sacred Centre of the Society. *Media, Culture & Society* 31(1): 119–35. DOI: 10.1177/0163443708098251.

Discussion and exploration

1   Returning to the questions at the start of this chapter, what were your answers? Have your answers changed at all, having read this chapter? What further questions, if any, do the conclusions in this chapter raise for you?

2   Below is an online book blurb for the book *A Life Well Lived* by Jim Lucey, Medical Director of St Patrick's Mental Health Services and Clinical Professor of Psychiatry at Trinity College, Ireland (Table 8.2).

   a   What contextual information might you need to analyse this text?

   b   What religious language (both explicit and implicit) is used to construct the notion of a life well lived? Consider in particular any discourse strategies as well as uses of vocabulary, metaphor and intertextuality.

   c   What kind of life is made sacred in this blurb?

   d   To what extent does the notion of a life well lived in this text compare to the one which this chapter has presented?

Table 8.2 Online Book Summary for **The Life Well Lived** *by Jim Lucey*

We all long to live a fulfilled and happy life – a life that offers us love and opportunity, independence and hope. Sadly, for many people struggling with mental health problems such as anxiety, depression, eating disorders and addiction, recovery and a future full of potential may seem to be unachievable goals.

In *The Life Well Lived* Professor Jim Lucey focuses on how a range of contemporary therapies can provide pathways to recovery. Through insightful case histories, he also explores issues such as stigma and other barriers to recovery, the true meaning of wellness, and how the rediscovery of a life of independence and social connection is not only possible but entirely achievable.

Positive and optimistic, *The Life Well Lived* shines a light into the psychotherapeutic world – a world which is so often feared and

misunderstood.

Source: (Lucey, 2017).

3   Find a text that uses the phrase 'waste my life'. You may want to find your own text using a web search, but you can also find a text by entering the search string 'waste * life' into GloWbE or another corpus at English-corpora.org.

    a   What does it mean to waste a life, according to the text you selected?

    b   What explicit or implicit religious language, if any, does the author use to create this meaning?

    c   In short, what additional meaning, if any, does this text offer to the sacred notion of a life well lived?

9

Religious language here, there and everywhere

FIGURE 9.1 *Bite Me, 2005.*

Advertising and religious imagery and language have a long history, as we've seen in previous chapters. Together, these create sacred brands. As you did in Chapter 2, create a story that explores the meaning of the billboard in Figure 9.1. In particular, consider what roles the religious language plays, alongside religious symbolism, in creating a sacred brand.

This chapter aims to give you a taste of the many other contexts in which religious language is likely to occur. I'll begin with moments of conflict and high stakes, considering religious language in politics, sport and advertising in various parts of the world. Within politics, for example, I'll not only be looking at obvious political scenes like the United States but considering evidence for religious language in what we think of as the most secular countries in the world. After that, I'll discuss serious illness as a moment of crisis, looking especially at the ways religious metaphor affects how we experience cancer. Finally, I'll look at one of the most common human experiences, conversion, as a significant moment of life transition. This is the last of three chapters which looks at language in various contexts through the lens of a functional theory of religious language. In all, my goal is to answer the question: What are some of the many ways that we use language for sacred-making?

Moments of conflict and high stakes: Politics

Few would be surprised that I begin this section on religious language and politics with American President Donald Trump. His inaugural address in 2017, with its intertextual references to the Bible and use of religious metaphor, was perhaps his most overtly religious speech to date. But of course Trump's use of explicit religious language is nothing new when it comes to American presidents. 'History is littered with presidents who claim divine sanction for their agenda' (O'Connell, 2017: xx). Explicit religious language has nevertheless ebbed and flowed in American politics. Ronald Reagan's presidency was a watershed moment for presidential public invocations of religion. In fact, invocations of God, broader religious and moral references and mentions of prayer by the last four presidents (Reagan to George W. Bush) averaged 4.5 references per address, more than double the 2.0 mean for presidents Roosevelt to Carter (Coe and Domke, 2006). But US presidents also used much more explicit Christian religious language in smaller speaking venues than when speaking to the nation as a whole. Reagan's explicit religious language increased by 25 per cent in smaller venues, George Bush's by 55 per cent and George W. Bush's by 44 per cent. Barack Obama's increased by 106 per cent in more private moments (Coe and Chenoweth, 2013).

The relationship between religion and politics is well documented among political scientists and historians. In 1967, sociologist Robert Bellah coined the term **civil religion** to refer to the United States's use of religious beliefs, symbols and rituals for its own purposes. Bellah writes,

> Behind the civil religion at every point lie biblical archetypes: Exodus, Chosen People, Promised Land, New Jerusalem, and Sacrificial Death and Rebirth. But it is also genuinely American and genuinely new. It has

its own prophets and its own martyrs, its own sacred events and sacred places, its own solemn rituals and symbols (Bellah, 1967: 18).

However, civil religion is by no means an American concept only. It takes different forms depending on the context, but its functions remain the same. It works as social glue, providing a sense of spiritual, national unity. It also positions politicians as sacred figures, the prophets and priests of a nation.

Beyond the United States, **politicians around the world rely on explicit and implicit religious language to claim moral meaning and authority for themselves and their political platforms and to establish in- and out-groups.** In 2018, the leader of Spain's far-right political party Vox, Santiago Abascal, released a campaign video that involved a re-enactment of Spain's medieval battle to end Muslim occupation.[1] Key to Abascal's Vox platform was a clampdown on fundamentalist Islam and 'military combat missions against the Jihadist threat' (JAR, 2018).

Elsewhere, in 1979, the late Iranian leader Ruhollah Khomeini used the metaphor 'The Great Satan' to describe the United States (Dabashi, 2015). Carrying on in this tradition more recently in 2015, Ayatolla Khamenei used the same metaphor along with 'Iblis' (the devil in Islam) as a derogatory epithet for the United States and other Western countries (Dabashi, 2015). And in the Egyptian context, as we saw in a previous chapter, the religion of Islam was prominent and significant in the political speeches of the third President of Egypt Anwar Sadat (1970–81). In another part of the world, East Asia, during the 1996 Taiwanese presidential election, Taiwanese President Lee Teng-hui told an interviewer that he saw himself as Moses leading the Taiwanese to their promised land (Tefft, 1996).

Reporting on the phenomenon of religious language and politics in Australia, Anna Crabb presents evidence from 2,422 political speeches that between 2000 and 2006 politicians doubled their use of Christian vocabulary like Christ, church, faith, pray, Jesus, Bible, spiritual, God and/ or religion (Crabb, 2009). She suggests from this that religion has played an increasingly prominent role in Australian political discourse in the early twenty-first century. And in the UK, though religious language is notably more subtle and indirect, the premiership of Margaret Thatcher marked the starting point of a rise in explicit religious language in the political rhetoric of British prime ministers (Crines and Theakston, 2015). Both Thatcher and David Cameron drew on the Bible to justify economic individualism and construct and further foster a romanticized Britain. Prime Ministers Tony Blair and Gordon Brown didn't directly quote the Bible, but they drew attention to the comparable values of different faiths in order to create a sense of unity and social democratic purpose. And of course British politician Boris Johnson, like the Taiwanese president, used a Moses metaphor in the run-up to Brexit when he urged Theresa May to say 'to the Pharaoh in Brussels – let my people go' (Johnson, 2019) (see Figure 9.2). Religion has also entered the political space in the UK much more visibly in recent

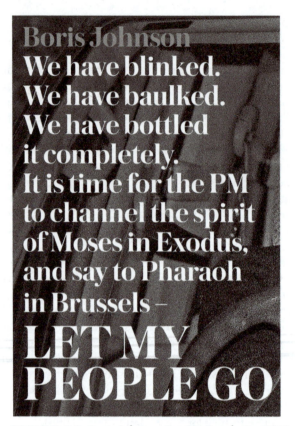

FIGURE 9.2 *Boris Johnson, Let My People Go, 2019.*

months as debate has circulated about anti-semitism in the Labour Party and specifically in connection with Jeremy Corbyn (Quinn, 2019).

Although all of this demonstrates that religious language remains a powerful political tool in a wide variety of political contexts, existing scholarship largely operates from a closed definition of religion. Most of the work on religious language of American presidents, for instance, has analysed political speeches at the level of words and phrases that are either distinctly religious in all contexts or likely to be imbued with institutionalized religious meaning (Coe and Domke, 2006; Coe and Chenoweth, 2013). Work like this has focused on words and phrases in the following categories:

1 god-talk: language that indicated the existence of a divine power, that is, God, the Almighty, Divine power, providence

2 Bible: references to the Bible itself

3 manifestations: physical or metaphysical manifestations of Christianity, that is, church, sermon, pulpit, bless, creed, eternity, faith, heaven, holy

4   people: those with a direct tie to Christianity, that is, priest, pope, saint, flock, worshipers

A notable exception is a recently published paper on the National Rifle Association (NRA)'s use of religious language to link nationalism with the political debate about gun rights in the United States. Jessica Dawson scrutinized a corpus containing every issue of *The American Rifleman* from 1975 to 2018 for explicit religious language like 'God' and 'God-given' rights (Dawson, 2019). But Dawson also coded for explicit religious metaphor, what she refers to as 'implicit discussion related to the religious nationalist discussion of the Second Amendment' (p. 5). This included metaphors of SACRIFICE and MOUNTAINS, even on occasion DEMONS.

Dawson concludes that the NRA uses religious metaphor, religious vocabulary and culturally sacred icons like the actor Charlton Heston to imbue the Second Amendment with sacred meaning, to be defended at all costs from a profane government. Still, Dawson's methods for identifying religious language aren't entirely clear, and this affects her analysis at times. For instance, she connects the gladiator imagery in the phrase 'come to the arena' to the biblical story of Daniel in the lion's den. Despite some shortcomings, Dawson's work pushes our understanding beyond the explicit religious language of elected politicians to consider the ways powerful lobbying groups likewise wield the power of the sacred.

We've seen that existing scholarship gives us part of the picture. What we still lack is full and rightly nuanced understanding of the relationship between religion and politics and likewise other aspects of culture and society. Kjell Lejon and Marcus Agnafors make this point in reference to religion and politics in Scandinavian countries, widely considered to be among the most secular in the world (Lejon and Agnafors, 2011). They refer to recent published conversion stories to Christianity of several high-profile individuals in Sweden and argue that religion and faith are still engaging Scandinavians. Conversions to Christianity like these, they write, do not constitute a return to religion but rather a shift of interest in a fairly stable religious realm. They go on to make the case that the political realm, rather than being largely secular, is in fact manifestly Lutheran. They acknowledge that religion may look different in Scandinavia and specifically in its politics than elsewhere. Here, organized religion, particularly 'uncontrolled religion', is viewed suspiciously. But what they argue fairly convincingly is that closed and otherwise narrow definitions of religion simply fail to account for the complexities of religion in politics and other aspects of society.

Returning to the UK, Veronika Koller has keenly observed the use of the phrase 'clean Brexit' instead of 'no Brexit' in the run-up to the UK's exit from the European Union. You might remember that in Chapter 4, I talked about links between soap and morality which helped pave the way for all sorts of aspects of life to be imbued with moral meaning, using the metaphor of cleanliness. As Koller points out,

> The metaphor suggests purity and, though a secondary metaphor, moral purity. Whoever came up with it knew what they were doing. (Koller, 2019)

I've barely scratched the surface of religious language in politics here. There is much room for linguists to explore in more depth the linguistic features used by politicians to invoke religion. We must look beyond explicit religious vocabulary to other features of religious language, both macro and micro. As a site of conflict involving high stakes, politics will always be a place where political leaders will vie to present themselves as exemplifications of sacred texts and ideals (Alexander, 2006), whether these are overtly religious or not.

Moments of conflict and high stakes: Sport

On 6 March 2019, Tom Brady, Michael Strahan and Gotham Chopra released a trailer connected to their project called *Religion of Sports* ('Religion of Sports - Official Trailer', 2019). In the video, just over one minute in length, various athletes at the top of their game talk about their relationship to sport, against a backdrop of videos of football, climbing, rowing and more. They say,

> Spirituality means a lot of different things to different people. And I think, for me, it's your deepest purpose.
> What are you willing to give up to be the best that you can be?
> Someone is out there working really hard, and they're working to beat me.
> I'm not a player that's just going to come and go. I'm here to be an all-time great.
> You need something that brings your community together and there are a lot of places that that's church but for this part of the world, your church is on Saturday night [at the stock car races].
> It's like that single moment when everything magically happens the right way.
> If I were a religious person, this would be like going to the cathedral.[2]

Within this short video are explicit and implicit religious vocabulary, religious metaphor, and even religious parallelism. The website connected to the project is likewise rich with religious language. At the top of the 'About Us' page, the founders state provocatively, 'Sports are not *like* religion. **Sports are religion**' ('About Us', 2019, emphasis original).

Work by linguists on sport and religion includes Saija Peuronen's study on the use of religious language among Christian snowboarders in Finland. Peuronen concludes that snowboarders create a unique space which combines overtly Christian vocabulary with the language of snowboarding (Peuronen, 2013). She presents a scene where some of the community members sit together and talk about worship in their various churches. Eventually, some of the participants begin discussing their conclusions about what the Bible has to say about women participating in extreme sports. For these snowboarders, snowboarding is not itself a religion. Instead, the sport is functioning as the activity that the snowboarders participate in while they discuss matters of faith.

We can contrast this with Todd Vernon Lewis's article on religious metaphor in American college football (Lewis, 2013). The religious language is not incidental to the practice of sport. Rather the use of metaphor both relates and constructs a sacred space for sports fans and competitors. Among the many examples he gives, Lewis identifies four key metaphors – CATHEDRAL, WORSHIP, GLORY and SACRED – which powerfully imbue sport with religious meaning. Lewis's methodology isn't clear in the article, but his work is a useful reference point for those investigating sport and religion.

The powerful link between religion and sport is thoroughly corroborated, just not by linguists. Indeed, sport as religion has a long history. Arthur Remillard documents, for example, the origins of lacrosse among Native Americans in the early fifteenth century. He recounts one Cherokee myth involving the ball as a sacred object which a lacrosse player hit into the sky with his hand in an act of frustration. That ball became the moon. The Cherokee tribe repeats this myth as a means to achieve social order (Remillard, 2016). And of course we can take these links back much further, to the ancient Greek Olympic Games.

As a context involving conflict and high stakes, religious language is frequent in sport. An area my students often work in is European football, whether it's Pele's famous quote 'Football is like a religion to me. I worship the ball and treat it like a god', the use of Christian hymns and other religious songs among fans or the deification of footballers like Stephen Gerrard. But whatever the sport, for those interested in investigating this rich area of inquiry, we are spoilt for choice.

Moments of conflict and high stakes: Advertising

My first formal, paid job as a teenager was for a consumer research centre. My job involved presenting consumers with advertisements for films, for crackers, for soap, for soda, for sunglasses, for whatever product you can think of. I then had to ask them a series of questions about whether the advertisement made them more or less likely to buy, to use, to vote, to watch, to choose that product or that person. I often saw explicitly religious imagery and language in the advertisements I worked with, but there was a great deal of implicit religion as well.

We as consumers are manipulated into certain choices, often unconsciously. Certainly, it's no secret that advertising is ultimately a form of proselytizing, the act of converting someone from one belief or opinion to another. The goals of advertising are, put simply, to communicate information, to sell a product and to create a community of loyal consumers. Religious language, therefore, has a happy home in advertising. As we saw in the case of the soap advertisement in Chapter 4, advertisers often rely on religious language and symbols, both explicit and implicit, to communicate the nature of value, who we are and how we should live our lives. One could argue that implicit in every instance of advertising is an act of sacred-making.

Just as in the other areas I've covered so far, there are few linguists looking at religious language in advertising. Not even biblical scholars have paid much attention to this area. One place worth starting is Katie Edwards's book *Admen and Eve: The Bible in Contemporary Advertising* (Edwards, 2012a). Although not from a linguistic point of view, her work confirms just how pervasive the biblical Garden of Eden symbolism is within advertising, particularly aimed at women. Her work introduces us to frequently used Discourses surrounding women in advertising, including the 'ultimate postfeminist' who 'exercises her power through her female sexuality, which is maintained or boosted through her consumer spending power' (p. 38). Furthermore, Edwards equips her readers with tools to analyse images. Particularly useful is her discussion of Eve's apple as a metaphor for women's bodies. Edwards writes,

> Eve is quite a money-maker, and so long as she can bring in the revenue she will be out there in cinemas and magazines with her trusty apple and snake to lure in consumers to take a bit of whatever produce she is selling.
>
> (p. 34)

Advertisers tend to rely on certain common religious narratives, including creation as Katie Edwards discusses, but also resurrection, Messiah and Satan (Belk and Tumbat, 2005). The messianic narrative is a particularly productive one and involves the deification of products and celebrity endorsers, particularly men. An example is when the iPhone became the 'Jesus phone' (Campbell and La Pastina, 2010). Apple CEO Steve Jobs himself achieved a level of sainthood in death comparable to a prophet. Many members of the public held candlelight vigils and created shrines, re-appropriating numerous religious symbols to sacralize both him and the technology he created (Bell and Taylor, 2016). Figure 9.3 shows some of the language common during that time. Although not always explicitly religious, such language communicates sacred beliefs, implicitly connected to the notion of a life well lived. Numerous other advertising firms and the brands they represent have similarly capitalized on a Messiah narrative,

FIGURE 9.3 *Remembering Steve, 2011.*

including Sony PlayStation, the ESPN sports channel and Eshe Streetwear (Edwards, 2012b).

A particularly potent Messiah narrative is Nike's portrayal of American basketball player LeBron James. Scholars Richard Mocarski and Andrew Billings point us to three Discourses that Nike has used to sell LeBron James as King James (Mocarski and Billings, 2014). First, advertisers rely on stereotypes of black bodies, rooted in racism. Although black athletes are associated with muscular strength and speed, they are also frequently portrayed as servile, anonymous, selfish and lazy. These racist stereotypes also associate black bodies with cheaters and drug dealers. Second, advertisers tap into hegemonic masculinity, which includes maleness as power and control, occupational achievement, familial patriarchy, frontiersmanship and heterosexuality. Finally, they draw on the established power of branding, which fosters loyalty and creates a sacred entity. We can draw connections here to Rihanna as a sacred brand, whom you can worship not least by purchasing a prayer candle for the low price of £19.99. Crucially, these hegemonic Discourses exist in tension. Mocarski and Billings argue that the branding of LeBron James is shown to endorse parts of these tenets while challenging others, 'producing a brand of James that is both raced through the body and de-raced through the normative understandings of Blackness' (Mocarski and Billings, 2014: 6).

The chronology of the Messiah narrative began early in James's career, in 2002, where he was headlined as 'the chosen one' for Sports Illustrated. This prompted him to tattoo 'Chosen 1' from shoulder to shoulder, followed by another tattoo reading 'King James'. In 2003, James further contributed to the growing hype, in an interview for *The Village Voice* magazine. 'Jesus

Christ made me famous', he said (St. John, 2003). International brand Nike quickly seized on that narrative. Their first commercial about LeBron James depicts him as totally in control not only of the basketball court but also of the spectators around him (Nike, 2006). This demonstrated his power, affirming all three Discourses, of stereotypical black bodies, of hegemonic masculinity and of heterosexuality.

Nike went on to air another LeBron James ad campaign using the concept of 'witness' (Nike, 2008). The religious connotations were obvious. In the commercial, black comedian Bernie Mac stands at a pulpit, preaching to a crowd, 'Let us read from the playbook, the King James playbook'. The commercial contains further explicit religious vocabulary, intertextuality and archaism. Eventually, we witness James passing the ball and imbuing his 'power' to members of the congregation. The choir sings his praises throughout his appearance in the church.

Mocarski and Billings trace the narrative through James's allegorical connection with the Holy Trinity in 2009 and the 'Rise' and 'The Decision' campaigns in 2010 and 2011. The effect of Nike's use of a Christian Messiah narrative to frame James is compelling. It allows Nike to ingratiate James to the audience, ultimately to separate him from his Blackness. They write that 'the overt use of the Messiah narrative accelerated the racial neutering of James'. We might ask ourselves how the Messiah narrative works in other contexts, to make marginalized people more acceptable to mainstream hegemonic society, reinforcing racism and other forms of discrimination.

As in other sections, I've provided here just a taste of the significant presence of religious language and imagery in advertising. In a world constantly bombarding us with advertising in every imaginable form and context, religion is among the last great taboos. Advertisers have demonstrated eagerness to exploit the sacred in order to achieve surprise and obtain shock value. There is indeed enormous potential for linguistic analysis of religious language within advertising.

Moments of crisis: Healthcare

Illness, particularly life-threatening illness, prompts reflection on fundamental questions about life, death and where we are all headed (Seibaek et al., 2013). Whereas the Enlightenment fostered a suspicion of religion in discussion about health, scholars are recognizing that science need not pretend to be secular. As we emerge from the myth of objectivity, scholarship on religion and health has recently exploded. Much of this work wrestles with questions like: Does religion decrease suffering? Does it result in stronger mental health? Does prayer work? Do religious people outlive non-religious people? However, again, much of the research in this area has historically neglected people who don't consider themselves religious. One provocative question that some are beginning to ask is this:

Are there health consequences for specific comprehensive worldviews, be they secularism, Marxism, Christianity, or any other?'

(Hall, Koenig and Meador, 2004: 397)

But of course there is also much scope to look at the ways people talk about their illness and how others talk to them. The wealth of scholarship on language and cancer gives us a good place to begin.

Understandably, metaphor plays a significant role in language around illness as well as death. Remember that metaphor is one means of acknowledging our cognitive limitations, of articulating things we can't fully make sense of. The metaphor of BATTLE and other language of struggle are particularly prominent in discourses around cancer. Language like 'She lost her battle to cancer' or 'Don't fear Cancer. Fight it!' is likely familiar to us all. We talk about cancer as an act of warfare on the body by invisible forces that we defeat by strength, strategy and will. In the image in Figure 9.4 of a poster produced by the United States Health Service, the BATTLE metaphor is used alongside visual imagery of a (male) ancient warrior carrying a sword. If we die from cancer, we've lost. Perhaps we

FIGURE 9.4 *Don't Fear Cancer. Fight It! 1938.*

were too weak, not worthy enough as warriors. Although scholars have not talked about this kind of language as religious, there's no escaping the connection here between cancer and evil, a kind of holy war. As warfare is a common theme in explicitly religious discourse, this isn't a far leap to take. And indeed, medical practitioners are now regularly advised to be aware that people use more than just explicit religious language to articulate what they hold sacred (Baldacchino and Draper, 2001).

Many are beginning to challenge language that connects cancer with warfare, however. More and more, we now 'race for the cure'. Cancer is now a journey, but it is also a sporting event (Seale, 2001). The warfare imagery may be waning, but a race nevertheless requires stamina and strength, what some feminist scholars see as evidence of a male-dominant society (Lumby, 1994). Metaphors like this, they argue, demonstrate that even in women's most vulnerable times, society encourages them to view their experiences through the lens of hegomonic masculinity. Such language shapes how women view themselves and their bodies and thus constitutes an act of sacred-making.

Religious language at times of illness is often more explicit, however. Medical practitioners' lack of understanding of such language can often have terrible consequences. Tia Powell reports the case of LJ, an 86-year old African American Pentecostal woman who refused to have her melanoma treated by amputation of her leg. She insisted, 'Jesus will save me if I am to be saved, not you.' The doctors were not proficient in LJ's religious language in connection with her health and were unable to meet LJ on her own terms (Powell, 1995: 74). In a report commissioned by The European Observatory on Health Systems and Policies, Sophie Durieux-Paillard outlines the need for medical practitioners, including those providing end of life care, to become more familiar with culturally specific expressions of pain, distress and comfort, including religious expressions as well as the sacred notions that underlie them (Durieux-Paillard, 2011). Although there is still plenty of work for linguists to do in this area, there is increasing recognition of the significance of religious language during serious illness, as a site of crisis.

Moments of significant life transition: Conversion

The last context I'll look at in this chapter is one that every person, at least once in their lifetime, is likely to undergo and tell others about. That moment is conversion. Whether it is a conversion to a world religion (Ammerman, 1994), to veganism (Haidrani, 2018; Malesh, 2009), to vegetarianism (Towns and Towns, 2001), to feminism (Magnanti, 2014) or to abstinence from alcohol (Galanter, Dermatis and Sampson, 2014;

Greil and Rudy, 1983), the conversion experience seems to be a universally human experience. All kinds of people in different situations have told their stories-of-becoming, from backpackers (Noy, 2004) to volunteer overseas development workers (Hudson and Inkson, 2006), from therapists (Kottler and Carlson, 2005) to teachers (Carter, 2012).

I have on occasion used examples of conversion narratives in this book to argue for an open definition of religion and to talk about the push-pull strategy. Since conversion has come up multiple times already, it may seem odd to discuss it more fully now. It's worth revisiting, however. This is not only because of how common it is in the human experience but also because there is a considerable literature on conversion for religious language enthusiasts to engage with.

There are many names for conversion narratives. They have been called change narratives, stories-of-becoming, religious experience, spiritual awakening or simply experiences of personal transformation. A conversion narrative is a kind of religious movement activity where people talk about their own and sometimes another person's life-changing experiences. Patricia Malesh writes that in a conversion narrative, a person tells a story which speaks 'to a moment or event, or series of moments or events, that transform those who experience them' (Malesh, 2009: 133). These may be stories about encounters with injustice and other moments of crisis, stories expressing moral outrage in situations of conflict or threats to a way of life or a person's well-being. People may tell stories of empowerment, recounting how and why they rejected an old way of life and embraced a new one. Ultimately, they are stories which speak to who people are and who they are not (Benford, 2002). Whatever these stories are about, they all speak of a significant life transition. 'To change one's religion is to change one's world' (Buckser and Glazier, 2003: xi).

Conversion narratives have multiple functions. Like other forms of sacred community activities, conversion stories mark people out as members of that community. They are shared between insiders to build community. They reaffirm beliefs, articulate shared experiences and bring comfort. They help narrators to make sense of what they have experienced, to articulate and justify their beliefs. But conversion stories can also be shared with outsiders in the hopes that they will experience a conversion of their own. Sharing a conversion story can in this way be an act of proselytizing.

The different contexts in which conversion narratives take place may shape what the narratives actually look like, the form that they take. These stories do not operate in isolation. Various conversion stories or participant narratives bundle together and help to construct the culture of a sacred community. Over time, they function as models for experience of sacred group insiders. Many religious communities even publish what they consider best versions of conversion narratives. In 2017, for example, the magazine *Christianity Today* published 'The Top 10 Testimonies of 2016' (Editors,

2017). I had to wonder about those that didn't make the cut. What was unacceptable about them?

According to Massimo Leone, although conversion stories may differ in structure depending on context, most involve six factors:

1 the encounter with a different system of (religious) ideas
2 the discomfort of (spiritual) uncertainty
3 the loss of personal and social identity
4 the anxiety of destabilization
5 the reconstitution of the self
6 the discovery of a new language of the soul (Leone, 2004).

We've already seen in Chapter 4 that conversion narratives tend to feature a push-pull narrative or a dichotomous worldview strategy. Robert Priest looked at word choice in conversion narratives among Aguarana men and women in Peru (Priest, 2003). He writes that these narratives construct a vision of two alternative ways of life. In one narrative, a grandmother called Ducitak says,

> I used to be tudau (sinful), pegkegchau (bad). I did many bad things Apajui (God) does not like. When I heard the word of Apajui, I discovered my sin, what I am. I said, 'truly I am going to the place of fire'. Thinking of this, I wept much. And so I contracted myself to Jisucristui (Jesus Christ). Then I began to obey the word.
>
> (p. 95)

Priest says that the Aguarana people already have vocabulary related to evil. Their conversion story involves reframing the old way of life using words they already possess, such as tudau (sinful) and pegkegchau (bad). In this way, significant life transition entails rejecting and reframing an old way of doing things, an old set of beliefs, and embracing what is new.

For this reason, conversion narratives often rely on the metaphor of a JOURNEY down a good path. In her work on conversion stories of adolescent Singaporeans, Phyllis Chew documents the JOURNEY metaphor as well as other related ones, like conversion as a BREAKTHROUGH, a LIGHT AT THE END OF A TUNNEL, an ESCAPE ROUTE or a TIME OF GROWTH (Chew, 2010). In each, there is movement of some kind. But beyond these larger structures, conversion narratives within every sacred community tend to have a particular vocabulary. In order to mark oneself as a member of a new sacred community, a person should display not just an awareness of how their story should be structured but also proficiency in the insider vocabulary and sacred texts of that community.

Compared to other domains where religious language appears, conversion is frequently talked and written about among scholars. However, as in other areas, linguists have done limited work. Systematic linguistic analysis of conversion stories in various contexts, using an open perspective on religion, will enrich our understanding of this widespread phenomenon.

Chapter summary

In this chapter, I've covered some of the areas where religious language plays a common role. These are moments we can gain something significant by affirming our deepest-held beliefs and commitments. I've given an overview of religious language in politics, sport, advertising, healthcare and conversion, but there are numerous other contexts and events I could have chosen. Every year, my students surprise me with the texts they've found that use religious language in ways I'd never imagined. I hope this chapter has demonstrated the vast power and potential of religious language. It appears on the world's stages, but it is also whispered in our most private moments. It is the language of our deepest selves.

Further reading

Chilton P and Schäffner C (2002) *Politics as Text and Talk: Analytic Approaches to Political Discourse*. Philadelphia, PA: John Benjamins.

Crines AS and Theakston K (2015) 'Doing God' in Number 10: British Prime Ministers, Religion, and Political Rhetoric. *Politics and Religion* 8(1): 155–77. DOI: 10.1017/S1755048315000036.

Koller V (2009) Missions and Empires: Religious and Political Metaphors in Corporate Discourse. In: Musolff A and Zinken J (eds.) *Metaphor and Discourse*. London: Palgrave Macmillan, pp. 116–34. DOI: 10.1057/9780230594647_8.

Koller V, Kopf S and Miglbauer M (2019) *Discourses of Brexit*. London: Routledge.

Sheffield T (2006) *The Religious Dimensions of Advertising*. New York: Palgrave Macmillan. DOI: 10.1057/9780230601406.

Stromberg P G (2014) The Role of Language in Religious Conversion. In: Rambo L R and Farhadian C E (eds.) *The Oxford Handbook of Religious Conversion*. Oxford: Oxford University Press, pp. 117–39.

Discussion and exploration

1   Some scholars argue that at least some of the uses of religious language I've presented in this chapter are abuses or at least misappropriations.

Would you agree with them? Why or why not? Consider, for example, the use of religious language to buttress racism or anti-blasphemy laws, which declare it illegal to insult a particular religion or deity. What would count as a proper use of religious language? Why?

2 Some called American President Donald Trump's 2017 inauguration speech his most religious speech to date. Read the transcript of it, found here: https://www.bartleby.com/124/pres70.html.

   a Choose one or more feature of religious language (intertextuality, for instance) and trace its use across the text. Note: Trump's explicit religious language begins in earnest in section 9 and intensifies further in section 17 and following.

   b What religious discursive strategy, if any, does the religious language create? What does Trump accomplishes in his reliance on religious language? Ultimately, he is making himself and his policies sacred. But which policies? In short, what sacred political message is he communicating?

10

Religious language: An open horizon

We've both made it to the end of this book. Thank you for sticking with me. I hope it's been worth it. In this final chapter, I will give an overview of the key points in this book and close by reflecting on the importance of work on religious language and where scholarship in this area might next be headed.

Summary of the book

Over the last nine chapters, I have argued that all humans participate in sacred-making. The sacred is anything or anyone that is set apart from the ordinary, treated with reverence or disdain. Any material or immaterial entity can be sacred, from the seemingly mundane to the more visibly significant. The sacred flows out of answers to fundamental questions about knowledge, ourselves and the world around us, our worldview. The sacred is always connected to these understandings of the greater world. It substantially affects the way we view ourselves, how we live our lives, how we spend our time and our money, how we relate to others and to the world.

But sacred entities are not typically constructed by individual people. They are rather frequently connected to dominant Discourses or resistance to dominant Discourses. These include sacred notions related to immaterial realities like supernatural beings, the origins of the universe and the afterlife. But they are also attached to material realities like food, music, human and animal life, loyalty to one's country, one's community, what it is to be human. The natural world can be made sacred, as can marriage, art, science fiction, children, physical fitness, sex, sexuality, gender, consumer brands, employment, comic books, technology, civil law, romance and sport. These are just a few! And any number of these can combine and be prioritized in any way that suits the sacred community. We can learn a great deal about a community's sacred ideals by which ideals that community considers negotiable and non-negotiable, what marks a person as in or out. Although I haven't discussed blasphemy in much detail in this book, a further way to identify what is sacred in any community is considering what its members are not allowed to say or to question and whether the penalties are mild (gasp!) or severe (death!). Blasphemy itself creates a site of conflict. For example, the caption for Figure 10.1 is almost certainly tongue-in-cheek but nevertheless taps into and preserves a concept of fashion as sacred. This Discourse was recently dramatically manifested in the 2018 Met Gala in New York, whose theme was 'Heavenly Bodies: Fashion and the Catholic Imagination' (Edwards, 2018).

Although sacred entities tend to be communally constructed and form the centre of those communities, as individuals our sacred notions are also incredibly complex. They are often contradictory, comprising a tangled web of intersections between the various people, places, things and ideas we interact with throughout our lives. Few of us live consistently.

Religious language is a significant part of the way we make something sacred or acknowledge it as sacred and perpetuate its sacred status. Religious language assists us in sacred-making by articulating our deepest beliefs and longings, our connections with and distance from others within and outside

FIGURE 10.1 *Blasphemy! Chanel Bag on the Street, 2011.*

the world, and a sense of our human limitations, of mystery, wonder and joy but also grief, pain and confusion. Put simply, religion and religious language function axiomatically, social cohesively and emotively.

The religious language we (often unconsciously) choose to mark out what we hold sacred is a combination of explicit and implicit forms. Explicit religious language is language that is frequently used in and associated with a world religion. Implicit religious language is any other language that we use to construct Discourses connected to the sacred. Religious language is constructed using some, perhaps even all of the following resources:

1   world religions we are associated and/or familiar with and their specialized language and texts,

2   specialized language and texts connected to other sacred belief systems we are associated and/or familiar with (including prominent Discourses around us) and

3   texts and people whose authority we hold sacred (perhaps even unconsciously so), who shape our language choices.

We can expect to encounter religious language in certain contexts. Of course these include contexts connected not only to institutionalized religion, formal rituals, worship and religious education but also to the everyday lives of people of faith. I talked about some of these contexts in Chapter 4, giving particular detail about sermons as authoritative teaching in the lives of people of faith.

Beyond these overtly religious contexts, we are likely to find religious language at moments of conflict, times of crisis, moments involving high stakes and significant life transition events. All of these are places where it becomes necessary to articulate our most fundamental beliefs and our loyalties. Throughout the book, I introduced many examples of these kinds of events, focusing in particular in Chapters 7 and 8 on a parody of the Lord's Prayer as a site of conflict and on the ways we mark certain lives as sacred, particularly when talking about death.

Within all of the contexts I've mentioned (and more), texts can perform religion in a variety of ways, both macro and micro. A text that is involved in sacred-making can sometimes be spotted by its information structure. Does it mimic the structure of an explicitly religious text, for example? This can tell us that a text is functioning religiously, as we saw in the parody of the Lord's Prayer. But information structure can also point us to sacred beliefs about what is important and what is not. We saw this in the example of the wedding invitations, where parents are often mentioned first.

There are also particular discourse strategies associated with sacred-making. A dichotomous worldview strategy reveals and enforces sacred boundaries, and a push-pull strategy signals movement from an old (bad) way of life to a new (good) way of life. The use of a sacred external legitimating authority like a text, a person or a deity signals legitimacy (or illegitimacy) and allows a sacred community to claim that authority for themselves.

Language features in a text help to construct these discourse strategies. In Chapters 5 and 6, I introduced religious vocabulary, archaism, parallelism, metaphor and intertextuality. These are common features used to communicate religious meaning, but they are by no means an exhaustive list. Work on language and ideology points us to further language features that signal deeply held beliefs. I recommend in particular the work of Teun A. van Dijk, whose article 'Ideology and Discourse Analysis' contains a helpful table summarizing some expressions of ideology in discourse (van Dijk, 2006: 125–6). This is just a starting point, however. We have only begun to understand the many ways that language encodes the sacred.

Also in Chapters 5 and 6, I talked about tools that can help us identify and analyse religious language. I spent some time on corpus linguistics as well as metaphor vehicle identification. I gave an extended example of religious intertextuality in an employment text that relied heavily on witness statements to support a religious seminary board's decision not to renew a professor's contract.

Chapters 7 to 9 looked at religious language in specific text types and contexts. Chapter 7 considered the language of prayer. This was a difficult task since prayer is such a hugely diverse set of practices done by many different people all over the world, often in private. I chose to consider one of the most famous Christian prayers in the world, the Lord's Prayer, found in Matthew 6.9-13. This prayer has been parodied many times, and I looked closely at one such parody, the Atheist's Prayer. These two prayers taken together constitute a site of conflict, and I considered the structural and linguistic choices each make and what this reveals about underlying sacred notions.

In Chapter 8, I looked at a much larger set of texts, studying language at a significant life transition point: human death. I traced patterns across these texts and looked at some of the texts in more detail. Through this, I came to a greater understanding of the idea of a 'life well lived' and how it is used to mark certain lives as sacred and others as not so. A life well lived is ultimately a life of privilege.

Finally, Chapter 9 summarized some of the many additional contexts in which religious language has a happy home. I began with sites of conflict and high stakes, such as politics, sport and advertising. I moved on to discuss a moment of crisis, serious illness. The chapter ended with an overview of a significant life transition, conversion, what is possibly a universal human experience.

In taking this approach, I have challenged some of the existing work on religious language. My aim has been to propose a theory of religious language which extends beyond the language of devotion for a sacred supernatural to the depth and breadth of language that encodes what we value and what we hate and fear the most, both as individuals and as communities.

What's next?

Our understanding of religious language is growing but held back by closed definitions of religion and lack of cross-fertilization between scholarship on ideology, on community and on religion traditionally understood. Closed definitions consider religion to be primarily connected to beliefs about the immaterial world and/or organized world religion. These definitions don't account for the widespread use of both explicit and implicit religious language. But more worryingly, definitions like these perpetuate the othering of institutionalized religion and hinder self-reflection and dialogue among different sacred communities.

This self-reflection and dialogue are as pressing as ever. For at least the past decade, sectarian violence has engulfed parts of the Middle East, China, Myanmar and many parts of the African continent. Religious conflict is on the rise in French workplaces as is violence against Jews and Muslims. Indeed, the upsurge in sectarian violence is global. Whether a country is at war or not, mass killings and other bloody encounters are mounting (Muggah and Velshi, 2019). And if trends in politics are any predictor, we can expect more of the same. Restrictions on expressions of organized religion around the world increased in 55 of the world's 198 countries in 2016, largely fuelled by political parties and other social groups with nationalist views (Kishi, 2018). We also know that deprivation and marginalization often underscore violence (Canetti, Hobfoll and Pedahzur et al., 2010).

Some would have us believe that such violence is a natural product of organized world religion. There are many studies making this claim, that organized religion is more likely to provoke violence than so-called secular ideology. But when we examine these claims closely, the picture is more complex. First, there are also many studies which suggest that overt religious involvement is unrelated to acts of aggression (Wright and Khoo, 2019). In fact, belief in the supernatural appears to correlate with reduced aggression. Second, violence consistently happens outside of institutionalized religion, at times when people of other opposing sacred belief systems meet and conflict. In Australia, for example, people both for and against same-sex marriage have physically attacked one another (Mercer, 2017). In October 2019, supporters of England's national football team The Lions clashed with Czech supporters of other football clubs in Prague, a fairly common scene in football and other sport (Tait, 2019). In my own city of Sheffield in South Yorkshire in the UK, violent clashes broke out during a long-running dispute between Sheffield City Council and local protestors over the felling of thousands of trees across the city (BBC News, 2018). What we can learn from violence is that it has roots in worldview and perceived threats to that worldview.

> Aggressive responses to threats exist as ways of bolstering the positive value of one's social identity when the group's value is impeded in some way.
>
> (Wright and Khoo, 2019: 3)

We need to pay attention to religious language, both the language that we encounter and the language that we ourselves use. Much is at stake, if we are truly to understand ourselves and one another. Many conflicts are due to forces we can and should mitigate, like psychological and economic loss (Canetti, Hobfoll and Pedahzur et al., 2010). And many conflicts are also due simply to failure to listen, leading to misunderstanding.

However, fundamentally, there is little evidence that understanding and education will eradicate violence. For example, people disagree even with respect to who suffers from inequality. Men's rights movements deny that women in particular are held back by sexist and misogynist systems. They assert, instead, that men are the real victims of a misandrist culture. Even people looking at the same evidence come to different conclusions. So-called objective facts will always require interpretation. And even when there is agreement regarding who suffers the most from inequality, some people disavow responsibility for righting the wrongs of economic and social inequality. People come to the table with different questions and seek different answers. Even mutual understanding does not lead to perfect peace. Evidence is not the issue that divides us but rather something much more profound.

What I am saying here is that the world will always contain competing notions of the sacred, which will sometimes lead to conflict, even violence. Matters of conflict often have little to do with empirical evidence. Even violence itself is a highly disputed activity. We may see certain acts of resistance or even violence as necessary, where others might argue that violence can never be justified. We may believe God created the world or that what exists is only that which we can ourselves empirically and materially encounter. What unites us is that we all argue from a first principle, a basic assumption from which we begin. Concrete evidence for these basic assumptions are beyond our grasp. We all live by faith. So what faith are you?

A question that follows is whether our differing notions of the sacred allow us to live in peace. A society must itself determine what notions of the sacred it allows and protects within its borders. Consideration of religious language is one piece of the puzzle towards making informed judgements in this regard. The hope is that in understanding more about religious language, in plumbing the depths of ourselves and ideas we encounter, some of us might develop greater empathy, might choose to live in peace with others with whom we disagree, as far as it is within our power to do so.

Insofar as we can, perhaps we might become more willing to acknowledge the importance of freedom to articulate what we hold sacred and to live in ways consistent with sacred beliefs. We may have loftier goals still yet. We may want to reject certain sacred notions, even our own, having critically examined them. We may want to convince others that our version of the sacred is the truth. Barring that, perhaps we can learn to disagree with greater kindness and understanding.

I've packed a great deal into this book. Sometimes I've wondered if it was too much, but the reality is that I could have done much more. The field of religious language is one of open horizons. For the religious language enthusiast, the sky's the limit! In the last five years, the journal of *Implicit Religion* has published articles on right-wing British politics, scientific fundamentalism, science fiction, religious freedom, paganism, international human rights law, atheism, royal weddings, magic, art and performance festivals, video games and robot theists. These are just a few of the many social and cultural arenas where scholars argue religion plays a role. And few of these scholars are linguists. Truly, there are opportunities for investigation of religious language in almost any area which commands your attention.

This is where I leave you. I hope I've captured your imagination. But more importantly, I hope that in reading this book, you've begun to reflect on what you hold sacred. Why do you believe what you believe? What is worth defending? What is worth compromising on? What is worth reconsidering? These are important questions that we all benefit from reflecting on and, more importantly, acting on.

APPENDICES

Appendix 1 Top 100 Keywords in W_religion and S_sermon Sections of the BNC

1	ESAU	35	ORGANISTS	68	1:8
2	MATT.	36	ISRAELITE	69	EARTHED
3	RAASAY	37	SCIAF	70	NON-CHRISTIANS
4	MIDLIFE	38	PASSOVER	71	JESUS
5	BOAZ	39	THOREAU	72	UNBELIEVER
6	DUNVEGAN	40	EXORCISMS	73	TRANSCENDENT
7	LEVITICUS	41	JUDAEO-CHRISTIAN	74	GOSPELS
8	THEISM	42	PHARISEES	75	DISCIPLES
9	EPHESIANS	43	ENCYCLICAL	76	ABRAM
10	ZEALOTS	44	PARABLE	77	MENSTRUATING
11	YAHWEH	45	IRENAEUS	78	HEBREWS
12	UNBELIEF	46	CAESAREA	79	PSALMIST
13	PARACLETE	47	LAMPITT	80	RABBINIC
14	THRALE	48	JUDAH	81	BULTMANN
15	NICODEMUS	49	OUIJA	82	ORDINANDS
16	JUDAIC	50	HAGAR	83	SAMARIA
17	BOSWELL	51	ISAIAH	84	BHAGAVAD
18	COR.	52	TABERNACLE	85	KOLBE
19	DATA-GATHERING	53	IMMANENCE	86	SECULARISATION
20	PENTECOST	54	DAMNATION	87	ELISHA
21	DISCIPLESHIP	55	COVETOUSNESS	88	GALATIANS
22	DEUTERONOMY	56	ECCLESIAL	89	EVANGELISE
23	CULTIC	57	MASADA	90	NAG

24	QUMRAN	58	SHEKELS	91	CORINTHIANS
25	PATRISTIC	59	CANAAN	92	SINFULNESS
26	PARABLES	60	DOUBTER	93	ISHMAEL
27	DV	61	REDEEMER	94	MESSIAH
28	GODHEAD	62	UNLEAVENED	95	LOGOS
29	GENTILES	63	EVANGELISM	96	GITA
30	ELI	64	PHILISTINES	97	ECUMENISM
31	CRANHAM	65	NAZARETH	98	POLYTHEISTIC
32	PILATE	66	CONCILIAR	99	JUDAS
33	HEROD	67	GETHSEMANE	100	AYER
34	ISRAELITES				

Note: Reference corpus: Rest of the BNC; minimum frequency of five occurrences in both corpora; 1,194,827 words in W_religion and S_sermon; 95,068,572 in the remainder of the corpus.
Source: The British National Corpus (2007).

Appendix 2 The complete theological wordlist

amen	evangelical	patristic
apologetics	evil*	pelagianism
apostle	exegesis	perichoresis
apostolic	expiation	pietism
appropriation	fideism	pneumatology
Arminianism	filioque	polytheism
atheism	foreknowledge	predestination
atonement	foreordination	prolegomena
authority*	fundamentalism	protestant
baptism	glorify	providence
bible	gnosticism	redemption
calvinism	gospel	resurrection
canon	hamartiology	revelation*
catechism	heresy	righteous
chalcedonian	hermeneutic	sacrament
charismatic	homiletic	salvation
christian	homoousion	sanctification
christological	illumination*	scripture
confession *	immanence	seminary

conversion*	immutability	Septuagint
cosmological	incarnation	sermon
covenant	inerrancy	sin
creation*	infallibility	soteriology
creationist	inspiration	sovereign**
creed	interpretation*	subordinationism
decree	justification*	teleological
deism	kerygma	testament
deity	liturgical	theism
dialectical	messiah	theodicy
dispensationalism	ministry	theology
doctrine*	modalism	transcendence
dogmatics	monotheism	trichotomy
ecclesiology	omnipotence	trinity
ecumenical	omniscience	triune
election*	ontological	vulgate
enlightenment**	orthodox	worldview
epistemology	pantheism	worshipper
eschatology	pastor	

Source: Lessard-Clouston (2010). Reprinted with permission.

* words that also occur in the GSL
** words that also occur in the UWL

Appendix 3 The USAS S9 'Religious and the Supernatural' Lexicon

abbess	celebrate	evangelical	matthew	reverend doctor
abbey	celebrating	evangelise	maundy thursday	revival
abbey church	celebration	evangelism	meditation	rite
abbeys	celestial	evangelist	medium	ritual
abbot	cell	evangelists	medium ship	ritual
abbott	chalice	evangelization	meeting	ritualised
ablution	chalices	evangelize	memorial service	ritualized
abracadabra	chancel	evangelizing	mercury	ritually

absolution	chantries	even-service	merlin	roman catholic
absolutism	chantry	evil eye	mermaid	rosary
accursed	chapel	exalted	mermaids	rudolf
achilles	chaplain	ex-nun	mesmerise	sabbath
act of contrition	chapter	exodus	mesmerised	sacrament
act of faith	charism	exorcise	messiah	sacramental
act of god	charismatic	exorcised	messiahs	sacraments
acts	charm	exorcism	methodist	sacred
acts of the apostles	charmed	extreme unction	methodist minister	sacrifice
adonis	charming	fable	methodists	sacrificed
advent	cherub	fabled	minister	sacrificing
advent sunday	cherubim	fairies	minister of religion	sacrilege
adventism	christen	fairy	ministers	sacrilegious
adventist	christendom	fairy godmother	ministry	sacristan
afterlife	christened	fairy stories	minotaur	sacristy
after-life	christening	fairy story	minster	sagittarius
afterworld	christening gown	fairy tale	miracle	saint
agnostic	christening name	fairyland	miraculous	salesian
agnosticism	christening robe	fairytale	mission	salvation
ahmadiyya	christenings	fairy-tale	missionary	salvationist
air sign	christian	faith	missions	sanctification
akashic	christian centre	faithful	mitre	sanctified
akashic record	christian science	faithfully	mohammedans	sanctify
al qaeda	christian scientist	faithfulness	monastery	sanctimonious
alchemical	christian union	faithless	monastic	sanctity
alchemist	christianity	fall	monk	sanctuary
alchemy	christian-like	familiar	monster	santa
all hallows 'day	christians	family service	moon sign	satan
all saints 'day	christian-type	fate	mormon	satanic
allah	christmas	father	mormons	savable
alleluia	christmas cake	father christmas	moslem	save
almighty	christmas carol	father of the church	mosque	saved

altar

altar boy

altar rail

ambrosia

ambrosian chant

ammonite

amulet

angel

angelic

angelical

angelically

angel-like

anglican

anglican chant

anglicanism

anglo-catholic

animism

annunciation

anoint

anointed

anointing of the sick

anti-catholic

anti-catholicism

antichrist

antichristian

anti-christian

antichrists

anti-church

anticlerical

anti-clerical

anticlericalism

christmas day

christmas dinner

christmas eve

christmas party

christmas present

christmas pudding

christmas stocking

christmas tree

christmases

christmastime

church

church goer

church going

church group

church hall

church leader

church music

church school

church service

church warden

church wedding

church worker

church-house

churchman

churchmen

churchwarden

churchwardens

churchy

churchyard

circumcised

cistercian

feast

feast day

feng

festival

fetishism

firmament

flock

font

fonts

foretell

foretelling

foretells

foretold

fortune

fortune teller

fortune-teller

freemason

friar

friars

friary

fundamentalism

fundamentalist

fury

gemini

geminian

genie

gentile

ghost

ghostly

ghosts

ghoul

mullah

muller

muslim

muslims

mystic

mystical

mysticism

myth

mythic

mythical

mythological

mythology

nativity

nave

near death experience

near-religious

neptune

new age

new age traveller

new testament

new-age

nirvana

non christian

non jew

non-catholic

non-christian

non-christians

nonconformist

non-conformist

non-conformists

novena

saving

saviour

scientologist

scopola

scorpio

scribe

scribes

scriptural

scripture

scriptures church

sd

sectarian

secular

see

seer

seminarian

seminary

sequence

sermon

sermonette

sermons

serpent

serpents

servers

service

services

shades

shakra

shakras

shari'ah

shepherd people

anti-cult
clairvoyance
ghoulish
noviciate
shepherd person

anti-muslim
clairvoyant
giant-killer
novitiate
shi'a

anti-religious
clergy
giant-killers
nt
shi'as

anti-semitic
clergyman
gloria
nun
shi'ite

anti-semitism
clergymen
glorified
nunnery
shi'ite muslim

aphrodite
cleric
glorify
nuns
shi'ites

apocalypse
clerical
gnome
nymph
shintoism

apostasy
clerics
gnomes
oblate
shintoist

apostate
cloister
go down in the holy spirit
occult
shintoists

apostle
cloth
goblin
offertory
shrine

apostolate
collect
goblins
office
shui

apostolic
collection plate
god
ogre
sign

apparition
comforter
god fearing
old testament
signed

aquarian
coming
god fearing
old wives thing
signing

aquarians
commandments
god given
omen
signs

aquarius
communicant
goddess
ominous
sikh

archangel
communion
god-given
omniscient
sikhism

archbishop
communion rail
godliness
once-sacrosanct
simesta

archbishopric
communion service
godly
oratory
sin

archbishopric
communion table
gods
ordain
sins

archbishops
compline
goes down in the holy spirit
ordained
sister

archdeacon
concelebrate
going down in the holy spirit
ordains
sixth sense

archdeaconeries
concelebrating
gone down in the holy spirit
ordination
slight of hand k

archdeaconery
conclave
good friday
orthodox
soothsayer

archdeaconry
confession
gospel
orthodoxy
soothsayers

archdiocesan
confessional
gospel message
ot
sorcerer

archdiocese
confessor
gospel song
otherworldly
sorcerers

archiepiscopal
confirm
grace
ouija-board
sorceress

archimandrite
confirmation
graceless
our father
sorcery

archimandrite
confirmed
greek-catholic
our lady
soul

archpriest
confirming
gregorian chant
out of body experience
souls

ardor
confiteor
guru
pagan
spectre

ardour
confucianist
gurus
paganism
spectres

aries
ark
article of faith
asb

ascendant

ascendants
ascendent
ascension
ascension day
ascetic
ascetical

ash wednesday
assumption

assumptionist
astral
astral
    projection
astrologer
astrological
astrology
atheism
atheist
atheistic
atone
atone for
atonement
augustinian
aureole

ayatollah
backslide
backsliding
bahais
banns
bans
banshee

baptise
baptised

congregant
congregation
congregational
congregational
    church
congregation-
    house
conjure up
conjuration
conjurations
conjure
conjurer
consecrate

consecrated
consecrating

consecration
consecrations
consistory

convent
convent school
conversion
convert
converted
converts
convocation
cope
copt
copts
council of
    christians
    and jews
coven
covens
creature
creatures
creed
crescent
cross

crossed
crosses

hades
hail mary
half-reformed
hall

hallelujah

hallow
hallowed
halloween
hallowe'en
hallows
halo

haunt
haunted

haunting
haunts
heathen

heathenism
heaven
heavenly
hell
heresy
heretic
heretical
heretics
high
higher
highest

hindu
hinduism
hindus
hocus
hocus pocus
holiness
holy

holy communion
holy day

palm read
palm reader
palm reading
pancake day

pantheon

papacy
papal
paradise
parish
parish church
parish council

parish priest
parish records

parishioner
parishioners
parishoners

parochial
parson
parsonage
parsons
parthenon
passion
passion play
passionist
passover
pastor
pastoral

pastoral unit
pastors
pegasus
penance
pentecost
pentecostal
pentecostal
    church
pentecostals
phantom

spell
spellbound
spells
sphinx

spirit

spirit child
spirit realm
spirit world
spirits
spiritual
spiritual
    director
spiritual healer
spiritual
    healing
spiritualism
spiritualist
spirituality

spiritually
sprite
sprites
sr
st
st patrick's day
st patricks day
st.
st.*'s day
standing stone
star sign

star sign
stars
stigmata
stigmatic
stigmatise
stigmatised
stigmatist

stoic
sun astrology

baptism
baptismal
baptist
baptist church
baptistry
baptists
baptize
baptizing
barmitzvah
basilica
bcp

beatification
beatify

beatitude
belfry
belief

believe
believed
believer
believes
believing
bell ringer
bell-ringer
bell-ringers

benedictine
benediction
benedictus
bible

bible class
bible college

bible reading
bible school

bible story
bible studies
bible study
bible study

crossing
crucifix
crusade
crusader
crystal healer
cult
curate
curse
cursed
curses
cyber-christmas

cyclops
daily/weekly
    prayer

damnation
damned
day of
    judgement

deacon
deaconess
dean
deanery
deanery synod
deifies
deity
deliver

deliverance
delivered
deliveries
delivering

delivers
delivery

demi god
demi-god

demi-gods
demon
demonic
demonically

holy ghost
holy spirit
horoscope
horror stories
horror story
host
house group
huguenot
huguenots
humanism
humanist

humanists
hymn

icon
icons
idol

idols
imam
imman
impious
incantation
incantations
incarnate
incarnation

incarnations
incumbent
induct
inducted

indulgence
intercession

intercessions
inter-
    denominational

inter-religious
introit
introits
invocation

pharisee
pharisees
phoenix
piety
pilgrim
pilgrimage
pious
piously
pisces
pixie
place of
    worship
pluto
pocus

poltergeist
poltergeists
pontiff

pontifical
pope
popish
possess
possessed
possession
post-easter
postulant

practitioner
pray
prayer
prayer book

prayer meeting
prayerful

praying
prays

preacher
pre-christian
pre-christmas
pre-clerical

sunday school
sunni
sunnis
superhuman
supernatural
superstition
superstitions
superstitious
superstitiously
synagogue
synagogue
    council
synagogues
synod

tabernacle
talisman
taoism

taoist
taoists
tarot
tarot card
tarot reader
tarot reading
taurus
tell a
    fortune
temple
temporal
thanksgiving
the
    abominable
    snowman 1
theocratic
theocratic
    school
theologian
theological

theology
tithe
tithes
tonsure

bible teaching	demonise	islam	pre-ordained	totem
bible thumper	demonised	islamic	presbyterian	totem pole
biblical	denomination	islamist	presbyteries	transcendental
bionic	descendent	jainism	presbytery	transcendental meditation
birth chart	deus	jains	presence	transfiguration
birth sign	devil	jamad al	priest	transfixed
bishop	devils	jehovah	priesthood	transmigration
bishopric	devotion	jehovah 's witness	priestly	trappist
bishops	devotions	jehovah-nissi	priests	travelers
bl	devout	jehovahs witnesses	primate	traveller
black magic	devoutly	jesuit	primates	travellers
blaspheme	diabolical	jesus	prior	trinity
blasphemer	dildo	jew	priory	troll
blasphemous	dioc	jewess	procurator	trolls
blasphemy	diocesan	jewish	procurators	unbelief
bless	diocese	jewry	prognostics	under-shepherd
blessed	disciple	jews	proper	under-shepherds
blessing	disciples	john	prophecy	underworld
bogey	divinas	judaism	prophesy	unearthly
bogeyman	divination	juggernaut	prophet	unfaithful
boogeyman	divine	jupiter	prophetess	ungodly
book of common prayer	divine right	king james version	prophetic	unholy
book of mormon	divinely	kirk	prophets	unicorn
born again	divineness	knell	proselytizers	unorthodox
born again christian	divines	kosher	protestant	unrepentant
born-again	divinity	laity	protestantism	untouchable
brat pack	doctor of divinity	lama	protestants	vampire
breastplate	doctrinal	lamaism	proverb	verger
breast-plate	doctrine	lamaist	psalm	vespers
brimstone	dog collar	lamaists	psalms	vestment
broomstick	dom	lapse	psychic	vestments
brother	dominican	lapsed	psychical	vestries
brothers	doomsday	lar	psychically	vestry
buddha	doppelganger	last supper	pulpit	vicar
buddhism	dowse	laud	purgatory	vicarage
buddhist	dowsing	lauds	puritan	vigil

buddhist	dowsing rod	lay on hands	puritanism	village church
buddhists	dragon	lay preacher	put a curse on	virgin birth
burial service	dragons	lecture divinas	quaker	virgo
call	druid	legate	quakers	vision
calling	druze	legates	rabbi	vocation
calls	druzes	legend	rabbi	voodoo
calvinist	earth-mother	legendary	rabbinic	vow
camelot	easter	legends	rabbis	vows
cancerian	easter bonnet	lent	rain dance	wafer
canon	easter day	leo	ramadan	wand
canon law	easter monday	lesson	re	water sign
canonical	easter parade	levellers	reconciliation	water symbol
canonisation	easter saturday	leviticus	rector	went down in the holy spirit
canonisations	easter sunday	libra	rectory	werewolf
canonise	easter sunday	limbo	redeem	whit
canonised	easter vigil	litany	redeemer	whit sunday
canonises	easter week	liturgical	redemption	whitsun
canonize	easter week	liturgy	redemptorist	whitsunday parade
canonized	ecclesiastic	living	reformation	witch
canticle	ecclesiastical	lord	reincarnate	witch finder general
capricorn	ecclesiastically	lord bishop	reincarnation	witchcraft
capuchin	ecumenical	lord 's prayer	relic	witness
cardinal	ecumenically	lucifer	relics	witness
cardinals	ecumenism	luke	religion	witnessed
carmelite	eden	lutheran	religiosity	witnesses
carol	elder	lutherans	religious	witnessing
carol service	electoral roll	magic	religious affairs committee	wizard
cassock	elf	magical	religious community	wom*n priest
cassocks	elves	magically	religious education	word
cast	emir	magician	religious festival	word of wisdom
casting	emmanuel	magicians	religious institution	worship
catechesis	enchant	magnificat	religious school	worshipped

catechising	enchanted	manna	religious studies	worshipper
catechism	enchanting	mantra	religiously	worships
catechist	enchantment	mark	remonstrant	zen
catechize	enchantments	mars	repent	zen buddhism
catechumens	encyclical	martyr	repentance	zen buddhist
cathedral	enshrines	martyrdom	requiem	zodiac
cathedral church	epiphany	martyred	respond	zoroastrian
cathedral cit	episcopacy	mason	responds	zoroastrianism
catholic	episcopal	mass	restored gospel	zoroastrians
catholic church	episcopalian	mass goer	resurrection	
catholicism	episcopate	master	rev	
catholics	eucharist	matin	revd	
celebrant	eucharistic	matins	reverend	

Source: Paul Rayson (private communication). Used with permission.

Appendix 4 GloWbE-UK Corpus Contents

1	http://www.bbc.co.uk/blogs/newsnight/paulmason/2011/02/twenty_reasons_why_its_kicking.html
2	http://hat4uk.wordpress.com/2012/08/10/at-the-end-of-the-day-176/
3	http://www.acgrayling.com/the-meaning-of-things
4	http://www.dailymail.co.uk/debate/article-2004515/Terry-Pratchett-euthanasia-debate-Dont-fall-idea-old-disposable.html
5	http://www.creativereview.co.uk/cr-blog/2011/october/steve-jobs
6	http://www.sagepub.net/tcs/default.aspx?page=interviewee25
7	http://www.dailymail.co.uk/femail/article-2130239/Daphne-Selfe-83-worlds-oldest-supermodels-secret-botox.html
8	http://www.telegraph.co.uk/news/religion/8975721/Why-the-lowly-shepherd-is-the-one-who-gets-to-hear-the-angels.html
9	http://alexlesterspersonalblog.blogspot.com/
10	http://newhumanist.org.uk/2828/hope-against-hope
11	http://literateur.com/the-other-achilles/
12	http://agirlastyle.com/2012/02/30-things-to-do-before-im-30/
13	http://www.belfasttelegraph.co.uk/business/opinion/big-interview/government-needs-to-make-it-easier-for-our-entrepreneurs-15150284.html
14	http://www.bigissue.com/features/columnists/1566/samira-ahmed-urge-succeed-young-has-been-curse-us-all

15   http://www.christianfocus.com/item/show/1482/-

16   http://www.guardian.co.uk/books/2011/jul/06/jennifer-worth-obituary

17   http://www.telegraph.co.uk/travel/9411305/Band-on-the-run-Larmer-
      Tree-Festival.html

18   http://www.thecentenarian.co.uk/stress-in-the-lives-of-people-who-live-
      to-hundred.html

19   http://almostalwaysthinking.com/2012/10/11/life-itself-can-be-an-
      awfully-big-adventure/

20   http://cornwalllocalnews.co.uk/2012/11/19/tributes-paid-to-a-cricket-
      legend-an-inspirational-headmaster-and-preacher/

21   http://jonlord.org/2012/07/16/jon-lord-has-sadly-passed-away/

22   http://stephencherry1.wordpress.com/2012/11/18/sermon-for-2nd-
      sunday-before-advent-cathedral-university-and-prison/

23   http://thereandbackbytricycle.blogspot.com/2012/05/it-was-celebration-
      of.html

24   http://www.lawandreligionuk.com/2012/11/09/ten-further-questions-for-
      the-new-archbishop-of-canterbury/

25   http://www.samiraahmed.co.uk/?p=2688

26   http://hawesps.posterous.com/harrys-house

27   http://www.theloomroom.co.uk/wordpress/?p=655

28   http://www.lawandreligionuk.com/2012/08/10/parliamentary-reform-
      and-the-bishops/

29   http://www.thisisfakediy.co.uk/articles/film/amour/

NOTES

Chapter 2

1   This is what some scholars refer to as the moment when religion becomes ideology. Christopher Hart explains it like this: 'Language is ideological when it is used to promote one perspective over another' (Hart, 2014: 2).
2   It's very difficult to trace or even affirm the existence of boundaries between religious language and language that is not religious, for this reason.
3   For a discussion of the legal case for ethical veganism as a religion, see Page (2005).

Chapter 3

1   See Geoff Thompson's further example of three meta-functions of language encoded in one question, 'Did Jim take her calculator?' (Thompson, 2013: 31).

Chapter 4

1   https://twitter.com/FrankCogliano/status/963804772682911745
2   https://twitter.com/anne_goldgar/status/968436730121654272
3   https://twitter.com/UCUVP/status/994129601210343426
4   Linda Zagzebski proposes a General Justification of Authority thesis (GJA) which is: 'The authority of another person is justified for me by my conscientious judgement that if I do what the authority directs (or believe what the authority tells me), the result will survive my own conscientious self-reflection better than if I try to figure out what to do/believe myself' (Zagzebski, 2017: 98).

Chapter 5

1   W stands for written and S stands for spoken. See David Lee's Genre Classification Scheme ('David Lee's Genre Classification Scheme,' n.d.).
2   A 100-million-word collection of written and spoken text samples from late twentieth-century Britain.
3   David Evans at the University of Nottingham has published a helpful online guide to compiling a corpus. It contains not only the basic corpus construction

concepts below but also how to convert your corpus into an electronic form readable by corpus tools and other issues (Evans, n.d.).

4 'Pray earnestly' is a collocation with an MI score of 6.87 in the GloWbE Corpus (Davies, 2013).

5 These are words that appear in the NGSL (Charlie Browne, Culligan and Phillips, 2013).

6 These are words that are keywords in the religious genre sub-section of the BNC (The British National Corpus, 2007) but which do not appear in the NGSL (Browne, Culligan and Phillips, 2013).

7 These are words that appear in lists of technical religious vocabulary derived from study of overtly religious texts used in Christianity and Islam (Al-Faruqi, 1988; Lessard-Clouston, 2010).

8 http://ucrel-api.lancaster.ac.uk/usas/tagger.html.

9 Subjunctives are expressions of wished-for, hypothetical or tentatively assumed events.

Chapter 6

1 British politician, leader of the Brexit party, former leader of UK Independent Party.

2 A useful place to start for an explanation of grammatical metaphor is Miriam Taverniers 'Grammatical Metaphors in English' (Taverniers, 2004).

3 Thanks to Emily Hughes for her insight on this use of intertextuality.

4 http://www.hawaiifreepress.com/ArticlesMain/tabid/56/ID/2818/Crichton-Environmentalism-is-a-religion.aspx

Chapter 7

1 The Authorized (King James) Version of the Bible ('the KJV'), the rights which are vested in the Crown in the UK, is reproduced here by permission of the Crown's patentee, Cambridge University Press.

2 This would be an interesting research study, looking at the use of religious language and imagery in food banks and other forms of assistance to vulnerable people.

Chapter 8

1 By way of comparison, the 15-billion-word English Web 2015 corpus, also known as enTenTen15 (Sketch Engine, 2015), contains 1,306 instances of 'life well lived,' 129 instances of 'life well-lived' and 289 instances of 'well-lived life'.

2 https://www.theguardian.com/uk/2008/apr/07/britishidentity.immigration

3 https://hat4uk.wordpress.com/2012/08/10/at-the-end-of-the-day-176/

4 http://agirlastyle.com/2012/02/30-things-to-do-before-im-30/

5 https://www.telegraph.co.uk/news/health/news/9451734/Anorexia-You-cant-force-me-to-live.html
6 https://www.dailymail.co.uk/femail/article-2130239/Daphne-Selfe-83-worlds-oldest-supermodels-secret-botox.html
7 https://catholicherald.co.uk/news/2010/09/17/papal-visit-2010-archbishop-of-canterburys-speech-full-text/
8 https://www.telegraph.co.uk/news/health/news/9451734/Anorexia-You-cant-force-me-to-live.html

Chapter 9

1 https://twitter.com/matthewbennett/status/1061949276950065153.
2 Transcription my own.

REFERENCES

#LancsBox: Lancaster University Corpus Toolbox (n.d.) Available at: http:// corpora.lancs.ac.uk/lancsbox/ (accessed 24 October 2019).

12 Weird and Wonderful Gifts for Pop-Culture Fanatics (n.d.) Available at: https:// mom.com/momlife/272292-weird-wacky-wonderful-gifts-pop-culture-fanatics (accessed 11 September 2019).

Abdul-Latif E (2011) Interdiscursivity between Political and Religious Discourses in a Speech by Sadat. *Journal of Language and Politics* 10(1): 50–67. DOI: 10.1075/jlp.10.1.03abd.

About Patheos (n.d.). Available at: https://www.patheos.com/about-patheos (accessed 5 September 2019).

Aburrow Y (2016) Metaphors for Religion. Available at: https://www.patheos. com/blogs/sermonsfromthemound/2016/05/metaphors-for-religion/ (accessed 29 October 2019).

Ads of the World (2012) Jesus, Mary! What a style! Available at: https://www. adsoftheworld.com/media/outdoor/robert_kalinkin_jesus_mary_what_a_style_2 (accessed 9 October 2019).

Ahmed S (2017) *Living a Feminist Life*. Durham, NC: Duke University Press.

Al-Ali M N (2005) Communicating Messages of Solidarity, Promotion and Pride in Death Announcements Genre in Jordanian Newspapers. *Discourse and Society*. DOI: 10.1177/0957926505048228.

Al-Ali M N (2006) Religious Affiliations and Masculine Power in Jordanian Wedding Invitation Genre. *Discourse & Society* 17(6): 691–714. DOI: 10.1177/0957926506068428.

Alexander J (2006) Cultural Pragmatics: Social Performance between Ritual and Strategy. In: Alexander J C, Giesen B and Mast J L (eds.) *Social Performance: Symbolic Action, Cultural Pragmatics, and Ritual*. Cambridge: Cambridge University Press, pp. 29–90.

Al-Faruqi I R (1988) *Toward Islāmic English*. Riyadh: International Institute of Islamic Thought.

Ali Official (2017) Things Muslims Say in Ramadan. Available at: https://www. facebook.com/AliOfficialUK/videos/1317648441664174/ (accessed 16 July 2019).

Al-Kharabsheh A (2011) Arabic Death Discourse in Translation: Euphemism and Metaphorical Conceptualization in Jordanian Obituaries. *Across Languages and Cultures* 12(1). Akadémiai Kiadó: 19–48. DOI: 10.1556/Acr.12.2011.1.2.

Ammerman N T (1994) Telling Congregational Stories. *Review of Religious Research* 35(4): 289. DOI: 10.2307/3511731.

Anthony L (2014) *AntConc (Windows, Macintosh OS X, and Linux) Build 3.4.1*. Tokyo, Japan: Waseda University.

Archer D, Wilson A and Rayson P (2002) Introduction to the USAS Category System. Available at: ucrel.lancs.ac.uk/usas/usas_guide.pdf (accessed 16 July 2019).

Aupers S and Houtman D (2011) Beyond the Spiritual Supermarket: The Social and Public Significance of New Age Spirituality. In: *New Age Spirituality: Rethinking Religion*. Acumen Publishing Limited, pp. 174–96. DOI: 10.1080/13537900600655894.

Bachman D W (1991) Sermon of Sermons. Available at: https://www.churchofjesuschrist.org/study/ensign/1991/03/sermon-of-sermons?lang=eng (accessed 9 October 2019).

Bailey E (1998) *Implicit Religion: An Introduction*. London: Middlesex University Press.

Bailey E (2010) Implicit Religion. *Religion* 40(4). Taylor & Francis Group: 271–8. DOI: 10.1016/j.religion.2010.07.002.

Baker P, Gabrielatos C, Khosravinik M et al. (2008) A Useful Methodological Synergy? Combining Critical Discourse Analysis and Corpus Linguistics to Examine Discourses of Refugees and Asylum Seekers in the UK Press. *Discourse and Society* 19(3): 273–306. DOI: 10.1177/0957926508088962.

Baldacchino D and Draper P (2001) Spiritual Coping Strategies: A Review of the Nursing Research Literature. *Journal of Advanced Nursing* 34(6): 833–41. DOI: 10.1046/j.1365-2648.2001.01814.x.

Baquedano-López P (1999) Prayer. *Journal of Linguistic Anthropology* 9(1): 197–200.

Barcelona A (2003) The Metaphorical and Metonymic Understanding of the Trinitarian Dogma. *International Journal of English Studies* 3(1): 1–27.

Barth S, van Hoof J J and Beldad A D (2014) Reading between the Lines: A Comparison of 480 German and Dutch Obituaries. *OMEGA – Journal of Death and Dying* 68(2). SAGE Publications Sage CA: Los Angeles, CA: 161–81. DOI: 10.2190/OM.68.2.e.

BBC (2003) *Rough Guide to Prayer. CBBC – KS3 Curriculum Bites*. Available at: https://www.bbc.co.uk/programmes/p01111df (accessed 12 September 2019).

BBC News (2018) Sheffield Tree Felling: More Saved after Deal Brokered. 24 October. Available at: https://www.bbc.co.uk/news/uk-england-south-yorkshire-45958502 (accessed 13 November 2019).

Beck G L (1995) *Sonic Theology: Hinduism and Sacred Sound*. New Delhi: Shri Jainendra Press.

Belk R and Tumbat G (2005) The Cult of Macintosh. *Consumption Markets & Culture* 8(3). Informa UK Limited: 205–17. DOI: 10.1080/10253860500160403.

Bell E and Taylor S (2016) Vernacular Mourning and Corporate Memorialization. In: Cutcher L, Dale K, Hancock P et al. (eds.) Framing the Death of Steve Jobs. *Organization* 23(1): 114–32. DOI: 10.1177/1350508415605109.

Bellah R N (1967) Civil Religion in America. *Journal of the American Academy of Arts and Sciences* 96(1): 1–21. Available at: http://www.robertbellah.com/articles_5.htm (accessed 11 November 2019).

Bellah R N (2005) Civil religion in America. *Daedalus* 134(4): 40–55. DOI: 10.1162/001152605774431464.

Benford R D (2002) Controlling Narratives and Narratives as Control within Social Movements. In: Davis J E (eds.) *Stories of Change: Narrative and Social Movements*. Albany: State University of New York Press, pp. 53–76.

The Bible: Authorized King James Version (2012) *The Bible: Authorized King James Version.* Cambridge: Cambridge University Press. DOI: 10.1093/actrade/9780199535941.book.1.

Binkley L J and Hick J H (1962) What Characterizes Religious Language? *Journal for the Scientific Study of Religion* 2(1): 18–24. DOI: 10.2307/1384089.

Blackburn S (2005) *The Oxford Dictionary of Philosophy.* Oxford: Oxford University Press.

Bohlman P V, Blumhofer E L and Chow M M (eds.) (2006) *Music in American Religious Experience.* Oxford: Oxford University Press.

Bonsu S K (2007) The Presentation of Dead Selves in Everyday Life: Obituaries and Impression Management. *Symbolic Interaction* 30(2). John Wiley & Sons, Ltd: 199–219. DOI: 10.1525/si.2007.30.2.199.

Books – Friendly Atheist (n.d.) Available at: https://friendlyatheist.patheos.com/publications/ (accessed 5 September 2019).

The British National Corpus (2007) 3 (BNC XML Edition). Oxford University Computing Services. Available at: http://www.natcorp.ox.ac.uk/ (accessed 14 January 2019).

Browne C, Culligan B and Phillips J (2013) New General Service List. Available at: http://www.newgeneralservicelist.org (accessed 16 July 2019).

Buckser A and Glazier S D (2003) *The Anthropology of Religious Conversion.* Oxford: Rowman & Littlefield.

Bugajski J (2011) Early Warning, Conflict Prevention, Crisis Management, Conflict Resolution and Postconflict Rehabilitation: Lessons Learned and Way Ahead. In: *2011 Annual Security Review Conference*, 2011. Available at: https://www.osce.org/cio/80530?download=true (accessed 15 November 2019).

Burning Man (n.d.a) Glossary. Available at: https://burningman.org/culture/glossary/ (accessed 30 September 2019a).

Burning Man (n.d.b) First-Timer's Guide. Available at: https://burningman.org/event/preparation/first-timers-guide/ (accessed 5 November 2019).

Burning Man (n.d.c) The 10 Principles of Burning Man. Available at: https://burningman.org/culture/philosophical-center/10-principles/ (accessed 27 September 2019).

Callahan R J, Lofton K and Seales C E (2010) Allegories of Progress: Industrial Religion in the United States. *Journal of the American Academy of Religion* 78(1): 1–39. DOI: 10.1093/jaarel/lfp076.

Cameron L (2008) Metaphor Shifting in the Dynamics of Talk. In: Zanatto M S, Cameron L and Cavalcanti M C (eds.) *Confronting Metaphor in Use: An Applied Linguistic Approach.* Amsterdam: John Benjamins, pp. 45–62. DOI: 10.1075/pbns.173.04cam.

Campbell H A and La Pastina A C (2010) How the iPhone Became Divine: New Media, Religion and the Intertextual Circulation of Meaning. *New Media & Society* 12(7): 1191–207. DOI: 10.1177/1461444810362204.

Campbell J (2001) *Thou Art That: Transforming Religious Metaphor.* Novato, CA: New World Library. DOI: 10.5860/choice.39-5759.

Canetti D, Hobfoll S E, Pedahzur A et al. (2010) Much Ado about Religion: Religiosity, Resource Loss, and Support for Political Violence. *Journal of Peace Research* 47(5): 575–87. DOI: 10.1177/0022343310368009.

Carter M R (2012) *The Teacher Monologues: Exploring the Experiences and Identities of Artist-Teachers.* University of British Columbia. DOI: 10.14288/1.0055366.

Charteris-Black J (2004) *Corpus Approaches to Critical Metaphor Analysis*. London: Palgrave Macmillan. DOI: 10.1057/9780230000612.

Chase T (1988) *The English Religious Lexis*. Lewiston, NY; Queenston, ON: Edwin Mellen Press.

Cheong E-Y (1999) Analysis of Sermons Delivered by Korean, Filipino and American Pastors: The View of Genre Analysis. *RELC Journal* 30(2). Sage Publications Sage CA: Thousand Oaks, CA: 44–60. DOI: 10.1177/003368829903000203.

Chew P G-L (2010) Metaphors of Change: Adolescent Singaporeans Switching Religion. In: Omoniyi T (eds.) *The Sociology of Language and Religion*. London: Palgrave Macmillan, pp. 156–89. DOI: 10.1057/9780230304710_8.

Chilton P and Kopytowska M (eds.) (2018) *Religion, Language, and the Human Mind*. Oxford University Press. DOI: 10.1093/oso/9780190636647.001.0001.

The Church of Scotland (2019) Brexit Prayers. Available at: https://www.churchofscotland.org.uk/worship/prayers/brexit_prayers (accessed 30 September 2019).

Cipriani R (2003) Invisible Religion or Diffused Religion in Italy? *Social Compass* 50(3). SAGE Publications: 311–20. DOI: 10.1177/00377686030503005.

Clowney E P and Clowney Jones R (2007) *How Jesus Transforms the Ten Commandments*. Philipsburg, NJ: P&R.

Coe K and Chenoweth S (2013) Presidents as Priests: Toward a Typology of Christian Discourse in the American Presidency. *Communication Theory* 23(4). John Wiley & Sons, Ltd (10.1111): 375–94. DOI: 10.1111/comt.12020.

Coe K and Domke D (2006) Petitioners or Prophets? Presidential Discourse, God, and the Ascendancy of Religious Conservatives. *Journal of Communication* 56(2): 309–30. DOI: 10.1111/j.1460-2466.2006.00021.x.

Comstock W R (1984) Toward Open Definitions of Religion. *Journal of the American Academy of Religion* 52(3): 499–517.

Cook G and Walter T (2005) Rewritten Rites: Language and Social Relations in Traditional and Contemporary Funerals. *Discourse & Society* 16(3). Sage Publications Sage CA: Thousand Oaks, CA: 365–91. DOI: 10.1177/0957926505051171.

Corry K (2019) We Asked Religious Experts about Kanye West's 'Jesus Is King'. Available at: https://www.vice.com/en_uk/article/j5ynv3/we-asked-religious-experts-about-kanye-wests-new-church-album-jesus-is-king (accessed 1 November 2019).

Couture B (1991) Functional Theory, Scientism, and Altruism: A Critique of Functional Linguistics and Its Applications to Writing. In: Ventola E (eds.) *Functional and Systemic Linguistics: Approaches and Uses*. Berlin: De Gruyter Mouton, pp. 259–80. DOI: 10.1515/9783110883527.259.

Crabb A (2009) Invoking Religion in Australian Politics. *Australian Journal of Political Science* 44(2): 259–79. DOI: https://doi.org/10.1080/10361140902862784.

Crines A S and Theakston K (2015) 'Doing God' in Number 10: British Prime Ministers, Religion, and Political Rhetoric. *Politics and Religion* 8(1). Cambridge University Press: 155–77. DOI: 10.1017/S1755048315000036.

Crossley J (2018) *Cults, Martyrs and Good Samaritans: Religion in Contemporary English Political Discourse*. London: Pluto Press.

Crystal D (1964) A Liturgical Language in a Linguistic Perspective. *New Blackfriars* 46(534). John Wiley & Sons, Ltd (10.1111): 148–56. DOI: 10.1111/j.1741-2005.1964.tb07472.x.

Crystal D (2018) Whatever Happened to Theolinguistics? In: *Religion, Language, and the Human Mind*. Oxford, UK: Oxford University Press, pp. 3–18. DOI: 10.1093/oso/9780190636647.003.0001.

Dabashi H (2015) Who Is the 'Great Satan'? *Al Jazeera*, 20 September. Available at: https://www.aljazeera.com/indepth/opinion/2015/09/great-satan-150920072643884.html (accessed 23 March 2020).

David Lee's Genre Classification Scheme (n.d.) Available at: http://rdues.bcu.ac.uk/bncweb/manual/genres.html (accessed 18 October 2019).

David M K and Yong J Y (2000) Even Obituaries Reflect Cultural Norms and Values. In: Kirkpatrick A (eds.) *Englishes in Asia: Communication*, Identity, *Power and Education*. Perth, Western Australia: Language Australia Ltd, pp. 169–78.

Davies M (2008) The Corpus of Contemporary American English (COCA): 520 Million Words, 1990–Present. Available at: http://corpus.byu.edu/coca.

Davies M (2013) Corpus of Global Web-Based English: 1.9 Billion Words from Speakers in 20 Countries (GloWbE). Available at: https://corpus.byu.edu/glowbe/.

Davies M (2018) iWeb: The 14 Billion Word Web Corpus. Available at: https://www.english-corpora.org/iweb/.

Davies M (n.d.) English-Corpora.org. Available at: https://www.english-corpora.org/ (accessed 24 October 2019).

Dawood T by NJ (ed.) (1990) *The Qur'an*. New York: Penguin.

Dawson J (2019) Shall Not Be Infringed: How the NRA Used Religious Language to Transform the Meaning of the Second Amendment. *Palgrave Communications* 5(1). DOI: https://doi.org/10.1057/s41599-019-0276-z.

Dillistone F W (1981) Attitudes to Religious Language. In: van Noppen J P (eds.) *Theolinguistics*. Brussels: Studiereeks Tijdschrift Vrije Universiteit Brussel, pp. 5–21.

Dobbelaere K (2011) The Contextualization of Definitions of Religion. *International Review of Sociology* 21(1). Taylor & Francis Group: 191–204. DOI: 10.1080/03906701.2011.544199.

Draper P (2017) Atheism and Agnosticism. In: Zalta E N (ed.) The Stanford Encyclopedia of Philosophy. Available at: https://plato.stanford.edu/archives/fall2017/entries/atheism-agnosticism/ (accessed 1 September 2020).

Duff B (2010) Confession, Sexuality and Pornography as Sacred Language. *Sexualities* 13(6). SAGE Publications Sage UK: London, England: 685–98. DOI: 10.1177/1363460710384557.

Durieux-Paillard S (2011) Differences in Language, Religious Beliefs and Culture: The Need for Culturally Responsive Health Service. In: Rechel B, Mladovsky P, Deville W et al. (eds.) *Migration and Health in the European Union*. Maidenhead: McGraw-Hill, pp. 203–12. DOI: 10.1046/j.1365-3156.1998.00337.x.

Durkheim E (1976) *The Elementary Forms of the Religious Life*. 2nd Edition. London: Allen and Unwin.

Dzameshi A K (1995) Social Motivations for Politeness Behavior in Christian Sermonic Discourse. *Anthropological Linguistics* 37(2): 192–215.

Eden O of (n.d.) Eden Pleat Wrap Soap. Available at: https://www.outofeden.co.uk/products/1412-20/eden-pleat-wrap-soap?incvat=true&gclid=EAIaIQobChMIlt GcraXp5AIVw7TtCh049Qo_EAQYAiABEgIJ6vD_BwE (accessed 24 September 2019).

Editors C (2017) The Top 10 Testimonies of 2016. *Christianity Today*, 28 December. Available at: https://www.christianitytoday.com/news/2016/december/top-10-testimonies-of-2016.html (accessed 13 November 2019).

Edwards K B (2012a) *Admen and Eve: The Bible in Contemporary Advertising*. Sheffield: Sheffield Phoenix Press.

Edwards K B (2012b) Sporting Messiah: Hypermasculinity and Nationhood in Male-targeted Sports Imagery. In: Exum C and Clines D A (eds.) *Biblical Reception*. Sheffield: Sheffield Phoenix Press, pp. 323–46. Available at: http://eprints.whiterose.ac.uk/96438/ (accessed 12 November 2019).

Edwards K B (2018) The Pope Wears Prada: How Religion and Fashion Connected at Met Gala 2018. *The Conversation*, 8 May. Available at: https://theconversation.com/the-pope-wears-prada-how-religion-and-fashion-connected-at-met-gala-2018-96290 (accessed 13 November 2019).

Esimaje A U (2014) A Descriptive Survey of the Character of English Lexis in Sermons. *SAGE Open* 4(4). SAGE Publications Sage CA: Los Angeles, CA: 1–16. DOI: 10.1177/2158244014563044.

Eslami Z R, Ribeiro A, Snow M et al. (2016) Exploring Discourse Practices in American Wedding Invitations. *Lodz Papers in Pragmatics* 12(2). De Gruyter Mouton: 135–51. DOI: 10.1515/lpp-2016-0009.

Ethelston G (2009) Appraisal in Evangelical Sermons: The Projection and Functions of Misguided Voices. *Text & Talk – An Interdisciplinary Journal of Language, Discourse & Communication Studies* 29(6). Walter de Gruyter GmbH & Co. KG: 683–704. DOI: 10.1515/TEXT.2009.035.

European Social Survey (ESS) (2016) Available at: https://www.europeansocialsurvey.org/ (accessed 12 September 2019).

Evans D (n.d.) Unit 2: Compiling a Corpus. Available at: https://www.birmingham.ac.uk/Documents/college-artslaw/corpus/Intro/Unit2.pdf (accessed 30 September 2019).

Evert S and Hoffmann S (2006) BNCweb. Available at: http://corpora.lancs.ac.uk/BNCweb/ (accessed 24 October 2019).

Fairclough N (2003) *Analyzing Discourse: Textual Analysis for Social Research*. New York: Routledge. DOI: 10.5354/0716-3991.2013.29147.

Fairman N, Knapp P and Martin A (2005) Flourishing: Positive Psychology and the Life Well-Lived. *Journal of the American Academy of Child & Adolescent Psychiatry* 44(8): 834–5. DOI: 10.1097/01.chi.0000166150.20764.37.

Farrelly M (2019) Rethinking Intertextuality in CDA. *Critical Discourse Studies*. Routledge: 1–18. DOI: 10.1080/17405904.2019.1609538.

Fernández E C (2007) Linguistic Devices Coping with Death in Victorian Obituaries. *Revista Alicantina de Estudios Ingleses* 20: 7–21.

Field M and Blackhorse T (2002) The Dual Role of Metonymy in Navajo Prayer. *Anthropological Linguistics* 44(3): 217–30. DOI: 10.2307/30028848.

Francis M and Knott K (2011) Return? It Never Left. Exploring the 'Sacred' as a Resource for Bridging the Gap between the Religious and the Secular. In: Kutz C, Riss H and Roy O (eds.) *Religious Norms in the Public Sphere: The Challenge*. European University Institute, Robert Schuman Centre for Advanced

Studies, ReligioWes, pp. 44–8. Available at: http://igov.berkeley.edu/sites/default/files/francis-matthew.docx (accessed 29 November 2018).

Francis W N and Kučera H (1964) Brown Corpus: Corpus of American English. Available at: https://www.sketchengine.eu/brown-corpus/ (accessed 24 October 2019).

Friedland R and Mohr J (2004) *Matters of Culture: Cultural Sociology in Practice.* Cambridge: Cambridge University Press.

Gaffney P D (1994) *The Prophet's Pulpit: Islamic Preaching in Contemporary Egypt.* Berkeley: University of California Press.

Galanter M, Dermatis H and Sampson C (2014) Spiritual Awakening in Alcoholics Anonymous: Empirical Findings. *Alcoholism Treatment Quarterly* 32(2–3). Routledge: 319–34. DOI: 10.1080/07347324.2014.907058.

Gee J P (2004) *An Introduction to Discourse Analysis: Theory and Method.* London: Routledge. DOI: 10.4324/9780203005675.

Giebels E, Ufkes E G and van Erp K J P M (2014) Understanding High-stakes Conflicts. In: Ayoko O B, Ashkanasy N M and Jehn K A (eds.) *Handbook of Conflict Management Research.* Cheltenham, UK: Edward Elgar, pp. 66–78. Available at: https://www.elgaronline.com/view/edcoll/9781781006931/9781781006931.00011.xml (accessed 23 March 2020).

Glover J (2015) Why We Need Mother God on Mother's Day. Available at: https://s3.amazonaws.com/storage.nm-storage.com/pilgrimchurchucc/files/sermons/sermon_mothers_day.pdf (accessed 9 October 2019).

Goodman F D (1972) *Speaking in Tongues: A Cross-Cultural Study of Glossolalia.* Chicago: Chicago University Press.

Gottlieb R S (1995) *This Sacred Earth: Religion, Nature, Environment.* New York: Routledge. DOI: 10.1093/isle/5.1.134.

GPTS (2000) *Partners in Training: Field Education Handbook.* Taylors, SC: GPTS. DOI: 10.1080/02615470601036492.

GPTS (2013) *Summary of the Proceedings of the Board of Trustees of Greenville Presbyterian Theological Seminary in Not Renewing the Contract of Dr [Smith].* Taylors, SC: GPTS.

Greil A L (1993) Exploration along the Sacred Frontier: Notes on Para-Religions, Quasi-Religions, and Other Boundary Phenomena. In: Bromley D G and Hadden J K (eds.) *The Handbook on Cults and Sects in America.* JAI Press.

Greil A L and Rudy D R (1983) Conversion to the World View of Alcoholics Anonymous: A Refinement of Conversion Theory. *Qualitative Sociology* 6(1). Kluwer Academic Publishers-Human Sciences Press: 5–28. DOI: 10.1007/BF00987195.

The Guardian (2019a) Donald Trump Says He Is 'the Chosen One' to Take on China. 22 August. Available at: https://www.theguardian.com/us-news/video/2019/aug/22/trump-says-he-is-the-chosen-one-to-take-on-china-video (accessed 23 August 2019).

The Guardian (2019b) 'Let My People Go:' What the Papers Said about the Chequers Summit. 25 March. Available at: https://www.theguardian.com/media/2019/mar/25/let-my-people-go-what-the-papers-said-about-the-chequers-summit (accessed 23 August 2019).

Haeri N (2003) *Sacred Language, Ordinary People: Dilemmas of Culture and Politics in Egypt.* New York: Palgrave Macmillan.

Haidrani S (2018) We Asked Vegans if They Should Be Given the Same Protections as Religious People. *Vice*, December. Available at: https://www.vice.com/en_uk/

article/8xpbvb/we-asked-vegans-if-they-should-be-given-the-same-protections-as-religious-people (accessed 12 November 2019).

Hall D E, Koenig H G and Meador K G (2004) Conceptualizing 'Religion': How Language Shapes and Constrains Knowledge in the Study of Religion and Health. *Perspectives in Biology and Medicine*. DOI: 10.1353/pbm.2004.0050.

Halliday M A and Matthiessen C M (2014) *An Introduction to Functional Grammar*. London, UK: Routledge.

Hari J (2007) The Last Gasp of the Global Warming Deniers. *The Independent*, 25 January. Available at: https://advance.lexis.com/api/permalink/1d1d2eb7-258e-4222-b9f5-232a60d0f749/?context=1519360.

Harkness G (n.d.) Chapter 10: We Believe in the Kingdom of God. Available at: https://www.religion-online.org/book-chapter/chapter-10b-bwe-believe-in-the-kingdom-of-god/ (accessed 9 October 2019).

Harper R F (ed.) (1901) *Assyrian and Babylonian Literature*. New York: D. Appleton and Company. Available at: https://archive.org/details/assyrianandbaby11harpgoog/page/n9 (accessed 11 September 2019).

Hart C (2014) *Discourse, Grammar and Ideology: Functional and Cognitive Perspectives*. London: Bloomsbury. DOI: 10.11606/issn.2236-4242.v30i1p159-167.

Hategan E (2015) Journey to Judaism: The Day I Became a Jew. Available at: https://incognitopress.wordpress.com/2015/08/10/journey-to-judaism/ (accessed 28 August 2019).

Heather N (2000) *Religious Language and Critical Discourse Analysis: Ideology and Identity in Christian Discourse Today*. Bern, Switzerland: Peter Lang.

Hernando B (2001) La Muerte Mensajera. Las Esquelas de Defunción Como Elemento Informativo. *Estudios sobre el Mensaje Periodístico* 7: 221–39. Available at: http://revistas.ucm.es/index.php/esmp/article/download/esmp0101110221a/12842 (accessed 17 April 2019).

The Historical Thesaurus of English (n.d.) 4. 21.2019. Glasgow: University of Glasgow. Available at: https://ht.ac.uk/ (accessed 11 September 2019).

The Historical Thesaurus of English, version 4.2.1 (n.d.a) 03.06 (n.) Morality. 4. 21.2019. University of Glasgow. Available at: https://ht.ac.uk/category/#id=169954.

The Historical Thesaurus of English, version 4.2.1 (n.d.b) 03.08 (n.) Faith. 4. 21.2019. Glasgow: University of Glasgow. Available at: https://ht.ac.uk/category/?id=173497 (accessed 11 September 2019b).

The Historical Thesaurus of English, version 4.2.1.2019 (n.d.) Historical Thesaurus: Search. Available at: https://ht.ac.uk/search/ (accessed 11 September 2019).

Hobbs A (2009) Response: Ethics and Money Part 1. Available at: https://blogs.warwick.ac.uk/drangiehobbs/entry/response_ethics_and/ (accessed 1 May 2019).

Hobbs V (2015) Characterizations of Feminism in Reformed Christian Online Media. *Journal of Media and Religion* 14(4). Taylor & Francis: 211–29.

Hobbs V (2018a) Disability, the 'Good Family' and Discrimination in the Dismissal of a Presbyterian Seminar Professor. *Journal of Language and Discrimination* 2(2): 133–61.

Hobbs V (2018b) Rape Culture in Sermons on Divorce. In: *Rape Culture, Gender Violence, and Religion*. Cham: Springer International Publishing, pp. 87–110. DOI: 10.1007/978-3-319-72224-5_6.

Hobbs V (2019) The Discourse of Divorce in Conservative Christian Sermons. *Critical Discourse Studies*. Informa UK Limited: 1–18. DOI: 10.1080/17405904.2019.1665079.

Hobbs V and Miller R (2015) The Subordinate Place of Supreme Honor: A Response to Douglas Wilson. Available at: https://www.patheos.com/blogs/jesuscreed/2015/09/02/the-subordinate-place-of-supreme-honor-response-to-douglas-wilson/ (accessed 13 November 2019).

Hsieh H-F and Shannon S E (2005) Three Approaches to Qualitative Content Analysis. *Qualitative Health Research* 15(9): 1277–88. DOI: 10.1177/1049732305276687.

Hudson S and Inkson K (2006) Volunteer Overseas Development Workers: The Hero's Adventure and Personal Transformation. *Career Development International* 11(4): 304–20. DOI: 10.1108/13620430610672522.

Hume J (2000) *Obituaries in American Culture*. Jackson: University Press of Mississippi.

Hyland K (2005) Stance and Engagement: A Model of Interaction in Academic Discourse. *Discourse Studies* 7(2): 173–92. DOI: 10.1177/1461445605050365.

Hylén T (2014) Closed and Open Conceptions of Religion: The Problem of Essentialism in Teaching about Religion. In: Andreassen B-O and Lewis J R (eds.) *Textbook Gods: Genre, Text and Teaching Religious Studies*. Sheffield: Equinox, pp. 16–42. DOI: 10.1558/equinox.23872.

Ingold R (2014) God, the Devil and You: A Systemic Functional Linguistic Analysis of the Language of Hillsong. *Literature and Aesthetics* 24(1): 85. Available at: https://openjournals.library.sydney.edu.au/index.php/LA/article/viewFile/8332/8470 (accessed 8 August 2019).

The International Churchill Society (1940) We Shall Fight on the Beaches. Available at: https://winstonchurchill.org/resources/speeches/1940-the-finest-hour/we-shall-fight-on-the-beaches/ (accessed 27 September 2019).

Irving K (2012) The Financial Life Well-Lived: Psychological Benefits of Financial Planning. *SSRN Electronic Journal* 6(4): 47–59. DOI: 10.2139/ssrn.1927110.

Ishii S (1992) Buddhist Preaching: The Persistent Main Undercurrent of Japanese Traditional Rhetorical Communication. *Communication Quarterly* 40(4). Taylor & Francis Group: 391–7. DOI: 10.1080/01463379209369856.

Jacoby S (2018) The White House Is Tearing Down the Wall between Church and State. *The New York Times*, 5 July. Available at: https://www.nytimes.com/2018/07/05/opinion/sunday/church-state-supreme-court-religion.html.

James W (1987) *Writings, 1902–1910*. New York: The Library of America.

JAR (2018) Far-right Spanish Political Party Vox: What Are Its Policies? *El Pais*, 3 December. Available at: https://elpais.com/elpais/2018/12/03/inenglish/1543832942_674971.html (accessed 13 November 2019).

Jensen J S (2014) *What Is Religion?* New York: Routledge.

Johnson B (2019) Theresa May Is a Chicken Who's Bottled Brexit. The Only Way Forward Is to Come Out of the EU Now. *The Telegraph*, 24 March. Available at: https://www.telegraph.co.uk/politics/2019/03/24/theresa-may-chicken-bottled-brexit-way-forward-come-eu-now/?hootPostID=c3649b85d453225656c152044601c079 (accessed 11 November 2019).

Johnson L (2015) The Religion of Ethical Veganism. *Journal of Animal Ethics* 5(1). University of Illinois Press Ferrater Mora Oxford Centre for Animal Ethics: 31. DOI: 10.5406/janimalethics.5.1.0031.

Jordan D K (2019) Catholic Religious Vocabulary. Available at: http://pages.ucsd.
edu/~dkjordan/xy/xydocs/CatholicTerms.html#l (accessed 3 May 2019).

Kant I (1987) *Critique of Judgment*. Indianapolis, IA: Hackett Pub. Co.

Kapaló J A (2011) Genre and Authority in the Scholarly Construction of Charm
and Prayer: A View from the Margins. *Incantatio. An International Journal on
Charms, Charmers and Charming* 1: 79–101. DOI: 10.7592/incantatio2011_1_
kapalo.

Kashdan T and Steger M (2007) Curiosity and Pathways to Well-being and
Meaning in Life: Traits, States, and Everyday Behaviors. *Motivation and
Emotion* 31(3): 159–73. DOI: 10.1007/s11031-007-9068-7.

Keane W (1997) Religious Language. *Annual Review of Anthropology* 26(1):
47–71. DOI: 10.1146/annurev.anthro.26.1.47.

Keane W (2008) The Evidence of the Senses and the Materiality of Religion.
Journal of the Royal Anthropological Institute 14(SUPPL. 1): S110–S127. DOI:
https://doi.org/10.1111/j.1467-9655.2008.00496.x.

Kelsey D (2017) *Media and Affective Mythologies: Discourse, Archetypes
and Ideology in Contemporary Politics. Media and Affective Mythologies:
Discourse, Archetypes and Ideology.* In: *Contemporary Politics.* Cham: Springer
International Publishing. DOI: 10.1007/978-3-319-60759-7.

Kilgarriff A, Baisa V, Bušta J et al. (2014) The Sketch Engine: Ten Years On.
Lexicography 1(1). Springer Berlin Heidelberg: 7–36. DOI: 10.1007/s40607-
014-0009-9.

Kishi K (2018) Key Findings on the Global Rise in Religious Restrictions. Available
at: https://www.pewresearch.org/fact-tank/2018/06/21/key-findings-on-the-
global-rise-in-religious-restrictions/ (accessed 13 November 2019).

Knott K (2013) The Secular Sacred: In-between or Both/And? In: Day A, Cotter C
and Vincett G (eds.) *Social Identities between the Sacred and the Secular.* New
York: Routledge, pp. 145–60.

Kohnen T (2012) Prayers in the History of English: A Corpus-based
Study. *Language and Computers* 76(1). Brill | Rodopi: 165–80. DOI:
10.1163/9789401207935_009.

Koller V (2012) How to Analyse Collective Identity in Discourse-Textual and
Contextual Parameters. *Critical Approaches to Discourse Analysis across
Disciplines* 5(2): 19–36.

Koller V (2019) Clean Brexit. Available at: https://twitter.com/VeronikaKoller/
status/1085536598912045056 (accessed 2 December 2019).

Končar A B (2008) Contemporary Sermons: From Grammatical Annotation to
Rhetorical Design. *Systemic Functional Linguistics in Use: Odense Working
Papers in Language and Communication* 29: 503–21.

Kottler J and Carlson J (2005) *The Client Who Changed Me: Stories of Therapist
Personal Transformation.* New York: Routledge.

Kristeva J (1986) Word, Dialogue and Novel. In: Moi T (eds.) *The Kristeva Reader.*
Oxford: Basil Blackwell.

Ladd KL and Spilka B (2006) Inward, Outward, Upward Prayer: Scale Reliability
and Validation. *Journal for the Scientific Study of Religion* 45(2): 233–251.

Leech G, Johansoon S, Hofland K et al. (1986) The Lancaster-Oslo/Bergen Corpus
(LOB). Available at: http://www.helsinki.fi/varieng/CoRD/corpora/LOB/index.
html#manuals (accessed 24 October 2019).

Legacy.com (2018) Stephen Hawking Obituary. Available at: https://www.legacy.com/obituaries/name/stephen-hawking-obituary?pid=188446071 (accessed 14 October 2019).

Legacy.com (n.d.a) About Us. Available at: https://www.legacy.com/about/about-us (accessed 17 April 2019a).

Legacy.com (n.d.b) Legacy.com – Where Life Stories Live On. Available at: https://www.legacy.com/ (accessed 3 May 2019b).

Lejon K and Agnafors M (2011) Less Religion, Better Society? On Religion, Secularity, and Prosperity in Scandinavia. *Dialog* 50(3): 297–307. DOI: 10.1111/j.1540-6385.2011.00619.x.

Leone M (2004) *Religious Conversion and Identity: The Semiotic Analysis of Texts.* Abingdon: Routledge.

Lessard-Clouston M A (2009) *Specialized Vocabulary Learning and Use in Theology: Native and Non-Native English-Speaking Students in a Graduate School.* Koln, Germany: Lambert Academic Publishing.

Lessard-Clouston M A (2010) Theology Lectures as Lexical Environments: A Case Study of Technical Vocabulary Use. *Journal of English for Academic Purposes* 9(4). Pergamon: 308–21. DOI: 10.1016/J.JEAP.2010.09.001.

Lewis T V (2013) Religious Rhetoric in Southern College Football: New Uses for Religious Metaphors. *Southern Communication Journal* 78(3): 202–14. DOI: 10.1080/1041794X.2013.770064.

LexisNexis (n.d.) Finding Obituaries. Available at: http://lexisnexis.custhelp.com/app/answers/answer_view/a_id/1085470/~/-finding-obituaries- (accessed 17 April 2019).

Locke T (2004) *Critical Discourse Analysis.* London: Continuum.

Lopez-Sanchez J (2013) A Night on Mount Yeezus: The Kanye West Experience. *Dead Curious*, November. Available at: http://deadcurious.com/2013/11/25/a-night-on-mount-yeezus-the-kanye-west-experience/ (accessed 1 November 2019).

Lowth R (1825) *Isaiah: A New Translation, with a Preliminary Dissertation and Notes.* Edinburgh: W. Baynes and Son.

Lucey J (2017) The Life Well Lived. Available at: https://www.penguin.co.uk/books/111/1112191/the-life-well-lived/9781848272330.html (accessed 28 October 2019).

Luckmann T (1967) *The Invisible Religion: The Problem of Religion in Modern Society - Thomas Luckmann - Google Books.* New York: Macmillan.

Lukes S (1986) *Power.* New York: New York University Press.

Lumby C (1994) Feminism and the Media: The Biggest Fantasy of All. *Media Information Australia* 72: 49–54. Available at: https://search.informit.com.au/documentSummary;dn=147859294737972;res=IELLCC (accessed 12 November 2019).

Lynch G (2014) *On the Sacred.* Durham: Routledge.

Lyons I (2018) Ethical Veganism Could Be Considered 'Protected Belief' Akin to Religion in Landmark Case. *The Telegraph*, 12 December. Available at: https://www.telegraph.co.uk/news/2018/12/03/ethical-veganism-could-considered-religion-landmark-tribunal/.

MacGregor N (2018) Belief Is Back: Why the World Is Putting Its Faith in Religion. *The Guardian*, 5 October. Available at: https://www.theguardian.com/books/2018/oct/05/belief-is-back-societies-worldwide-faith-religion.

Machin D and Mayr A (2012) *How to Do Critical Discourse Analysis*. London: Sage.

Magnanti B (2014) Russell Brand's Hollow Conversion from Sexist to Feminist. *Telegraph*, 16 January. Available at: https://www.telegraph.co.uk/women/sex/10576993/Russell-Brands-hollow-conversion-from-sexist-to-feminist.html (accessed 12 November 2019).

Malesh P (2009) Sharing Our Recipes: Vegan Conversion Narratives as Social Praxis. In: McKenzie Stevens S and Malesh P M (eds.) *Active Voices: Composing a Rhetoric of Social Movements*. Albany: State University of New York Press, pp. 131–45.

Mallia K L (2009) From the Sacred to the Profane: A Critical Analysis of the Changing Nature of Religious Imagery in Advertising. *Journal of Media and Religion* 8(3). Informa UK Limited: 172–90. DOI: 10.1080/15348420903091162.

Malmström H (2016) Engaging the Congregation: The Place of Metadiscourse in Contemporary Preaching. *Applied Linguistics* 37(4). University of California Press: 561–82. DOI: 10.1093/applin/amu052.

Mansour R (2016) Glenn Beck Invites America to Join Him in Another Fast. Available at: https://www.breitbart.com/politics/2016/05/02/glenn-beck-invites-america-join-another-fast/ (accessed 26 November 2018).

Martin M W (2015) The Poetry of the Lord's Prayer: A Study in Poetic Device. *Journal of Biblical Literature* 134(2). Society of Biblical Literature: 347–72. DOI: 10.15699/jbl.1342.2015.2804.

Matisoff J A (1991) Syntactic Parallelism and Morphological Elaboration in Lahu Religious Poetry. In: Shipley W (eds.) *A Festschrift for William F. Shipley*. Santa Cruz, CA: Syntax Research Center, pp. 83–103.

McCarron K (2006) Alcoholism and Authority. In: Omoniyi T and Fishman J A (eds.) *Explorations in the Sociology of Language and Religion*. Amsterdam: John Benjamins, pp. 68–78.

McEnery T (2006) *Swearing in English*. London, UK: Routledge.

McKay B (2015) More-Than-Human Life Well-Lived? Available at: http://sheffieldanimals.group.shef.ac.uk/more-than-human-life-well-lived/ (accessed 25 April 2019).

McNamara P H (1984) *Religion North American Style*. Belmont, CA: Wadsworth Pub. Co.

Mehta H (2013) Prayer Is Useless, and Has a Downside. *The New York Times*, 27 June. Available at: https://www.nytimes.com/roomfordebate/2013/06/27/should-atheists-pray/prayer-is-useless-and-has-a-downside (accessed 8 November 2019).

Mercer P (2017) Australia's Heated Same-sex Marriage Debate. *BBC News*, 24 September. Available at: https://www.bbc.co.uk/news/world-australia-41362445 (accessed 13 November 2019).

Micklethwait J and Wooldridge A (2010) *God Is Back: How the Global Rise of Faith Is Changing the World*. London: Penguin.

Miles J (2019) Pete Buttigieg Has Called Climate Change a Religious Crisis – But Is He Brave Enough to Do It in Evangelical Texas? *The Independent*, 11 September. Available at: https://www.independent.co.uk/voices/pete-buttigieg-religion-democratic-debate-texas-climate-change-a9101531.html (accessed 15 November 2019).

Mocarski R and Billings A C (2014) Manufacturing a Messiah: How Nike and LeBron James co-Constructed the Legend of King James. *Communication & Sport* 2(1): 3–23. DOI: 10.1177/2167479513481456.

Mohammed Sawalmeh M H (2014) A Sociolinguistic Study of Muslim and Christian Wedding Invitation Genre in the Jordanian Society. *Journal of Advances in Linguistics* 5(1). CIRWOLRD: 448–62. DOI: 10.24297/jal. v5i1.2731.

Moore S H (2002) Disinterring Ideology from a Corpus of Obituaries: A Critical Post Mortem. *Discourse & Society* 13(4): 495–536. DOI: 10.1177/0957926502013004071.

Moyer J D (n.d.) Nontheistic Prayer: Why I (as an atheist) Pray. Available at: https://www.snsociety.org/nontheistic-prayer/ (accessed 11 September 2019).

Muggah R and Velshi A (2019) Religious Violence Is on the Rise. What Can Faith-based Communities Do about It? Available at: https://www.weforum. org/agenda/2019/02/how-should-faith-communities-halt-the-rise-in-religious-violence/ (accessed 13 November 2019).

MyVocabulary.com (n.d.) Religion, Spiritual Inspiration Word List. Available at: https://myvocabulary.com/word-list/religion-spiritual-inspiration-vocabulary/ (accessed 3 May 2019).

Nickel S (2015) Intertextuality as a Means of Negotiating Authority, Status, and Place-Forms, Contexts, and Effects of Quotations of Christian Texts in Nineteenth-Century Missionary Correspondence from Yorùbáland. *Source: Journal of Religion in Africa* 45(2): 119–49. DOI: 10.1163/15700666-12340039.

Niemiec C P and Ryan R M (2013) What Makes for a Life Well Lived? Autonomy and Its Relation to Full Functioning and Organismic Wellness. In: *The Oxford Handbook of Happiness*. Oxford, pp. 1–11. DOI: 10.1093/oxfordhb/9780199557257.013.0016.

Nietzsche F W (2001) *Dithyrambs of Dionysus*. Hollingdale R J (ed.) London: Anvil Press Poetry.

Nike (2006) LeBron James Pressure. Available at: https://www.youtube.com/watch?v=Rv3niQ-w3y0&feature=youtu.be (accessed 11 November 2019).

Nike (2008) Bernie Mack LeBron James Commercial. Available at: https://www. youtube.com/watch?v=bT4tAltJ6oc&feature=youtu.be (accessed 11 November 2019).

Noy C (2004) This Trip Really Changed Me: Backpackers' Narratives of Self-change. *Annals of Tourism Research* 31(1). Elsevier Ltd: 78–102. DOI: 10.1016/j.annals.2003.08.004.

O'Connell D (2017) *God Wills It: Presidents and the Political Use of Religion. God Wills It: Presidents and the Political Use of Religion*. London: Routledge. DOI: 10.4324/9780203790595.

Obama B (2015) Obama Amazing Grace Clip. Available at: https://www.c-span. org/video/?c4544050/obama-amazing-grace-clip (accessed 9 October 2019).

Omoniyi T (ed.) (2010) *The Sociology of Language and Religion: Change, Conflict and Accommodation. The Sociology of Language and Religion: Change, Conflict and Accommodation*. Basingstoke: Palgrave Macmillan. DOI: 10.1057/9780230304710.

Omoniyi T and Fishman J (eds.) (2006) *Explorations in the Sociology of Language and Religion*. Amsterdam: John Benjamins.

Opie I A and Opie P (2001) *The Lore and Language of Schoolchildren.* New York: New York Review Books.

Ostenfeld E (1994) Aristotle on the Good Life and Quality of Life. In: *Concepts and Measurement of Quality of Life in Health Care.* Dordrecht: Springer Netherlands, pp. 19–34. DOI: 10.1007/978-94-015-8344-2_2.

Otnes C and Pleck E H (2003) *Cinderella Dreams: The Allure of the Lavish Wedding.* Oakland: University of California Press.

Owens P J (1898) We Have Heard the Joyful Sound. Available at: https://www.hymnal.net/en/hymn/h/991 (accessed 8 August 2019).

Oxford University Press (2007) Oxford English Dictionary. Available at: https://www.oed.com/ (accessed 24 October 2019).

Page D D (2005) Veganism and Sincerely Held Religious Beliefs in the Workplace: No Protection without Definition. *University of Pennsylvania Journal of Labor and Employment Law* 7(2): 363–408. Available at: https://heinonline.org/HOL/Page?handle=hein.journals/upjlel7&id=371&div=22&collection=journals (accessed 15 January 2019).

Petre J and Capon J (2001) Lord's Prayer Parody for Drinkers. *The Telegraph*, 5 August. Available at: https://www.telegraph.co.uk/news/uknews/1336437/Lords-Prayer-parody-for-drinkers.html (accessed 23 September 2019).

Peuronen S (2013) Heteroglossia as a Resource for Reflexive Participation in a Community of Christian Snowboarders in Finland. *Journal of Sociolinguistics* 17(3): 297–323. DOI: 10.1111/josl.12040.

Pew Research Center (2014) Frequency of Prayer – Religion in America: U.S. Religious Data, Demographics and Statistics. Available at: https://www.pewforum.org/religious-landscape-study/frequency-of-prayer/ (accessed 12 September 2019).

Pew Research Center (2017) The Changing Global Religious Landscape. Available at: http://www.pewforum.org/2017/04/05/the-changing-global-religious-landscape/ (accessed 12 November 2018).

Pew Research Center (2018) *The Age Gap in Religion around the World.* Available at: https://www.pewforum.org/2018/06/13/how-religious-commitment-varies-by-country-among-people-of-all-ages/.

Piferi R L and Lawler-Row K (2006) The Forgiving Personality: Describing a Life Well Lived? *Personality and Individual Differences* 41: 1009–20.

Pihlaja S (2014) *Antagonism on YouTube: Metaphor in Online Discourse.* London: Bloomsbury.

Pihlaja S (2018) *Religious Talk Online: The Evangelical Discourse of Muslims, Christians, and Atheists. Religious Talk Online: The Evangelical Discourse of Muslims, Christians, and Atheists.* Cambridge, UK: Cambridge University Press. DOI: 10.1017/9781316661963.

Pihlaja S (ed.) (n.d.) *Analysing Religious Discourse.* Cambridge: Cambridge University Press.

Powell R and Pepper M (2017) Local Churches in Australia: Research Findings from NCLS Research. *2016 NCLS Church Life Pack Seminar Presentations.* Sydney: NCLS Research.

Powell T (1995) Religion, Race, and Reason: The Case of LJ. *The Journal of Clinical Ethics* 6(1): 73–7. Available at: https://repository.library.georgetown.edu/handle/10822/745909 (accessed 12 November 2019).

Powers R (1991) *The Gold Bug Variations*. New York: William Morrow and Company.

Priest R J (2003) 'I Discovered My Sin!': Aguaruna Evangelical Conversion Narratives. In: Buckser A and Glazier S D (eds.) *The Anthropology of Religious Conversion*. Lanham, MD: Rowman & Littlefield, pp. 95–108.

Quinn B (2019) Jewish Labour Movement Passes No-confidence Motion on Corbyn. *The Guardian*, 7 April. Available at: https://www.theguardian.com/politics/2019/apr/07/labour-defends-antisemitism-response-after-documents-leak (accessed 11 November 2019).

Rachik H (2009) How Religion Turns into Ideology. *The Journal of North African Studies* 14(3/4): 347–58.

Rathbone Y (2009) Comment: Religion as Dance. The Stroppy Rabbit: Metaphors for Religion. Available at: http://stroppyrabbit.blogspot.com/2009/06/metaphors-for-religion.html.

Rayson P (2009) WMatrix. Lancaster: Computing Department, Lancaster University. Available at: http://ucrel.lancs.ac.uk/wmatrix3.html.

Rayson P and Garside R (1998) The CLAWS Web Tagger. *CAME Journal* 22: 121–3. Available at: http://www.comp.lancs.ac.uk/ucrel/claws/trial.html (accessed 28 October 2019).

Reichard G A (1944) *Prayer: The Compulsive Word*. New York: J. J. Augustin.

Religion of Sports (2019) About Us. Available at: https://www.religionofsports.com/about-us/ (accessed 11 November 2019).

Remillard A (2016) Sports and Religion in America. In: *Oxford Research Encyclopedia of Religion*. Oxford University Press. DOI: 10.1093/acrefore/9780199340378.013.145.

Resnicoff R A E (2014) Four Stories for Four Children. In: *Traditional Egalitarian Minyan, Adas Israel Congregation*. Washington, DC 2014. Try My Rabbi. Available at: http://trymyrabbi.com/jewish-holidays/rosh-hashanah/four-stories-for-four-children (accessed 9 October 2019).

Richardson P, Mueller C M and Pihlaja S (n.d.) *Cognitive Linguistics and Religious Language: An Introduction*. Abingdon: Routledge.

Robbins J (2001) God Is Nothing but Talk: Modernity, Language, and Prayer in a Papua New Guinea Society. *American Anthropologist* 103(4). Wiley-Blackwell: 901–12. DOI: 10.1525/aa.2001.103.4.901.

Robertson R (1970) *The Sociological Interpretation of Religion*. Oxford: Oxford University Press. Available at: https://www.encyclopedia.com/environment/encyclopedias-almanacs-transcripts-and-maps/implicit-religion (accessed 13 December 2018).

Roof W C (2010) Blood in the Barbecue? Food and Faith in the American South. In: Mazur E and McCarthy K (eds.) *God in the Details: American Religion in Popular Culture*. Routledge, pp. 126–37. Available at: https://www.taylorfrancis.com/books/e/9781136993138/chapters/10.4324%2F9780203854808-15 (accessed 6 February 2019).

Rose L A (1997) *Sharing the Word: Preaching in the Roundtable Church*. Louisville, KY: Westminster John Knox Press.

Ryken L (2011) *The Legacy of the King James Bible: Celebrating 400 Years of the Most Influential English Translation*. Wheaton, IL: Crossway.

Saler B (2000) *Conceptualizing Religion*. Leiden: Berghahn Books.

Samarin W J (1972) *Tongues of Men and Angels: The Religious Language of Pentecostalism*. New York: Macmillan.

Sawyer J F A and Simpson J M Y (2001) *Concise Encyclopedia of Language and Religion*. Oxford: Elsevier.

Scarre G (2012) Can There Be a Good Death? *Journal of Evaluation in Clinical Practice* 18(5). John Wiley & Sons, Ltd (10.1111): 1082–6. DOI: 10.1111/j.1365-2753.2012.01922.x.

Schaffalitzky De Muckadell C (2014) On Essentialism and Real Definitions of Religion. *Journal of the American Academy of Religion* 82(2): 495–520. DOI: 10.1093/jaarel/lfu015.

Schlehofer M M, Omoto A M and Adelman J R (2008) How Do 'Religion' and 'Spirituality' Differ? Lay Definitions among Older Adults. *Journal for the Scientific Study of Religion* 47(3). Wiley/Blackwell (10.1111): 411–25. DOI: 10.1111/j.1468-5906.2008.00418.x.

Schnell T and Becker P (2006) Personality and Meaning in Life. *Personality and Individual Differences* 41(1): 117–29. Available at: https://www.sciencedirect.com/science/article/pii/S0191886906000511 (accessed 12 September 2019).

Seale C (2001) Sporting Cancer: Struggle Language in News Reports of People with Cancer. *Sociology of Health & Illness* 23(3): 308–29. DOI: 10.1111/1467-9566.00254.

Seibaek L (2013) Hounsgaard L and Hvidt NC (2013) Secular, Spiritual, and Religious Existential Concerns of Women with Ovarian Cancer during Final Diagnostics and Start of Treatment. *Evidence-based Complementary and Alternative Medicine*. DOI: 10.1155/2013/765419.

SermonAudio.com (n.d.) Available at: https://www.sermonaudio.com/main.asp (accessed 8 August 2018).

Shoaps R A (2002) 'Pray Earnestly': The Textual Construction of Personal Involvement in Pentecostal Prayer and Song. *Journal of Linguistic Anthropology* 12(1): 34–71. DOI: 10.1525/jlin.2002.12.1.34.

Sigal S (2018) Atheists Are Sometimes More Religious than Christians. *The Atlantic*, May. Available at: https://www.theatlantic.com/international/archive/2018/05/american-atheists-religious-european-christians/560936/ (accessed 27 August 2019).

Singh P K H and Thuraisingam T (2011) Language for Reconciliation in Religious Discourse: A Critical Discourse Analysis of Contradictions in Sermons Explored through the Activity Theory Framework. *Multilingua - Journal of Cross-Cultural and Interlanguage Communication* 30(3–4): 391–404. DOI: 10.1515/mult.2011.019.

Sketch Engine (2015) TenTen Corpus Family. Available at: https://www.sketchengine.eu/documentation/tenten-corpora/ (accessed 3 May 2019).

Sketch Engine (n.d.) Word Sketch: A Summary of a Word's Behaviour. Available at: https://www.sketchengine.eu/user-guide/user-manual/word-sketch/ (accessed 8 August 2018).

Slaughter M M (1993) The Salman Rushdie Affair: Apostasy, Honor, and Freedom of Speech. *Virginia Law Review* 79(1): 153–204. DOI: 10.2307/1073409.

Smith J (1921) *The Book of Mormon: An Account Written by the Hand of Mormon upon Plates Taken from the Plates of Nephi*. Salt Lake City, UT: The Church of Jesus Christ of Latter Day Saints.

Smith J Z (1978) *Map Is Not Territory: Studies in the History of Religions.* Chicago, IL: Chicago University Press.

Smith W C (1991) *The Meaning and End of Religion.* Chicago: Fortress Press.

Soepriatmadji L (2009) Genre Analysis on English Friday Sermons Prepared by the Islamic Religious Council of Singapore. *Dinamika Bahasa Dan Budaya* 3(2): 171–84. Available at: https://www.unisbank.ac.id/ojs/index.php/fbib1/article/view/449 (accessed 22 August 2019).

Soskice J M (2007) *The Kindness of God: Metaphor, Gender, and Religious Language.* Oxford: Oxford University Press. DOI: 10.1111/j.1468-0025.2009.01546.x.

Spencer A B (1996) Father-Ruler : The Meaning of the Metaphor 'Father' for God in the Bible. *Journal of the Evangelical Theological Society* 39(3): 433–42.

St. John A (2003) The LeBron Road Show. *The Village Voice*, February. Available at: https://www.villagevoice.com/2003/02/11/the-lebron-road-show/ (accessed 11 November 2019).

Stephens R and Umland C (2011) Swearing as a Response to Pain – Effect of Daily Swearing Frequency. *The Journal of Pain* 12(12). Churchill Livingstone: 1274–81. DOI: 10.1016/J.JPAIN.2011.09.004.

Svenska Dagbladet (2010) Guds återkomst [The Return of God]. 23 February.

Tait R (2019) England Supporters Involved in Violent Clashes with Police in Prague. *The Guardian*, 11 October. Available at: https://www.theguardian.com/football/2019/oct/11/england-supporters-violent-clashes-police-prague (accessed 13 November 2019).

Taverniers M (2004) Grammatical Metaphors in English. *Moderna Språk* 98(1): 17–26.

Taylor R L (1990) *The Religious Dimensions of Confucianism.* Albany: State University of New York Press.

Tearfund (2018) Half of Adults in the UK Say That They Pray. Available at: https://www.tearfund.org/en/media/press_releases/half_of_adults_in_the_uk_say_that_they_pray/ (accessed 11 September 2019).

Tefft S (1996) Taiwan's Feisty 'Moses' Irritates China's Leaders. *The Christian Science Monitor*, 21 March. Available at: https://www.csmonitor.com/1996/0321/21013.html (accessed 11 November 2019).

Thomas J D (2010) Science and the Sacred: Intertextuality in Richard Powers's *The Gold Bug Variations*. *Critique: Studies in Contemporary Fiction* 51(1): 18–31. DOI: 10.1080/00111610903249831.

Thompson G (2013) *Introducing Functional Grammar.* London: Routledge.

Tillich P (1957) *Dynamics of Faith.* New York: Harper & Row.

Towler R (1974) *Homo Religious: Sociological Problems in the Study of Religion.* London: Constable. Available at: http://www.worldcat.org/title/homo-religiosus-sociological-problems-in-the-study-of-religion/oclc/1096836?page=citation (accessed 13 December 2018).

Towns D and Towns S (2001) *Voices from the Garden: Stories of Becoming a Vegetarian.* Herndon, VA: Lantern Books.

TripAdvisor (n.d.) In Cod We Trust – The Codmother Fish & Chips – San Francisco Traveller Reviews. Available at: https://www.tripadvisor.co.uk/ShowUserReviews-g60713-d2371705-r318193790-The_Codmother_Fish_Chips-San_Francisco_California.html (accessed 31 October 2019).

Tripp and Tyler (2013) Stuff Christians Say. Available at: https://www.youtube.com/watch?v=7Dxo0Yjno3I&feature=youtu.be (accessed 16 July 2019).

Tyler E B (1873) *Primitive Culture*. London: John Murray.

van Dierendonck D and Mohan K (2006) Some Thoughts on Spirituality and Eudaimonic Well-being. *Mental Health, Religion and Culture* 9(3): 227–38. DOI: 10.1080/13694670600615383.

van Dijk T A (2006) Ideology and Discourse Analysis. *Journal of Political Ideologies* 11(2). Taylor & Francis Group: 115–40. DOI: 10.1080/13569310600687908.

van Leeuwen T (2008) *Discourse and Practice: New Tools for Critical Discourse Analysis*. Oxford: Oxford University Press.

Van Nguyen D (2019) Kanye West: Jesus Is King Review – Rap Genius Can't See the Light. *The Guardian*, 26 October. Available at: https://www.theguardian.com/music/2019/oct/26/kanye-west-jesus-is-king-review (accessed 31 October 2019).

van Noppen J P (1980) *Spatial Theography: A Study in Linguistic* Expression *and* Communication in Contemporary *British Popular* Theology *(1960–1970)*. Université Libre de Bruxelles. Available at: http://difusion.ulb.ac.be/vufind/Record/ULB-DIPOT:oai:dipot.ulb.ac.be:2013/214005/Holdings (accessed 11 December 2018).

van Noppen J P (ed.) (1981) *Theolinguistics*. Brussels: Vrije Universiteit Brussel. Available at: http://difusion.ulb.ac.be/vufind/Record/ULB-DIPOT:oai:dipot.ulb.ac.be:2013/44718/TOC (accessed 11 December 2018).

van Noppen J P (2009) Prayers and the Presidency. In: Slembrouck S, Taverniers M and van Herreweghe M (eds.) *From Will to Well: Studies in Linguistics, Offered to Anne-Marie Simon*. Gent: Academia Press, pp. 451–60.

van Noppen J P (2011) Critical Theolinguistics vs. the Literalist Paradigm. *Sociolinguistica* 25: 28–40. Available at: https://www.academia.edu/1170082/Critical_Theolinguistics_vs._the_Literalist_Paradigm (accessed 13 November 2019).

van Noppen J P and Buscarlet J-M (eds.) (1983) *Metaphor and Religion*. Brussel: Vrije Universiteit Brussel. Available at: http://difusion.ulb.ac.be/vufind/Record/ULB-DIPOT:oai:dipot.ulb.ac.be:2013/44720/TOC (accessed 11 December 2018).

VoxEurop (2015) Salman Rushdie on Freedom of Expression: 'A Universal Right of the Human Race'. Available at: https://voxeurop.eu/en/content/blog/4997934-universal-right-human-race (accessed 29 August 2019).

Watkins B, Schoch A, Webb M et al. (2015) In Cod We Trust: Cod in Atlantic Canada | Student Research on Environment and Sustainability Issues. Available at: https://environment.geog.ubc.ca/in-cod-we-trust-cod-in-atlantic-canada/ (accessed 31 October 2019).

Wenham D (2010) The Sevenfold Form of the Lord's Prayer in Matthew's Gospel. *Expository Times*. DOI: 10.1177/0014524610364409.

Wolfram W (1974) Felicitas D. Goodman, *Speaking in Tongues: A Cross-cultural Study of Glossolalia*. Chicago: University of Chicago Press, 1972, pp. xxii and 175. *Language in Society* 3(1). Cambridge University Press: 123–6. DOI: 10.1017/S0047404500004218.

Wright J D and Khoo Y (2019) Empirical Perspectives on Religion and Violence. *Contemporary Voices: St. Andrews Journal of International Relations* 1(1). PsyArXiv: 1–26. DOI: 10.31234/OSF.IO/GZSPE.

Yinger J (1957) *Religion, Society and the Individual: An Introduction to the Sociology of Religion*. New York: Macmillan. Available at: http://psycnet.apa.org/record/1958-00415-000 (accessed 28 November 2018).

YouTube (2019) Religion of Sports – Official Trailer. Available at: https://www.youtube.com/channel/UCEX1TT5u8pUdfOau_wDgaKg (accessed 11 November 2019).

Zagzebski L (2017) Authority in Religious Communities. In: Abraham W J and Aquino F D (eds.) *The Oxford Handbook of the Epistemology of Theology*. Oxford: Oxford University Press, pp. 97–110.

INDEX